The Postmodern Sacred

The Postmodern Sacred

*Popular Culture Spirituality
in the Science Fiction, Fantasy
and Urban Fantasy Genres*

EMILY MCAVAN

McFarland & Company, Inc., Publishers
Jefferson, North Carolina, and London

Portions of the Introduction appeared in the *Journal of Religion and Popular Culture* 22:1 (Spring 2010).

LIBRARY OF CONGRESS CATALOGUING-IN-PUBLICATION DATA

McAvan, Emily.
 The postmodern sacred : popular culture spirituality in the science fiction, fantasy and urban fantasy genres / Emily McAvan.
   p.   cm.
 Includes bibliographical references and index.

 ISBN 978-0-7864-6388-6
 softcover : acid free paper ∞

 1. Fantasy literature — History and criticism.
 2. Spirituality in literature.   3. Popular culture —
 Religious aspects.   4. Postmodernism — Religious
 aspects.   5. Christianity in literature.   6. Mass
 media — Religious aspects.   I. Title.
 PN3435.M39 2012
 809.3'876209382 — dc23   2012034269

BRITISH LIBRARY CATALOGUING DATA ARE AVAILABLE

© 2012 Emily McAvan. All rights reserved

No part of this book may be reproduced or transmitted in any form or by any means, electronic or mechanical, including photocopying or recording, or by any information storage and retrieval system, without permission in writing from the publisher.

On the cover: *left to right* Carrie-Anne Moss as Trinity, Laurence Fishburne as Morpheus, Keanu Reeves as Neo in *The Matrix Reloaded*, 2003 (Warner Bros./Photofest); brick background (iStockphoto/Thinkstock)

Manufactured in the United States of America

McFarland & Company, Inc., Publishers
 Box 611, Jefferson, North Carolina 28640
  www.mcfarlandpub.com

Table of Contents

Acknowledgments	vi
Introduction: The Return of the Religious and the Postmodern Sacred	1
ONE • The Postmodern Sacred	21
TWO • Virtual Religion: Techniques of the Postmodern Sacred	31
THREE • "Something Up There": Transcendental Gesturing in New Age–Influenced Texts	43
FOUR • Of Gods and Monsters: Metaphor and the Postmodern Sacred	64
FIVE • Buffy and Xena: Polytheisms On-Screen	80
SIX • Whither Leonardo da Vinci? New Age Gnosticism	98
SEVEN • Christ Figures and the Messianic in *The Lord of the Rings*	108
EIGHT • The Cultural Logic of Postmodern Christianity: The Christian Right and Popular Culture	117
NINE • The Islamic Other and SFF Responses to 9/11	130
TEN • Good, Evil and Ethics: Morality and All That Stuff	143
Conclusion: Is There an Outside to Capital?	154
Chapter Notes	165
Bibliography	173
Index	187

Acknowledgments

I would like to dedicate this book to Margaret MacIntyre, teacher, mentor and friend, without whom I never would have gotten here.

I'd also like to thank:

My wife Suzan, for more than I could ever say. Every day is a gift with you.

My parents for their love and support, my sister Kristy and brothers Peter and Timothy. Fiona Hart and Noel Barrot for general amazingness. The rest of my family for being lovely. Brody Pilbeam for tunes and everything else.

Vijay Mishra and Wendy Parkins for their supervision of the Ph.D. dissertation this book is adapted from. Murdoch University provided a much needed scholarship and place to think. Candy Robinson took her kind, hard eye to a full manuscript and it is all the better for it. My friends at Murdoch: Rachel Shave, Julia Horncastle, Pamela Martin-Lynch, Michael Noble, Kathryn Imray, Kerry George, Alison Nichol, Carley Smith. Helen Merrick for fandom talk and being great to work for at Curtin.

Pia Valeen, Brett Potter and Rick Nelson for sharing their musical talents. Jess Cadwallader for helping me through the hardest day of my life. Charlene for coming through with books at the last minute. Sarah Jaffe for being a true friend, comrade and ever stimulating conversation partner, Aishwarya Subramanian for providing the squee, Arwyn Daemyir for being a delight. My QT sisters Helen, Lisa, Elena, Katherine, and finally Chally Kacelnik for talking religion with me.

Introduction: The Return of the Religious and the Postmodern Sacred

God is no longer dead. When Friedrich Nietzsche famously declared his death toward the end of the 19th century, it seemed possible, even inevitable, that God and religion would die under the rationalist atheist onslaught. That, however, was not to be the case. Religion has survived the atheist challenge, albeit profoundly changed. Although there are a number of contributing factors, the revival of the religious in the West has occurred partly as a result of the postmodernist collapse of the scientific meta-narratives that made atheism so powerful. The postmodern critique of Enlightenment universalism has had the unexpected result of fueling the resurgence of some forms of religion. The critiques of religion made by such modern luminaries as Nietzsche, Marx and Freud have been found to be "*also* perspectives, *also* constructions or fictions of grammar" (Caputo, 2001: 59). Postmodern writers have critiqued modern universalisms as contingent, historically produced and arbitrary, but they are unsurprisingly also often aware of the contingency of their own positions. Significant too, the state-sponsored multiculturalist respect for tolerance and diversity (however limited or facile this may be in practice) has meant that atheist dismissals of religion as "superstition" have become contested without recourse to some universal truth claim.

Concurrently, the postmodern skepticism toward scientific meta-narratives has meant the growth of all sorts of pseudo-science and New

Age medical and psychological practices. The apparent return of religion and/or pseudo-science are both unexpected considering the antipathy toward traditional religion by feminism and gay liberation, as well as the Marxist roots of the liberal Left, yet it emerges in part as a way of finding more female- and queer-friendly forms of spiritual practice. In practice, this respect for diversity is arguably oriented more toward the individualized practices of New Age "spirituality" than toward Christianity or Judaism (Islam arguably represents a rather different case post–September 11); however God figures and Christian symbols are nevertheless pervasive throughout popular culture. The return of the religious has been in two forms therefore, the rise of so-called fundamentalisms in the Abrahamic faiths—Christian, Jewish, Muslim — and the rise of New Age style spirituality.[1] It is in the interplay between traditional religions and New Age-ized spirituality that the stream of spiritual popular culture that I call the postmodern sacred finds itself.

Clearly after September 11, religion has become an ever-more vital, and contested, part of culture in the United States, and indeed across the world. The aftermath of September 11, however, has not been a reassessment of what legitimately constitutes the domain of the religious or the spiritual (and these two are not necessarily one and the same), but rather, the political implications that stem from religious belief. Debates over abortion, gay marriage, terror legislation, Israeli settlements, Middle East policy and so on are inflected with religious beliefs and practices, yet these debates all take religious positions as given. The terms shift depending on context, but all have a marked tendency to take religious beliefs as unified positions, static and fixed traditions—becoming, variously, religious/secular, Christianity/Islam, Judaism/Islam, East/West, and so on. This is, I should add, a presumption not only of atheistic disdain toward religion (as outmoded, for example), but one also made by religious adherents themselves, advocating their eternal, fixed truths. What I would like to do here is complicate the matter substantially, by pointing out how secular and profane are always-already entangled within one another.

I use popular culture as an entry point, an entry point *that can presume neither belief nor unbelief* in its audiences. In particular, I shall chiefly use explicitly unreal texts, texts in the science fiction, fantasy and urban fantasy (a kind of fantastic horror hybrid) genres. All of these, I argue, refract religious symbols and ideas through a postmodernist sensibility, with a complex and fraught relationship to "real world" epistemology. Even when Christian fundamentalists and evangelicals create their own popular culture, they do not so easily escape the postmodern condition. The science fiction/fantasy text produced for entertainment and the evangelical text produced for proselytizing are very much two sides of the same coin. The first is made for profane purposes and stages disavowed belief in an overtly fictional way, while the latter states overt belief in a disavowed fictional way.

Slavoj Žižek in *First as Tragedy, Then as Farce* has pointed out that we in the West believe much more than we think we do, that our ironic attachment to processes like democracy and financial capitalism are far more profound than they might seem on the surface (2010: 69). I would like to suggest a corollary for the fundamentalist subject — that the fundamentalist subject very often believes *much less than they believe they do*. Instead, fundamentalists unknowingly fold disbelief into their avowed beliefs, inhabiting a world irrevocably disenchanted in many ways (to use Max Weber's term) by modern science, medicine, and capitalism. As theologian Catherine Keller points out, "When it comes to the leaders (of our?) communities of faith [...] they are inevitably, for good or for ill, immersed in a secular culture. Both its habitual nihilism and healthy skepticism are part of us all" (2008: 17).

So although much of the rhetoric of the so-called "return of the religious" has been anti-modern (or anti-postmodern), this is in many ways a distraction from registering the true import of the cultural shifts of the last fifty years. We live in a world of the virtual, in which media permeates everything and everyone. The media shifts over the last fifty years, from the saturation of what is sometimes called "old media" and the development and convergence of new forms of media and distribution, have produced profound social changes. The task of analyzing what these changes are and mean is as important now as twenty years ago, when David Harvey (65) charged that the task of postmodern theory was to "trace the changes in the structure of feeling" in post-industrial society.[2] Contemporary culture is always-already mediated through a reign of simulacra best described as postmodern, and this is as true for the sacred as for the profane. The question we must ask ourselves is: how is the sacred modified through its interaction with virtual, media culture? Though one could undoubtedly use other theoretical terms such as "neo-liberalism" or "globalization" to describe the present-day regime, these economic-political terms do not capture the affective and cultural connotations that the term postmodern, especially in Fredric Jameson's hands, has gathered.

Postmodernism, as Jameson once rightly pointed out (1991: 6), constitutes a force field through which "very different cultural impulses must make their way." Subjectivity in the contemporary is clearly what Scott Bakutman (5) calls a "terminal identity," one formed in front of the computer, television and mobile screens, at the intersection of various information networks. Media "news" seems unable to relay "real" events without first mediating them through popular culture references from music, films or TV; indeed the lines between journalism, entertainment and advertising are blurry at best. This is the age of the spin-off, of product placement and infotainment. Symbols slide through different mediums, from the movie screen to the television to the computer to the mobile phone to the written page to the clothing with which we brand ourselves. Perhaps the decline of postmodern *theory* in the academy may, ironically, coincide with the utter victory of the cultural logic of postmodernism itself — a global, dispersed, virtual culture.

Postmodernity is very much about the virtual and electronic shift in political and aesthetic economies, though as Gayatri Spivak (317) rightly points out, this continues to make use of modern and even pre-modern forms of capitalist organization and exploitation. Indeed, as Michael Hardt and Antonio Negri (2000: 285) argue in their mammoth *Empire*, global capitalism notably makes a shift from industrial production to the production of networks of information and symbols, what they term "informatization." Indeed, for Hardt and Negri, "immaterial labor" with its colonization of images, linguistic forms, codes, and even affect (for instance, the bodily and emotional labor of flight assistants and fast food workers), can be seen as the paradigmatic form of labor in postmodern capitalist (2004: 108). With this commodification of the symbolic, there is little that escapes the decontextualized and deterritorialized lure of the marketplace, the sacred included. The science fiction author William Gibson has noted that the bohemian dreamscapes of modernism are no more, that (almost) every gesture comes pre-commodified in contemporary virtual culture (Parsons n.pag.).

Introduction

While information tends to flow from privileged positions within the network — particularly the U.S. in the texts I am analyzing — it flows from and through other points too. Texts from India or Japan are widely available in Western countries like the U.S. or Australia, along with what is marketed as "world" cinema (that is, anything from non–English speaking countries). The metaphors employed by global capitalism — the net, the web — suggest a different kind of spatialization at work, one without a center. Despite this shift, modernist top-down distribution has not been superseded by postmodern virtuality; rather it intersects with it, and supports it. Because of this shift in production, it is now perhaps impossible to underestimate the number of texts circulating in the culture now — in bookstores (on-line and off), on terrestrial television, cable or satellite TV, DVD.

This culture institutes a new mode of engagement with the spiritual — one that disconnects the sign from its context — and as such requires a mode of critical engagement adept at reading media culture. I use popular culture as an entry point, for popular culture both produces and exemplifies this process; it is a feedback loop. Arguably the symbolic, the virtual and the real have merged, irrevocably, into one. Given that the majority of texts are produced with mass-markets in mind, using popular culture as an entry point to postmodern spirituality can presume neither belief *nor* unbelief in its audiences. In particular, I shall chiefly use explicitly unreal texts, texts in the science fiction, fantasy and fantastic (*SFF*) horror genres. While there are undoubtedly Realist religious texts, from the burning bush to Revelations there is an element of the fantastic in Western religions that overlaps powerfully with more obviously "secular" fantastic texts.

The Postmodern Sacred

So what is the postmodern sacred? The postmodern sacred is a term I have coined to describe pop-culture spirituality, a strain of spiritually inflected unreal texts that have been remarkably central to the popular culture of the last decade or so which are marked by a number of postmodern characteristics,[3] movies like *The Matrix, Harry Potter, The Da Vinci Code* and Peter Jackson's adaptations of *Lord of the Rings*, TV series like *Stargate SG-1*, *Buffy the Vampire Slayer*, *The X-Files* and *Battlestar Galactica*. It is also *The Passion of the Christ* and *Left Behind*, two texts produced for and by Christian evangelicals that nevertheless have a significant correspondence with so-called secular entertainment. Though there is undoubtedly a great distance on some levels between *Buffy*'s lesbian witch Willow and Mel Gibson's *Passion*, I argue that both are marked by the traces of a New Age–ized postmodern cultural dominant. What these disparate texts share is a virtualization of the sacred, a foregrounding of the virtual as a legitimate form of experience, a pastiche of multiple traditions and generic tropes (if unknowing in the case of the *Passion of the Christ* and *Left Behind*) and lastly a consumptive approach to that sacred.

The postmodern sacred then consists of texts that are consumed in part for their spiritual content, for an experience of the transcendent ambivalently situated on the boundary of formal religious and spiritual traditions. The postmodern sacred is everywhere once one begins to look for it, for popular culture is rife with the detritus of millennia of religious tradition. Because of the suspension of the usual rules of the "real world" in their textual universes, the postmodern sacred occurs most of all in the literary and visual genres of science fiction, horror and fantasy (what I have termed the "fantastic postmodern sacred)" and it is those that I will be drawing on for some of my textual analysis. Although they are produced for the profane purposes of capitalism and entertainment, these texts are heavily packed with spiritual signifiers cobbled together from various religions and myths. All of these, I argue, refract religious symbols and ideas through a postmodernist sensibility, with little regard for the demands of "real world" epistemology.

The postmodern sacred emerges partly out of the various New Age movements that have become an increasingly acceptable part of hegemonic Western capitalism, championed and popularized by such people as the influential Oprah Winfrey. The contemporary landscape of the sacred has been profoundly marked by New Age beliefs and practices, though it is not necessarily produced by New Age practitioners nor always constrained by their need to justify their beliefs as epistemological "truth." Instead, it functions as the textual sedimentation of many New Age beliefs and practices. It takes from the New Age both its skepticism toward traditional institutions and a constant emphasis on the Self. In his compelling work on New Age movements, sociologist Paul Heelas (1996) argues that the New Age places the *experience* of the individual at its foreground as the sole arbiter of truth and authority. He says that "truth, not surprisingly for those who see themselves as spiritual beings, must — at least first-and-foremost — come by way of one's own experience. For this alone provides direct and uncontaminated access to the spiritual realm" (21). This becomes clear when one examines the Western embrace of Buddhism, which Slavoj Žižek has argued has come to function as the ideological supplement to late capitalism. Žižek points out that the Buddhist logic of "letting go" enables its practitioners to surrender to the inevitability of postmodern capital *and* to maintain the illusion of not participating in the game of capitalistic accumulation (2001: 12).

Rather than view their practices as religion, New Agers often use the term "spirituality" to more accurately capture what they consider to be more properly "lived" spiritual experiences. This shift in terminology is important. It foregrounds the break that New Agers see themselves as having made with traditional organized religion, which they considered a set of beliefs and practices that are "not lived" in the same way. "Religion" is considered to be tied to institutions such as the Catholic and Anglican Churches, to be disconnected from if not totally opposed to real-life spiritual practice. The New Age emphasis on lived experience means then that spiritual experience can just as easily occur in a popular culture context as in a yoga class or in meditation, for popular culture is experienced as a bodily experience — sound and spectacle on small and large screen. Similarly, too, popular culture is re-experienced as a common culture, from commodified aspects like clothing, figurines, etc., to the endless quoting of beloved series.

This shift in terminology is also important in that it often discards the notion of God. Recently, this New Age shift has been articulated by religious scholar Ray Billington (2002) (although he himself seems not to link his own ideas to the New Age, drawing instead on the writings of various mystics). Billington provocatively argues that God is antithetical to spirituality, that we need to "remove the concept of God. We need mysticism without theology" (8). Billington argues instead for a holistic, largely Eastern influenced spirituality, a "religion without god" as the title of his book goes. What replaces God in the New Age is the often nebulous idea of "spirit" or "energy." These ideas derive from Buddhism, Taoism and Hinduism but are largely disconnected from their traditions. The New Age appropriation of yoga or tantric sex, for instance, frequently refigure these practices as capitalist commodities, more reliant on racialized exoticism than true mysticism.

But while the New Age ideas of spirit are undeniably important to the landscape of the postmodern sacred, it is also important to note that the figure of God has not been completely abandoned. Similarly, figures like crosses, angels and the Devil abound, as do Christian tropes of redemption and sacrifice. It is interesting to see how Christianity and the New Age begin to incorporate elements of each other — Oprah's spirituality speaks of "'karma' and 'grace' in equal parts" (Parkins 2001: 149), while evangelical Rick Warren sounds remarkably New Age when he reassures Christians anxious about their body shape that "God wants you to enjoy using the shape he has given you" (Taylor 2009: 291). Even with their oft stated antipathy toward the New Age, it is not unusual to even hear evangelical Christian fundamentalists to speak of their faith in characteristically New Age terms (as "self-fulfillment" and so on). The postmodern sacred on the whole then makes use of Eastern and Christian ideas and symbols equally, in a sometimes jarring synthesis of disparate traditions. This eclecticism is a key feature of the New Age that fictional texts have taken for themselves. It is the interplay between the Jewish and Christian traditions and New Age spirituality that marks the postmodern sacred as a peculiarly contemporary form of popular culture. Ironically in incorporating Christian symbols, postmodern texts displace its singular purchase on spiritual truth.

But while its textual appropriations do not preclude the possibilities of the postmodern sacred functioning as a complement to traditional forms of institutional religion, the postmodern sacred arguably functions as *supplemental* in the sense that Derrida (1976: 144–145) describes it in *Of Grammatology*, an addition and a replacement. Though the pop-culture texts I've referred to have been praised in some religious quarters, it should be noted that evangelicals, for instance, largely loathe these texts, for a number of reasons. The critical stance on religious institutions in such paradigmatically postmodern sacred shows as *Buffy the Vampire Slayer* understandably alienates religious conservatives, as does an often ironic take on traditional religion. The practice of witchcraft in many texts has enraged evangelicals most, making that time-honored move of confusing Wicca or Merlinesque magic with Satan worship. A recent example of this is the ludicrous banning of J. K. Rowling's *Harry Potter* series in a number of school libraries in the United States. The outright fear and hostility toward *Harry Potter* is not by any means isolated; a fear of certain kinds of texts that involve the unreal or supernatural has long propelled evangelical disdain for the fantastic. Co-existent with this, however, is the popularity of the luridly supernatural *Left Behind* series among some Christian fundamentalists. The acceptability of *Left Behind*, a creatively embroidered take on Rapture theology with clear fantastic elements, suggests that the unreal is acceptable only if given a gloss of the "real."[4] The point is, then, if pop-culture spirituality functions as a supplement to traditional religious practice, it is, in some quarters at least, a *monstrous supplement*.

This supplementary nature brings into focus another facet of consumptive-based spirituality — it more frequently affirms the rights of people who have historically been marginalized by the Christian institutions, specifically, women, people of color and queers. This marks a significant departure from much of the religious history of the West, and in particular makes the postmodern sacred diametrically opposed to the rise of the Christian Right, which has been notable for its blatant hatred of queers, constant opposition to feminism and racial equality (taken in the form of, say, opposition to Equal Opportunity legislation). While conservative religious discourse takes the form of virulent denouncements of these marginalized positions, much of the postmodern sacred is notable for its inclusiveness and availability. Texts include fairly positive strong female characters (*Buffy*, Major Carter in *Stargate*, Scully in *The X-Files*), queers (Willow, Tara and Kennedy in *Buffy*, Captain Jack in *Torchwood*), and people of color (Teal'c in *Stargate*, Morpheus in *The Matrix*). While many of these representations are still problematic — this can at times be mere lip service to the idea of equality, not to mention Orientalist exoticism or sheer tokenism — it is noteworthy nevertheless and marks a shift from Eurocentric, patriarchal and homophobic religious traditions.

This does not mean, however, that the postmodern sacred cannot be criticized on the grounds of representations of race, gender or sexuality. Here a comparison with the recent work of Wendy Brown may be instructive. In *Regulating Aversion*, Brown argues that "tolerance" discourses for racial and sexual Others circulating through various forms of culture from the governmental to the museum function as a kind of supplement for unequal citizenship. Tolerance discourses work to add to those whose inequality is enshrined in law, but also to replace the idea of legal rights. If postmodern sacred texts function as supplemental to religious and spiritual practices, then it is not hard to see how the very premise of spiritual affirmation of marginalized identities through textual consumption is dubious to say the least. For the limited egalitarianism of the market, one does not need to be ideologically acceptable to engage with pop culture, one only needs media access and the ability to consume.

Hence because it is largely textually based, the postmodern sacred is necessarily and inextricably entangled with the mechanics of postmodern global capitalism. Though it makes the egalitarian call of all pop culture, it delivers the unequal products of classed economics. It is, first and foremost, a deinstitutional and individualized form as Ulrich Beck and Elisabeth Beck-Gernsheim (26) would describe it, a "choose-your-own" approach to spirituality, though that choice is necessarily curtailed by the products available in the market. Though the postmodern sacred can be criticized for its erasure of class, I find myself in agreement with philosopher Jane Bennett when she says that the commodity might embody several "dissonant possibilities" (127). These dissonant possibilities include producing a will to consume further, erasing the social inequities involved in the production of the commodity itself, and doing ideological work that can range from feminist to fundamentalist.

Methodology — Selections, Omissions

Film theorist Melanie J. Wright points out that, "for the most part, existing literature on religion-film relationships show little or no awareness of critical approaches in film and cinema studies, although it routinely expresses interest in those fields" (8). Wright rightly outs that new work in religion and film is regularly hailed as pioneering, precisely because of a lack of ongoing dialogue between the two fields (and, despite the fact that she points out research has been undergone since the 1920s,

Introduction

it is clearly too early to speak of an intersecting field possessing any degree of scholastic stability). For religious studies, often the problem has been a set of presumptions about the text that are clearly unworkable in present day cultural studies practice — of auteurism (in particular, using the "real" world belief of writer or director to validate religious readings), of a static method of interpreting religious symbols, of suggesting that consumption of a religiously inflected text necessarily entails religious belief of itself. These approaches suggest the kinds of passive audiences critiqued by such writers as Henry Jenkins. Jenkins suggests that fans engage with texts in a far more sophisticated, participatory fashion, discarding unwanted textual elements, foregrounding others, and sometimes rewriting popular culture texts into substantially new texts.

Wright suggests that "the territory of cultural studies, into which much film studies has been shifting, offers a discursive space in which the much-touted dialogue between religious (or theological) studies and film studies is perhaps newly possible" (27). Yet, this book is not chiefly intended to be a dialogue between theology, religious studies and cultural studies, although there are of course many references to theologians and sociological and other forms of religious study. Dialogue implies, I think, a certain minimal kind of ethical responsibility, of "doing justice" to a person, or in this case, discipline. I make no pretense as to being a theologian. Instead, I situate it squarely with contemporary cultural studies practice, and more broadly, within that body of work that has come to be tagged "theory." As such, one thing you will find here is a spirited defense of the continued relevance, and indeed in my opinion the increased applicability, of theory for contemporary cultural studies scholarship. So as the title suggests, this book draws heavily on postmodern theory, in particular that of Jean Baudrillard, Fredric Jameson and Jean-François Lyotard, as well as the deconstructionist theory of Jacques Derrida. Influential, too, have been the theological probings of Mark C. Taylor, whose own work creatively reads contemporary religious culture through the lens of postmodern and post-structuralist thought.

One approach I have largely avoided is the Jungian derived mythological approach to films, exemplified by such writers as Mircea Eliade and Joseph Campbell. Mythological criticism tends to posit a recurrence of archetypes and across cultures; the kind of universalizing theory film and cultural studies have long since discarded. Joel W. Martin rightly points out that "myth critics tend to focus on our psychological quest for meaning but ignore the way meaning is always politicized and historicized" (10). Mythological criticism has been clearly problematized by the insights of post-structuralism, from the Foucaultian focus on power (knowledge is never neutral, it works to privilege some positions and marginalize others) to the Derridean disruption of the text, and culture by extension, as a seamless whole. Mythological criticism is also problematic from a feminist perspective, since reading provisional historical constructs as universal and timeless seems to deny the capacity for change that underpins feminist thought and activism. Where I have referred to the mythological approach, it is not as much as a theoretical framework as to trace the emergence of these ideas[5] into New Age spiritualities and popular culture—for example, Joseph Campbell's work influencing George Lucas's *Star Wars*.

In keeping with current cultural studies practice, the ideological work that texts I have studied perform with regard with to race, class, gender and sexuality—what are sometimes dismissed as "identity politics"—is never far from my mind. Feminist, queer, liberation and postcolonial theology have shown the way in which religion is profoundly implicated in the construction and functioning of oppressive systems, yet may also provide us with the liberatory tools out of these systems. It's important to realize that while texts perform what Annette Kuhn terms "cultural instrumentalities" (1990: 1), these are necessarily multiple given the impossibility of truly definitive readings.[6] While for reasons of economy I have tried to confine my theorizing to the religious, it is nevertheless apparent that these texts may perform other, equally important, roles in the culture.

Generically, the texts I have chosen fit largely into the genres of fantasy, science fiction and fantastic horror, what I loosely call the unreal. I began writing this book as a study of the literary genre of fantasy. What became increasingly apparent over the course of writing, however, is how artificial the separations between fantasy, science fiction and horror are, and indeed how the different media of print, television and film are reliant upon one another when one is looking at these kinds of fandoms. While it is surely laziness that leads bookstores into lumping the three together, nevertheless there is a strong interrelationship among the three — science fiction and fantasy inevitably incorporate some form of horror, while some forms of horror at least incorporate some aspects of the fantastic, say in the forms of supernatural elements or creatures like ghosts, vampires and so on. The hybrid genre "urban fantasy" (for instance Charlaine Harris's *Sookie Stackhouse* mysteries) has recently been a much hyped bridge between fantasy and horror.

Critical approaches to these genres have frequently followed Russian structuralist Tvetzan Todorov's approach. Todorov divides unreal texts into uncanny ("the supernatural explained" 41), marvelous ("the supernatural accepted" 42) and fantastic. Those texts that introduce a moment of epistemological uncertainty — is this real or not — are what Todorov calls "the fantastic." While this approach has been immensely influential, particularly in psychoanalytically influenced theories such as Rosemary Jackson's, it is not particularly useful in understanding contemporary unreal genres, for these genres induce little of the hesitation that Todorov or Jackson describe. Indeed, there is a very definite confusion of terminology between Todorov's fantastic and what is commonly understood to be fantasy. The mostly Tolkien-derived fantasy genre sold in bookstores and the subversive literature Jackson affirms have little to do with one another, the latter being more applicable to writers like Kafka. Besides this, very few unreal texts, particularly visual film and TV texts, produce the kind of ontological hesitation described. Thus Jackson and Todorov's definitions are of little use to understanding the texts I have analyzed. Where I have used the term fantastic, it has generally been to mean, broadly, those texts with supernatural or otherwise unreal elements.

More recently than Todorov and Jackson's work, Alec Worley has suggested that fantasy might be defined by the presence of magic — "magic fuels fantasy, manifesting as miracles, mysterious forces or inexplicable events, none of which can be ascribed to the laws of rationality, nature or science" (10). Any text that offers a scientific explanation, however, falls into science fiction (hereafter SF) for Worley. While interesting, this approach proves problematic, given the rapid growth of pseudo-scientific explanations in fantasy texts (often in a genetic basis), and the miraculous events that periodically occur in otherwise scientific SF (say, for instance, the unexplainable revival of Neo in the first *Matrix* movie). Worley uses the classification "science fantasy" for texts like *Star Wars* which have implausible "scientific" explanations for their events—which seems a contradiction in terms. These are unrealistic (implausible) realistic (scientific) unrealistic (not reflecting real life) texts? At this point genre analysis begins to seem a little specialized, devising distinctions that have little to do with the way texts are consumed, let alone how they function culturally.

While I think a loose definition based upon a real/unreal binary is helpful in some sense—these texts are explicitly unreal—it is as useful to describe the genres by settings and tropes (medieval-styled worlds, wizards and dragons for fantasy; spaceships and aliens for SF; vampires, werewolves and so on for fantastic horror), while urban fantasy combines supernatural elements and creatures—vampires, werewolves, demons and so on. While these texts show a remarkable generic fluidity, there are two elements that have remained constant—the presence of some fantastic or supernatural element in the text, and religious iconography and significance. Some may consider this a rather broad, perhaps over generous, definition of SFF, though I hope it is also productive.

Classically, science fiction has tended to define itself against the real, or extrapolate from it. Marxist literary critic Darko Suvin argues that SF produces what he calls "cognitive estrangement." Suvin argues that SF includes a novum, a "strange newness" (4) that allows its readers to see the world through different eyes. SF, he says, "sees the norms of any age, including its own, as unique, changeable, and therefore subject to a *cognitive* view" (7, italics original). It is this critical capacity that Suvin argues distinguishes SF from other unreal genres like fantasy and fairy tales. But as Jean Baudrillard points out, the sense of real and unreal in the postmodern world becomes tenuous (1994: 124). When reality collapses into hyper-reality, it becomes too difficult to create the cognitive effects described by Suvin. In a cultural climate of pervasive nostalgia, it becomes difficult to separate SF's critical capacity from other similarly unreal genres—SF, particularly on television, becomes a set of familiar tropes rather than a practice of extrapolation and cognitive estrangement on the real world. So rather than spend time in tedious genre nit-picking, I have preferred to take my texts on the same terms as their viewer-readers, which seem far more aligned toward a real/unreal distinction than among the three. Genre in this sense, especially given the postmodern

Introduction

crossbreeding of texts, is marked as much by a history of readings and shared audiences than by any firm sense of textual contents.

So why these genres? Wright suggests that a "small number of critics have asked how film might move from trying to depict religion to 'doing' it" (4). In my opinion, these genres provide the flexibility necessary to depart from a Realist epistemology of the "real," and are thus best equipped to deal with many of the supernatural events we find in various religious traditions. New uses of CGI (Computer Generated Imagery) in particular make unreal genres able to depict the supernatural in hyper-real detail. Importantly, too, the departure from "real" history frees some texts to be able to construct alternative versions of spiritual experience, to make a disguised comment on current practices, and to combine various traditions together in interesting ways. The recurrence of religious tropes in these texts is often overlooked in critical accounts of their success. Instead, we see unreal texts dismissed as adolescent wish fulfillment. I shall argue instead, not for the intellectual seriousness of these texts (many are indeed quite silly), but for the importance of the religious element to their cultural functioning. I argue, against the backdrop of a postmodern world both estranged from reality and desperately seeking it, that consuming religiously inflected texts is a way of accessing spiritual experience divorced from real-world practice or belief.

When it comes to the criteria I have used in selecting my texts, contemporary impact and degree of visibility in the culture has usually been key. I have chosen therefore contemporary texts that have been consumed within the postmodern media culture. Texts like *Harry Potter*, *Lord of the Rings* and *The Matrix* have grossed billions of dollars in box office, DVD purchases and spin-off material. Within those mass audiences, all also feature devoted fan bases that one could arguably call cultish. I have also chosen TV series like *The X-Files*, too, which have been wildly successful. Other texts have been chosen for their cult status—*Buffy the Vampire Slayer*, for instance, has never been quite the massive hit it promised to be, yet it lasted seven seasons and spawned a spin-off called *Angel*. But Buffy's cultural impact, both in its immensely self-referential dialogue and butt-kicking post-feminist heroine, cannot be underestimated, as the series has been widely imitated. Some of the other selections have been perhaps more capricious on my part—for instance, the series *Dead Like Me*, which I analyze in Chapter Three, was canceled after two seasons but gained a devoted following on cable reruns. In this it lacks both popularity and cultural impact; however, it nevertheless provides a generic context for the other more popular unreal texts. The consumption of science fiction, fantasy and fantastic horror fans is, not surprisingly, often confined to those genres; however one often finds little discrimination among the three — the key determining factor being their recognizable unreality. As to the production of the texts, although many of these texts feature multinational casts, writers and production teams, they are nevertheless produced and distributed as global Americanized culture, and thus many national differences have been effaced. It is arguable that both production and consumption of the postmodern sacred occur in a virtual, postmodern world which more often makes distinctions based upon genre, special effect budget (how it *looks*), and the recognizability of the stars, than with nationality of production.

Because of my criteria in choosing texts because of their popularity and visibility within the culture, the majority of these have been films or TV series. This illustrates, I think, a cultural shift toward a post-literate society. Although texts like *Harry Potter*, *Lord of the Rings* and *Twilight* begin on the page, their reception has arguably been largely mediated through their filmic adaptations. Reception of these texts is marked by a tendency to slide between mediums, so I refer too to the written texts in order to demonstrate the slippages elided by postmodern readings (but not, one hopes, by postmodern theory itself).

Despite the backdrop of September 11, the most significant absence of mediated religion from this study is Islam. I suspect this is due to the fact that many Western writers and producers continue to be basically unaware of Islamic beliefs and practices, and thus unable to appropriate symbols or tropes for textual use. Given the prohibitions on representing Muhammad, references to Islamic beliefs in such texts could be problematic due to the possibility of causing offense to Muslims (most famously, the Salman Rushdie affair, which continues to be controversial a good two decades after the publication of *The Satanic Verses*). Another practical consideration would be the ability of the largely post Jewish or Christian audience to understand Islamic references. Of course, the repressed nevertheless returns, so we still see a refracted Islam appear in the familiar Orientalist guises of the "exotic" or the racialized, monstrous, often alien, Other—most especially after September 11. While there is one chapter devoted to this, I have also noted this elsewhere when it appears, in texts like Peter Jackson's films of *Lord of the Rings*.

The Argument

Chapter One traces the broad outlines of what I call the postmodern sacred, a strain of spiritually inflected unreal texts that have been remarkably central to the popular culture of the last decade or so. I begin by discussing the traditional sacred as analyzed by such scholars of religion as Mircea Eliade and Rudolph Otto. This establishes the continuities and discontinuities the postmodern sacred has with the traditions it draws on. I analyze the postmodern turn by engaging with three of the most influential theories of postmodernity—Jean-François Lyotard's idea of the collapse of the meta-narrative, Jean Baudrillard's ideas about hyperreality and simulation, and Fredric Jameson's theory that postmodern art is a theory of pastiche. I argue that the postmodern sacred exemplifies those three theorists' work in different ways. As a consequence of the postmodern turn, it is an individualized, consumerist approach to spirituality, pastiching together religious symbols into unreal texts. Given that texts like *Lord of the Rings* and *The Matrix* have been some of the most successful of the last decade or two, this appearance of spirituality in the midst of popular culture is an important cultural development. In Chapter Two I turn to the media technologies that have made some of this shift possible—CGI and 3D. I argue that CGI collapses the boundary between real and unreal, bringing the unreal into the realm of the real-appearing spectacle. Special effects of contemporary visual culture make the supernatural a visceral experience, a process that makes the sign appear almost corporeal. Paradoxically however, that process produces a hyperreality that makes the postmodern world highly *un*real.

Chapter Three analyzes the New Age usage of what I call transcendental signifier. Modifying Jacques Derrida's notion of the transcendental signified, I argue that New Age–influenced popular culture gestures to the transcendental as a way of signifying a spirituality distinguished from the monotheistic Jewish and Christian traditions. I argue that the transcendental signifier is reliant on a New Age approach to subjectivity—one that individualizes and detraditionalizes spiritual experience. I analyze the use of the transcendental signifier in such texts as *Dead Like Me* and *The X-Files*. In Chapter Four I discuss the literalization of metaphor in the postmodern sacred—the appearance of gods, monsters, heavens and hells. I analyze corporeal gods and monsters in such texts as *Stargate SG-1*, *Futurama*, and *Constantine*. I suggest that the corporeal gods may in fact be a way of staging belief safely in a secondary world, without entailing the need for real-world belief and practice. Moving on a little from that, I discuss the polytheisms of *Buffy the Vampire Slayer* and *Xena: Warrior Princess* in Chapter Five.

In Chapter Six I discuss Dan Brown's controversial *Da Vinci Code*. Though it contains minimal supernatural elements, its preface introduces a hesitation as to its epistemological status, Todorov's "fantastic." Brown weaves together aspects of Gnosticism and the New Age into a lurid reworking of the Christian tradition and a critique of the Catholic order Opus Dei. His version of the "sacred feminine" owes more to New Age handbooks on "sacred sex" than the patina of scholarly references in his novel. Staying in relation to Catholicism, I analyze the key text of Tolkien's *Lord of the Rings*. I discuss the ways in which Tolkien's text and Peter Jackson's film adaptations imagine multiple Christ figures in the forms of Gandalf, Aragorn and Frodo. None of these, I argue, provide any definitive form of closure or redemption, with Sauron's defeat and the disappearance of the Elves leaving only the melancholic coming of the Age of Men. Instead, in their multiplicity and ambiguity, they provide an analog for the "weak force" of the postmodern God.

In Chapter Eight I discuss several forms of evangelical pop culture made for explicit religious pedagogical purposes—the Mel Gibson–directed *Passion of the Christ* and the *Left Behind* series. I argue that these mix "popular entertainment" with religious messaging to further a radical neoliberal rightwing agenda but are always haunted by the possibility of their failure, of being aestheticized and consumed solely for pleasure without religious conversion. I then turn to the ostensibly secular *Twilight* series, which incorporates abstinence-only and pro-abortion motifs into its supernatural romance. I argue the series' conception of sexuality is a form of the death drive, in which Bella's desire for sex becomes entangled with her desire for death.

Introduction

In Chapter Nine, I discuss the responses to September 11 presented by *Stargate SG-1* and *Battlestar Galactica,* in which the War on Terror is estranged and extrapolated through the guise of the alien Other. In the rebooted *Battlestar Galactica*, the Cylons now appear perfectly human — the terrorist living among us, undetectable. As the series progresses into its third series however, the metaphor switches, with the humans becoming, metaphorically, Iraqi insurgents under a U.S.–coded Cylon occupation. In Chapter Ten, I argue that while the postmodern sacred appears to present heroic narratives that would confirm the "return of the real" argument, these are often diffused into the pleasures of postmodern textuality. I discuss the anti-postmodern heroes of *The Matrix* and *Harry Potter* and their morality in response to unjust systems—capitalism and a racist authoritarian state, respectively. How heroes conduct themselves in the face of oppression is a question with significant ethical and religious as well as political implications.

In summary, I will argue that the postmodern sacred is a paradoxical attempt at accessing spirituality, using the symbols contained in explicitly unreal texts to gain a secondhand experience of transcendence and belief. This second-hand experience displaces the need for belief or real-world practice into a textual world, requiring little of its consumers. While they seem to suggest a desire for a magical world outside of capitalism, the wonder produced by these texts, however, is only temporary; eventually the consumer must return again to purchase another text.

CHAPTER ONE

The Postmodern Sacred

The Postmodern

The term *postmodern* itself has a surprisingly long history, dating back as Perry Anderson notes, to Spanish writers in the 1930s (4). Its adoption in Anglophonic criticism therefore has been somewhat belated, growing in currency from the 1950s until its full blooming as a commonplace "school" of critical thought in the 1980s (if something so diverse may be called that). Postmodern thought has influenced a wide range of theorists in fields as diverse as architecture, economics,[1] critical geography[2] and literary theory.[3] Understandably, given its growth as a theoretical buzzword, there has been a growing backlash to the term. A number of contemporary theorists have discounted postmodern theory over the last few years, especially after September 11—for example, Terry Eagleton's *After Theory* (2004), much of Slavoj Žižek's recent work (2001), a collection entitled *After Postmodernism* (Lopez and Potter 2004) promoting "critical realism" and so on. Popularly, the deaths of Jacques Derrida and Jean Baudrillard provided a pretext for the media to ponder the death of postmodernism. But this is perhaps more indicative of an academy hungry for new theory than of any profound cultural shift. While other alternative terms such as *globalization* and *neo-liberalism* describe the economic elements of the contemporary world, these do not quite capture the same cultural and aesthetic dimensions. So one needs to weigh seriously the question of what realism exists now, and *how* have we truly moved past postmodernism? I do not believe the West has shifted in any significant way beyond the postmodern condition. If anything, the tendencies described in postmodern theory from the 1980s onward have only increased, and this has had a profound impact on the way the sacred is manifested in the culture.

So what is it that makes the postmodern sacred postmodern? My argument is therefore that the texts I analyze are produced under the cultural conditions of postmodernity and as such have a number of postmodern facets. Inevitably the postmodern sacred has continuities with traditional forms of the sacred as described by such religious scholars as Mircea Eliade, but just as surely it has significant differences. In the postmodern sacred, *the postmodern acts as a qualifier on the sacred*. This does not merely mean that this will be an investigation into how sacred might appear in this postmodern world, though it is that, but that the postmodern sacred is notable for a number of postmodern characteristics. The work of three of the most prominent postmodern theorists — Jean-François Lyotard, Jean Baudrillard and Fredric Jameson — are all instructive in conceptualizing the postmodern as it appears in the postmodern sacred.

The first key facet of the postmodern sacred is that it is arises out of a crisis of "grand" or meta-narratives. Jean-François Lyotard famously outlined the thesis in *The Postmodern Condition* (1984) that postmodern culture is marked by skepticism toward the Enlightenment grand narratives of science, rationality and so on. For Lyotard, postmodernism is in some ways about a crisis of belief. This is manifested by the "end of" debates that the academy has waged for some time — the end of history the author, God, theory and so on. There is often the sense in postmodernism that nothing can be relied on as true for very long. For instance, the crisis of belief in the State will often manifest itself in the form of a fantasmatic "conspiracy theory" in which the public face of the State is suggested to be façade run to cover up the traces of a hidden cabal running the world for their own nefarious purposes. The television series *The X-Files* ran with this premise — "The truth is out there" — and proved a barometer of the American public's distrust in its government, both real and as a pleasurable fantasy, as well as a measure of fin de siècle tension before the year 2000. The fact that the State has been publicly proven to have been untruthful (say for instance Watergate, Bill Clinton's economical use of the truth, the imaginary Weapons of Mass Destruction with which the Bush government justified the Iraq war) only adds fuel to the conspiracy theory fire, though I find myself in agreement with

Žižek when he argues that paranoia exists regardless of whether the subject of paranoia actually exists or not.

It should be fairly apparent what the postmodern disbelief in "grand" narratives would mean for religious narratives. The absence of belief in meta-narratives that Lyotard describes means that such a meta-narrative as the God of the traditional religions is treated with skepticism. Similarly, however, the death of the Enlightenment narratives of Science and Reason has meant that atheism too has been robbed of its cultural power. The postmodern sacred, then, is in an age of cultural agnosticism, in which "spirit" provides a useful medium between the two unsustainable poles of belief and total unbelief. "Spirit" suggests that we are on the terrain of the New Age, of Oprah and pop psychology, neither willing to commit to a meta-narrative of theology nor to entirely discard the idea of God (or Gods, or Goddesses). This is a point made strongly by postmodern a/theologian Mark C. Taylor (1984) — a large, growing group of people find themselves "suspended between the loss of old certainties and the discovery of new beliefs, these people constantly live on the border that joins and separates belief and unbelief" (5). It should not be surprising, therefore, that at the very least, the postmodern sacred is willing to *play* with the sacred, albeit situated at a safe distance in a secondary textual world often divorced from the need for real-world commitment and belief.[4]

While Lyotard's argument suggests that faith in rationalist science has faded, it is done so in an interesting fashion in the postmodern sacred. Far from simply disputing rationalism, the postmodern sacred seems to use it in order to confirm that the supernatural can exist alongside rationalism. The constant references to those magical things that live on the outskirts of our consciousness — Greek gods, fairy tales, mythic monsters and so on — introduce culturally familiar elements into the text, while the use of some kind of rationalism helps those improbable things re-enter the realm of the possible. The postmodern thus disrupts a modern rationalist narrative, emerging through it into a form of post-rationalism more akin to a religious sublime. As Vijay Mishra points out:

> Found in the postmodern is precisely an interest in the category of the sublime as a principle through which the "unpresentable" may be countenanced. Other discourses have used the word "numinous,"

> "mystical," "other-worldly," *mysterium tremendum*," even "hierophany," and "paranormal" to speak of the religious experience. Our age, in an uncanny echo of an earlier theorization (a theorization which dealt, in the main, with aesthetic matters) returns to the category of the sublime and forces us to think the religious sublime differently [n.pag.].

The postmodern sacred thus incorporates irrationalist forms of belief into rationalism — and in doing so collapses the border between the two, producing not a meta-narrative of scientific rationalism but an interplay between scientific and pseudo-scientific New Age language games.

One crisis of the postmodern meta-narrative is the very question of reality, and it is this point that is taken up by Jean Baudrillard (1995). Baudrillard argues that because of the immense saturation of media and the predominance of the sign, the distinction between real and not real has collapsed into what he calls the "hyper-real." What this means for the postmodern sacred is that the distinction has disintegrated between "real" religiosity (as practiced by the traditional sacred) and "fake" simulation in popular culture texts. While arguably Baudrillard overstates his case in some ways — people continue to make rather urgent distinctions between the real and the unreal — it is nevertheless clear that the relationship between the sign and the real-world referent has become fraught. What this means is that representation itself has become considered real, while our experiences of the real are mediated through textual representation, especially visual representation in advertising, television, movies and music videos.

Due to the fact that it is immersed in media, the postmodern sacred is inevitably a simulacra as Baudrillard would describe it. It is neither a real nor fake representation, it is instead the textual simulation of religious traditions. The postmodern sacred is, then, hyperreal, in that its representations seem *more real than religious tradition itself*. Part of this hyperreality is possibly due to the fact that through tools like CGI, texts of the postmodern sacred are able to graphically represent the spiritual as though it were literally real. The fact that the sacred is otherworldly necessarily means that it is necessary to suspend the "real-world" conditions of physics, etc., in order to represent the sacred, yet the postmodern sacred is able to present this unreality with far greater regularity and in greater hyperreal detail than the visual traditions of the world's religions. Ironically, the virtual has a kind of concreteness that the real sometimes lacks.

Baudrillard himself points out that the prohibition on representing the holy for religious fundamentalists stems from the fear that representation and its inevitably simulacral nature will ultimately point to the non existence of "real-world" religious referents like God, Allah, Jehovah, Muhammad or Buddha (4). The Danish cartoon controversy[5] of 2004 stemmed not just from the troubling racialization and absolute conflation between Muslim, terrorist and Muhammad but more basically from the violation of a generally accepted Muslim prohibition on representation of the Prophet. Even when directed at the faithful, however, the postmodern sacred has no such prohibitions on religious representation. Indeed, simulation is the very precondition for the postmodern sacred's occurrence. Religion must be simulated, must be aestheticized and break free of its contexts in order to be used and recontextualized as a textual signifier. It is precisely the simulacral nature of the postmodern sacred that makes it that monstrous supplement to traditional religious practice.

While Baurdillard's theories of the postmodern focus on the simulation of politics, recreation and indeed everyday life, Fredric Jameson (1991) has another take on postmodernism more focused on the postmodern text itself. He argues that one of the key features of postmodernism is its reduction to the play of surface aesthetics. In one of his most famous passages, he suggests that "the emergence of a new kind of flatness of depthlessness, a new kind of superficiality in the most literal sense [is] perhaps the supreme formal feature of all the postmodernisms" (5). Jameson argues that postmodern texts are marked by what he calls *pastiche*, the suturing together of texts from other texts. Pastiche, as a textual strategy, sees the postmodern text borrowing from other texts. It's easy to see how pastiche can fit in with Baudrillard's theory of simulation, for pastiche is the textual *result* of the contemporary disconnection between sign and referent. Pastiche asserts that there is nothing but the play of signs from which to assemble texts; the notion of a real world "outside" the text begins to retreat.

The point is, that postmodernism's textual games are not merely limited to the fictional, that they are in dialogue with real-world religious traditions. As I have argued, the postmodern sacred is entangled within

New Age spiritualities, and arguably much of its vocabulary is the language of the New Age, yet it also draws on a number of different, sometimes contradictory traditions and the world's great religious traditions as well — Christianity, Judaism, Hinduism, and especially Buddhism. What distinguishes the postmodern sacred from the New Age, however, is that it will take epistemological and ontological claims about the truth of the world, disconnect them from their context, and pastiche them together to form fictional texts. What we have, in a sense, is modern-day myth, which as Darko Suvin (2000: 216) argues is religion that one has ceased to believe in. The postmodern sacred's textual strategy of pastiching together signifiers from disparate sources makes it problematic for traditional forms of the sacred intent on maintaining the "purity" of the sacred traditions. It has instead a relativizing effect on the spiritual signifiers, presenting multiple versions of the sacred, or often even presenting a true "hidden" path to the sacred outside of the institutions that regulate religious practice. That postmodern skepticism toward metanarrative claims opens up many different avenues for its symbolic appropriation, while retaining an inability to ground itself in any one spiritual tradition.

The Traditional Sacred

It is worth comparing this postmodern sacred with more traditional forms of the sacred. Comparative religion scholar Mircea Eliade's (1959) concept of the hierophany proves especially useful in distinguishing the postmodern sacred from the traditional. The hierophany, as Eliade defines the term, is when "*something sacred shows itself to us*" (11). The hierophany stands out from the rest of the world in that it announces itself as sacred. It manifests itself, it is a revelation. The question of how to distinguish the sacred from the profane is thus answered by the hierophany, for the hierophany's "announcement" of itself *as sacred* makes the question meaningless. The hierophany is self-evidently sacred. This tautological definition is arguably insufficient for any skeptical, let alone atheistic, approach to the sacred. Suffice it to say that the hierophany is understood as *sui generis* in Eliade, it cannot be understood in any other terms.

One — The Postmodern Sacred

On a more sustained engagement with Eliade's work, we find that the hierophany works to construct a sacred/profane divide that reappears even more strongly than at first glance, since the split between "the sacred and profane is often expressed by the opposition between *real* and *unreal* or pseudoreal" (13). One way that opposition is expressed in Eliade's work is in his conceptualization of sacred space. Most fundamentally, manifestations of the sacred dramatize a cosmological act of creation, testifying to the presence of gods and otherworldly presences. Eliade says, "Every world is the work of the gods, for it was either created directly by the gods or was consecrated, hence cosmicized, by men [*sic*] ritually reactualizing the paradigmatic act of Creation" (64).

Though at first glance this seems to blur the lines of sacred and profane (or even entirely erase the profane), one finds on closer inspection that split is being made at the metaphysical level of Being. Eliade argues powerfully that religion not only organizes space into sacred and not-sacred but translates the sacred into absolute being and the profane into non-being. He says:

> There is [...] a sacred space, and hence a strong significant space; there are other spaces that are not sacred and so are without structure or consistency, amorphous.[...] For religious man, this spatial nonhomogeneity finds expression in the experience of an opposition between space that is sacred — the only *real* and *real-ly* existing space — and all other space, the formless expanse surrounding it [20].

Eliade argues that the manifestation of sacred space (the hierophany) ontologically founds the world, creating an absolute fixed point of reality. He points out that this sacred space is conceptualized as the "Centre of the World," for example Jerusalem is the center of the world in Christian tradition due to its associations with Christ and indeed the preexisting Hebrew tradition of it as a Holy City. This symbolism of the Centre of the World is invoked in many disparate ways, though, in the formation of not only obviously religious spaces like temples, (holy) cities and countries, but in the dwellings where people live — "every religious man places himself at the Centre of the World [...] as close as possible to the opening that ensures him communication with the gods" (64). The spatialization of the Sacred presents the illusory promise of absolute ontological foundation, a fixity of being.

Conversely, then, profane space appears to the religious to represent partial or even absolute non-being. It is Chaos, unknowable, terrifying. That opposition noticeably shows how the sacred/profane works not just to secure the space of the sacred, but as a projection of Otherness elsewhere, where everything outside the bounds of the sacred cannot be said to even properly exist. It's easy to see how problematic this opposition can be, meaning at the very least that profane space must be ritually "sanctified," and at worst that those who live *in that* profane space are dehumanized and denied the grounds of very existence.

So, Eliade's point about hierophany proves especially useful in distinguishing the postmodern sacred from the traditional. The modern and premodern sacred are understood as hierophany, fragments of absolute spirit that are the link to the otherworldly. This hierophanic relationship is an unmediated link between the believer and the sacred; the hierophany is a part of the whole revealed to the community of believers (in whatever tradition one looks at). In the postmodern sacred, however, there is no fragment of the whole, for indeed there is no hierophany in the sense that Eliade describes. The postmodern sacred is most clearly differentiated from Eliade's hierophanies because it does not (usually) announce itself *as* sacred. Indeed if pressed it would claim the profane — while collapsing the distinction between a sacred and profane itself. While many of the texts I will analyze as part of the postmodern sacred have content that mimics this traditional sacred, the *production* of the postmodern sacred most clearly is not a manifestation of a wholly different order — it is explicitly made primarily for the purposes of capitalistic consumption.

Since the postmodern sacred posits itself as wholly profane, it does not necessarily have the use value or ontological foundation which characterizes the traditional sacred. While Eliade's conception has been critiqued as problematically ahistorical and acultural, I would also argue that the postmodern sacred represents a profound rupture in that unified narrative. The postmodern death of the meta-narrative has meant that the postmodern is fundamentally different in not looking to a truth referent in which to ground its practices. The postmodern sacred remains ambivalent to the possibility of truth, any truth, and is instead a belief by proxy. It is characteristically postmodern in that it is virtual, pastiched together from the fragments of spiritual traditions that *do* have that ontological foundation. The postmodern sacred has a certain kind of belief, albeit sometimes ambivalent, that it is always diffused and mediated *through* texts. Writing about fantasy fiction, Darko Suvin (2000) points out that this kind of textual appropriation is "not thinkable before overriding mythological or religious belief suffers an epochal political breakdown, as a consequence of which some of its aspects and elements become available for fictional manipulation" (216). What this means, then, is that the postmodern sacred is only made possible by the disruption of religious meta-narratives that problematize straightforward belief.

Such classical notions of ontology as Eliade's become profoundly irrelevant when we consider the argument of Zygmunt Bauman (1997), for instance, who argues that postmodern identities are formed under a pleasure-seeking role. Of course, this shift to pleasure seeking, however, is not necessarily tied to the sacred, but it does maintain a relation to it. Bauman points out that "postmodern cultural pressures, while intensifying the search for 'peak-experiences,' have at the same time uncoupled it from religion-prone interests and concerns, privatized it, and cast mainly non-religious institutions in the role of purveyors of relevant services" (180). Paraphrasing Max Weber, Bauman calls this process "this worldly ecstasy" and argues that the postmodern version "abolish[es] the concept of 'non-peakers' altogether and declare[s] peak-experience a duty and realistic prospect for everybody" (180). He finds peak-experience to have been separated from "religion-inspired practices of self-denial and withdrawal from worldly attractions" (180). Postmodern textual producers deploy "peak-experience" to stimulate consumer desire, a peak suggested to increase in intensity and fulfillment, with the promise of complete and total ecstasy always just over the horizon.

But while Bauman maintains a distinction between traditional forms of religious peak-experience (say, the ecstasies of saints or whirling dervishes) and postmodern this-worldly ecstasy, the postmodern sacred maintains no such boundaries. As I have argued, the postmodern sacred contains both consumerist and non-consumerist implications—cognitively dissonant responses to the same cultural phenomena. The postmodern sacred is, above all, a corporeal experience, for popular culture is first and foremost physical—packed with sound and spectacle. As Tom Beaudoin (1998: 73) points out, "experience is key" for contemporary spirituality and it is this individualization of faith that underlines the postmodern sacred. In its focus on the visceral effects of popular culture, the postmodern sacred not only elides the distinction between sacred and profane; it relies on it, it revels in it. In my next chapter, I will move on to discussing the specific filmic and textual techniques by which the postmodern sacred collapses this boundary, and with it the boundaries between real and fictive, Christian and pagan.

CHAPTER TWO

Virtual Religion: Techniques of the Postmodern Sacred

God has become a sign; or, perhaps more precisely, the [...] sign has become God."
Taylor, 1993: 170

Jean Baudrillard's work compellingly argues that the camera in postmodernism flattens out the culture to a mere simulation. Fredric Jameson, too, points out that "the emergence of a new kind of flatness or depthlessness [is] perhaps the supreme formal feature of all the postmodernisms" (1991: 9). It is arguable that in many ways *the postmodern world has lost the ability to think metaphorically*. Recall the characteristic tic of TV chef Jamie Oliver ("the Naked Chef"), who describes practically everything as "literally," even though he is *already* discussing literal objects and subjects (e.g., you put it in the oven and it is literally 5 minutes before it's done). Indeed, it is unsurprising that the capacity for metaphor has been lost in a media which has seen the extraordinary boom of "reality" TV in the last decade or so. This is not to suggest that the "real" has returned in postmodernity, rather, that it is precisely in this extraordinary fidelity to the "real" that a hyperreality is introduced that paradoxically evaporates the real. As Baudrillard argues, "The collapse of reality into hyperrealism [occurs] in the minute duplication of the real" (1983: 141).

But while Baudrillard and Jameson trace this cultural movement much earlier, it is only through a number of digital technologies that this has truly flourished. Digital technologies like Photoshop "retouching" of photographs, Autotune pitch-correction in music illustrate this on a small scale. Both artificially remove the "blemishes" of the real, for by changing a person's appearance in retouching, and adjusting a singer's pitch to be more in tune with Autotune, the same end product is achieved—a hyperreal simulation of the real, smoothed out of the element of unpredictability that characterizes the human.

But it is with the judicious use of CGI technology that this has truly flourished on film, for with the rapid embrace of CGI in visual culture has arguably accelerated postmodern hyperreality. While bluescreens has been used since the 1950s, advances in CGI special effects have most notably transformed film and TV in the last several decades, with science fiction at the forefront of these innovations. George Lucas's *Star Wars* and the Wachowskis' *The Matrix* trilogies have been particularly influential in the development of new techniques. CGI has permeated the film industry; a great many contemporary films are filmed in front of blue screens and then have minor things like setting and even character added in post-production. Famously, George Lucas added the widely despised Jar Jar Binks CGI character in *Star Wars: The Phantom Menace*, an idea repeated in the form of the house-elf Dobby in the film version of *Harry Potter and the Chamber of Secrets* and taken to its logical conclusion in the seamless 12-foot-tall blue Na'vi aliens in James Cameron's *Avatar*. Cameron previously had employed CGI in *Titanic* to add passengers and ocean to the background. Importantly too, if less obviously, CGI has spread to other filmic techniques like the way the color palette is adjusted frame-by-frame in post-production — intensely green in the case of Peter Jackson's *Lord of the Rings*—and this is hardly confined to the explicitly unreal genres of science fiction and fantasy. And although often the domain of the expensive big budget films, many of these film techniques have spread to TV. *Babylon 5* was the first series in the United States to make use of CGI as its primary form of special effects in the early 90s. As well as the obvious use of CGI special effects for "unreal" elements (spaceships, monsters), many shows now employ CGI as a money- and time-saving technique, using CGI to simulate city streets, mountains, cars, and so on.

As well as CGI, 3D technology has made a strong return to screens. Once a 1950s gimmick, 3D has been revived by movie producers looking to secure audiences against the competition of "illegal" downloading and online streaming. Explicitly signaled in this turn is the desire for a size of spectacle unable to be reproduced at home or on mobile devices, less a text on literary terms (dialogue, plotting) than an immersive environment to be inhabited by the viewer. Film becomes ever more a vehicle to deliver high-quality sound and jaw-dropping visuals, with some cinemas even being equipped to deliver smells. James Cameron's *Avatar*, of course, has been the primary popularizer of the technology, with its stunning 3D landscapes of the alien world Pandora, while drawing thematically on New Age tropes from the Hindu referencing Na'vi aliens to the sacred Earth Mother Eywa.

Implications of Digital Technology

Quite clearly, one formal aspect that all of the visual texts of the postmodern sacred have in common is a reliance on special effects. CGI makes unreal texts, traditionally known for their unconvincing settings and models, appear far more "realistic." Alec Worley suggests that "CGI affects a realistic texture often indistinguishable from photographed reality, allowing the physical world the mutability of a cartoon" (80). CGI means that texts can depict the supernatural abilities of Gods and monsters, or the demonic imagery of hell or supernatural whites of heaven more convincingly or at least with more "realistic" detail. Alien or futuristic worlds, spaceships, magic spells, and all the rest are rendered spectacularly in CGI.

But while Baudrillard's version of hyperreality seems to make a certain kind of sense with regard to realistic texts—displacing reality through an extraordinary detailed simulacra—what effect could it have for texts that are explicitly unreal? Paradoxically, I think hyperreality makes unreal texts appear more "real" (fleshing out their details far more fully)—and in doing so confirms their own hyperreality. Unreal texts are no longer in opposition to a reality principle; the real/unreal opposition has become collapsed. What CGI means, therefore, is that texts are made very obviously simulacra; there is no real-world equivalent for the worlds these texts create, whether they are set in the "real world" or not. As well as the obvious postmodernist implications, what CGI means for the postmodern sacred is that texts are able to depict supernatural events in spectacular, hyperreal detail. The visual impact of the texts is inextricably tied with their use of special effects; it is part of what makes audiences affectively respond. Annette Kuhn suggests that

> in science fiction cinema, spectacle can become an end in itself: spectacular visual effects and sounds temporarily interrupt the flow of the narrative, inviting the spectator to contemplate, with awe and wonder the vastness of deep space or the technological miracles of future societies [1990: 7].

Now, this might seem to suggest a kind of pop sublime, but it is hardly psychological in the sense that the Romantics would assume. This is the sublime as mere spectacle, immediate and ultimately forgettable. It is arguable that this is one way, perhaps the key way, that the postmodern sacred "does" religion (instead of merely citing it), as an ecstatic, peak experience for its audience. But capitalist re-enchantment is necessarily a temporally limited one; it has the built-in obsolescence required for repeated consumption. The supernatural then becomes not a matter for imagination, or as something that cannot be quite grasped, it becomes very obviously, one more sign on the screen along with the setting and characters. The special effect, then, becomes supernatural in some sense; it makes the supernatural appear *real*.

Derrida points out that Christianity has a certain structural predisposition toward creating the religious image as concrete onscreen:

> During a Christian mass [...] the thing itself, the event takes place in front of the camera: communion, the coming of real presence, the Eucharist in a certain sense, even the miracles (miracles are produced on American television) — the thing actually takes place "live" *as* a religious event, *as* a sacred event. In other religions religion is *spoken about*, but the sacred event itself does not take place in the very flesh of those who present themselves before the camera [2001: 58].

It is for this reason that he considers Christianity to be the preeminently media-friendly religion, for it mediatizes itself from the beginning — a play between real and unreal, the unreal-becoming-real, the real-becoming-unreal. It is this movement that media stages in another way.

But this movement may itself become blocked — eventually, onscreen the supernatural may be just another special effect. What is awe-inducing one year becomes passé the next as the technology advances — and then there is the fact that at a certain limit spectacle becomes numbing rather than wondrous (for instance, the 20-minute-long freeway chase in *The Matrix Reloaded*). Textual producers thus have to continually up the ante, creating ever more epic sets and effects in an effort to reproduce the same awe. The recent reemergence of 3D films responds to this need, to overwhelm the audience experientially in ways that are not possible with the home theater experience. So, although hyperreality as described by Baudrillard clearly precedes CGI, CGI accelerates the cultural shift in postmodern approaches to the text. And by making the unreal appear *as* real, it expands the palette of the hyperreal.

Hell Is a Place on Earth

The movie *Constantine* exemplifies the tendency of postmodern texts to literalize metaphorical concepts, combining with the CGI techniques to produce a "place" "beyond" the everyday. Heaven, Hell, purgatory, even God, have always been ideas as much as literal places. At times, as *Constantine* shows, this seems a return to a medieval Christianity, snipping off half-remembered fragments of Roman Catholic theology to pastiche a thoroughly postmodern collage. The movie stars *The Matrix*'s Keanu Reeves, and is an interesting, if flawed, text that moves between cosmic "dimensions." Adapted to film from the comic book *Hellrazer*, *Constantine* is indicative of a supernatural comic book approach to the afterlife (see also *Hellboy*), giving a visual corporeality to heaven, hell, and purgatory. The titular character John Constantine is a supernatural detective, unable to enter heaven because of his own suicide. Constantine attempts to buy his way into heaven by killing as many demon "half-breeds" that crossover into the human dimension as possible. The movie states heaven and hell as literal places, dimensions of existence that both overlap with the human and that exist outside of it.

Like the TV series *Angel*, with which it shares some striking similarities, *Constantine*'s real-world setting is Los Angeles, the City of Angels. Interestingly, *Constantine* imagines hell as a version of a Los Angeles freeway. In the DVD extras for the film, the director points out the hell scenes were conceived as a perpetual version of the first seconds after a nuclear explosion, effectively conjured with judicious use of CGI.

Hell, then, could be considered a post-apocalyptic version of Los Angeles, or at the very least a Los Angeles in decay. In making Los Angeles hell, *Constantine* plays with some established conventions of religious visual texts. Throughout its history Los Angeles has been conceived as both heaven and hell, a place of eternal sunshine and apocalyptic disaster (especially in the form of earthquakes), the place where stars are born and dreams are shattered, and so on.

Naming is of some significance in *Constantine*, in suitably postmodern ways. We have of course the setting in Los Angeles, and to hammer the point home, John's client/love interest is called Angela (that is, *Angel*a). John's name, too, has religious connotations, recalling both Constantine and, in his initials, Jesus (JC). The Jesus coding is most striking in the scene in which John ascends to heaven, arms stretched out like an inverted Christ on the cross. This occurs after John's decision to sacrifice himself in order to secure Isobel's (Angela's dead sister) place in heaven. More interesting than the Jesus coding, which recurs in a number of other texts in the postmodern sacred, is the Constantine reference. Constantine, of course, was the Roman emperor who converted to Christianity in 312 and legalized Christianity the following year, in doing so ultimately prompting Christianity's move from marginal cult to state-sponsored religion. Yet John Constantine, who is written more in the mold of a hard-boiled noir character, is hardly helping to convert the world. Born with the powers to see the supernatural world, he is aware of the two worlds, yet he hardly believes. "God is a kid with an ant-farm," he says cynically. It's arguable then that the naming of *Constantine* is little more than a postmodern affectation, meant to signal a vague "religiousness" specifically linked to the Roman Catholicism it draws upon, but without any particular metaphorical resonance.

One influential text in this literalizing of metaphor has been *Buffy the Vampire Slayer*. Post-*Buffy*, fantastic texts tend to label a great many monsters as "demons" (see, for instance, *Charmed*) and to refer to hell and heaven "dimensions." Although it is hardly original in this, *Buffy* (and its spin-off, *Angel*) has certainly popularized the literal hells. With its TV budget, unlike *Constantine*, *Buffy* never manages to show us hell — though it depicts its threshold with various CGI created vortexes and electrical storms. Nevertheless, *Buffy* refers frequently to heaven and hell. For instance, Buffy sends Angel to hell at the end of the second sea-

Two — Virtual Religion

son, and goes to a heaven dimension after dying in "The Gift" (5.22). The high school setting itself is built over the literal boundary between Earth and hell ("The Hellmouth" as the show calls it). The heaven and hell "dimensions" show how *Buffy* and *Angel* combine Christian and New Age conceptions of the afterlife — the term "dimensions" is clearly New Age influenced.

The abiding metaphor of *Buffy the Vampire Slayer* reproduces the literality of the filmic techniques through which it is produced. *Buffy's* main conceit is that high school really *is* hell — your boyfriend really does turn into another person after you have sex ("Innocence" 2.13), mean kids really do hunt in packs ("The Pack" 1.06), the lunch lady really is trying to poison the students ("Earshot" 3.18), and so on. Bizarrely then, even as it entirely bends the idea of the real, this literality embodies a curiously naïve approach to the text, similar in some ways to literalist fundamentalisms. Literalist Christian fundamentalism emerges precisely at a time that the mainstream Christian denominations have made their religions metaphorical. "Hell is a state of mind," declared John Paul II. The cliché of the Anglican clergyman who doesn't actually believe in the specifics of the Virgin Birth and so on is certainly not entirely unfounded.

But this literality of place and supernatural creatures is, interestingly, not really at odds with the transcendental signifier of "spirit" that informs the New Age. The transcendental signifier is a way of gesturing "beyond" this existence; it is a signifier largely emptied of content. The New Age's perennialist habit of seeing disparate traditions as drawing on the same wisdom tends to disconnect signifiers from their ideological context. And as I have argued, the postmodern sacred occurs at the meeting point of New Age and Christianity (and less frequently drawing on Judaism and Islam), so inevitably different texts are bound to combine these aspects in different ways. It's not that surprising that the more Christian text of *Constantine* imagines the afterlife in far more corporeal terms than New Age-y texts gesturing to the transcendent. Significant too is the fact that the transcendental signifier is often gesturing toward an amorphous individualized transcendent — even those that are basically versions of the Christian heaven (modified, one imagines, to be more inclusive of marginalized groups, less judgmental and so forth). These rather more corporeal images however are more oriented toward the Christian hell than heaven. Edward J. Ingebretson has argued in *Maps of Heaven, Maps of Hell* that American Christian writers have often used the imagery of hell to chide the faithful toward the straight and narrow. Even without that moral purpose, it's not surprising that the hell appears rather more fleshed out in the postmodern sacred than the vague gestures toward heaven, since it has rather more of a cultural imaginary to draw on. This interplay between Christianity and the New Age plays itself out in numerous ways, for instance, sometimes in apocalyptic forms. Apocalypse is a recurrent trope throughout Western culture and is hardly restricted to religious belief — nuclear, environmental and viral civilization-destroying apocalypses[1] have all featured heavily in the recent imagination.

The Corporeal Image

This move toward the literal representation of the supernatural has inevitable philosophical consequences. In an interview with the formidable triangle of John D. Caputo, Kevin Hart and Yvonne Sherwood, Jacques Derrida asks a number of pertinent questions which can be adapted to the representation of God(s) and the supernatural. He says:

> What are we doing when we name God? What are the limits of this naming? Now we know that in many Abrahamic traditions God is nameless, beyond the name. In Jewish traditions, God is the empty place, beyond any name. But we name the nameless. We name what is nameless. And when we name "what is not," what is or is not nameless, what do we do? [Caputo et al. 2005: 37].

Derrida is, of course, talking here in a theological sense, concerned with the possibility of talking of God in a theological or philosophical sense, the possibility of God-as-truth. However, his questions illuminate a paradox of the postmodern sacred, the gap between the transcendental signifier and the frequent corporeal representation of Gods. To modify Derrida's question into a pop-culture context, what do we do when we name *and show* what is not?

What is or is not nameless is often also a question of what is or is not corporeal, the real-world referent to which the sign refers. Corporeality is, after all, often the precondition through which objects are presumed to exist (and hence become nameable). If one can see or touch a thing then it exists; if not, then one must see its effects (as with the wind). Typically theologians and lay people alike have used the second reasoning by which to "prove" God's existence, by pointing to his effect on the natural world, history and people. Of course, that proof lies largely in the eye of the beholder — the true believer might see God's wrathful punishment in the tragedy of Hurricane Katrina, while the skeptic might see a more prosaic combination of natural weather phenomena and human neglect.

Given that the literal presence of Gods (and their counterbalance monsters) has not been definitively proven to exist in the same way that, say, religious monuments dedicated to those Gods can be said to exist, it is arguable that Gods remain a construct of language and image. While theorists like Foucault, Derrida and Butler have in various ways theorized the textuality of the "real world," Gods remain as pure text — Baudrillardian simulations without a real-world referent. As Derrida's concept of the transcendental signified suggests, much of religious tradition can be defined only by what it is not, the world of the profane and the corporeal. However, as Derrida argues regarding negative theology, that evacuation of the knowable corporeal nevertheless grounds itself in a transcendental referent, a restatement of a real divine Being in a way that Baudrillard, for instance, would certainly refuse. The logic of negative theology is that we may not be able to describe God, since he is beyond our level of understanding and thus ultimately unknowable, but he nevertheless exists. For the secular West, however, and in this I would include people of religious belief as well, the possibility of a really existing divine is radically unthinkable in a certain sense, for if Jesus were to appear now, it is possible that he would be considered a cult leader, a charlatan or even a madman. Or, possibly, given the postmodern condition, Jesus would become a celebrity with a reality TV show.

While it is true that many people believe literally in their religions, it is also true that religion exists as much as a metaphor than as literality. The appearance of the "body of Christ" in the Eucharist, for instance, is a metaphor; the body of Christ does not literally appear. Similarly, religion is almost entirely articulated through ordinary people (say, the Pope); the era of Gods, prophets, disciples and saints[2] with supernatural abilities is long past. The appearance of a real, *undeniable* divinity — or even merely supernatural — would prove a massive rupture in the ontological foundation of reality, of scientific and philosophical knowledge.

The fact that the undeniable existence of the supernatural would considerably problematize our notions of "reality" is played out dramatically in the television series *The 4400*. The premise of the series is that 4400 people who have mysteriously disappeared over the last hundred years suddenly reappear on the shores of a lake in the American North-West. What makes this even more mysterious is that event begins by the tracking of what appears to be a comet, which then changes course and slows down until it appears as a ball of white light over the lake, then the ball seems to explode and a crowd of people appear through the mist. A conversation between two Homeland Security agents is suggestive of its *X-Files*-like slippage between the divine and the alien:

> DIANA SKOURIS: "There had to be some kind of intelligence behind it."
> TOM BALDWIN: "As in the hand of God? Or little green men?"
> SKOURIS: "I'm not discounting anything" ["Pilot" 1.01].

As the series progresses after this one, unexplainable event, it becomes apparent that the "returnees" have been endowed with superhuman abilities, such as healing, telekinesis, an ability to predict the future, and so on. In short, a not uncommon set of abilities of the sort often claimed in the real world by various prophets and holy figures. These abilities seem to have a largely positive, almost mystical, effect on the world; indeed one plot line centers on the immaculately conceived baby Isobel's extraordinary powers.

The series thus initially investigates the implications of what a real, measurable (notably we see the event relayed through TV news reporting) supernatural event would actually cause.[3] The uncertainty of the first episodes, however, is not sustained by the series, for by the end of the first season we find out that the 4400 were in fact taken by humans from the future and returned with superhuman powers in order to prevent the eventual demise of the human race. So what seems to be initially a radical rupture in Realist epistemology — the singular and unexplainable (re)appearance of the 4400 — ends with the reassuring affirmation of human capability, as the superhuman abilities of the 4400 become explained by a narrative of the advanced technology of the future. Even this, however, is given a mystical spin, as the 4400's abilities precipitate a kind of "butterfly effect" chain of events designed to improve the present.

Two — Virtual Religion

What should be apparent, then, from the fictional treatment of the supernatural in texts like *The 4400*, is that even though postmodernity is marked by a noticeable antirationalist swing, nevertheless the burden of Enlightenment skepticism and scientific rationalism remains heavy. There are many pre modern beliefs that have been irrevocably banished as "superstition" (for instance, the magic powers of witches). What the postmodern sacred does, though, is temporarily suspend the "rational" laws of the universe that prohibit Gods and monsters from existence, dramatizing for our pop-culture pleasure the possibility that such creatures can, in fact, really exist. It resuscitates some of those beliefs, albeit in modified ways, in the guise of the fictional (although if the texts themselves are fictional, the boundary between fact and fiction seems at times remarkably permeable in postmodern culture).

Of course, Baudrillard would insist that the postmodern pastiche of religious symbols in fact dramatizes the simulacral nature of religion. Paradoxically, in its seeming presence in the media, it exposes the death of God, for the divine has become just another symbol for appropriation. In that sense, Baudrillard is right, for the sacred has become another set of symbols for postmodern play. However, it does not therefore follow that postmodernism necessarily entails the death of belief — indeed it is arguable that religious fundamentalisms are inherently postmodern. Even as they rail against the postmodern world, they nevertheless use postmodernist strategies, relying on global media and the reign of the simulated symbol. However, the postmodern sacred is not to be confused with religious fundamentalisms, even as it is related to them in the same spiritual, post-rationalist postmodern turn. Unlike the various fundamentalisms which are marked by a seeming certainty, the postmodern sacred is caught somewhere between belief and unbelief, unwilling to discard or discount any symbolic tradition. The postmodern sacred, as I noted in my first chapter, is a play with belief, a belief by proxy diffused into a fictional text.

So that means of course that the postmodern sacred is different from religious texts such as the Torah or Qur'an in that it is not generally supposed to be believed in. For instance, the addition of "Jedi Knight" to the 2001 United Kingdom census list of religions[4] does not in any way presuppose belief or practice (although talking with some *Star Wars* fans might lead you to believe otherwise!), merely a passionate attachment to the *Star Wars* text and a carnivalesque inversion of the categories of religion and entertainment. So the postmodern sacred's representation of Gods and monsters must almost inevitably occur in non-realistic "secondary" worlds. This of course raises the question, is it now epistemologically possible to represent God in a Realist sense? Any postmodern representation must inevitably have to take into account the possibility, for instance, that the divine visitations of the past may have been undiagnosed mental illness (schizophrenia, for instance).[5]

CHAPTER THREE

"Something Up There": Transcendental Gesturing in New Age–Influenced Texts

"If only he'd joined a mainstream religion, like Oprahism, or voodoo."
Futurama, "Hell is Other Robots" (1.09)

Popularizing the New Age: Oprah and the New Age

The postmodern New Age shift arguably holds true for a significant part of the wider culture, more than merely those involved in New Age and/or Eastern practices like Buddhism, Taoism, yoga and meditation. Slavoj Žižek even goes so far as to call the New Age the hegemonic discourse of global postmodern capitalism (2001: 12).[1] While this overstates the case considerably — especially in an America where the religious Right has increasingly made its political and cultural presence known — it is nevertheless true that the New Age has become a significant part of the Western spiritual landscape.

New Age terminology has become part of the everyday discourse of the West, popularized by talk shows and a never-ending supply of self-help experts and pop psychologists — most significantly on Oprah Winfrey's talk show. While *Oprah* began as a sensationalist talk show not too dissimilar to modern day freak shows like *Donahue*, *Jerry Springer* and *Rikki Lake*, over the course of the 90s, *Oprah* began to evolve to become a more "quality" talk show. In 1997, she began what she called her "change-your-life" TV. *Oprah*, in the decade since, has specialized in the combination of New Age spirituality and self-help. Favored guests on *Oprah* have included Gary Zukav, author of *Spirit of the Soul*, and John Gray, author of self-help hetero-gender essentialist tract *Men Are from Mars, Women Are from Venus*.[2] Segments like "remembering your spirit" explicitly evoke New Age conceptualizations of the self as a spiritual being, usually one that has lost its way and been covered over by the "baggage" of late capitalism. This clearly recalls Paul Heelas's point that for New Agers "truth [...] come[s] by way of one's own experience. For this alone provides direct and uncontaminated access to the spiritual realm" (1996b: 21). Oprah and her assorted experts help her viewers get in touch with their "real" selves, in far greater numbers than any previous New Age group.

On one level, this emerges out of a dissatisfaction with consumer capitalism, but while projects like the "Angel Network" encourage community activism, this is still, as Kathryn Lofton points out, a highly consumerist version of spirituality. She points out caustically that "the only way religion or religious belief works for Oprah is if it is carefully coordinated with capitalist pleasure. Thus, the turn to 'spirituality': the non-dogmatic dogma that encourages an ambiguous theism alongside an exuberant consumerism"(616).

Indeed, as Lofton makes abundantly clear, Oprah's spirituality invariably comes attached to a product of some sort. There is Oprah's magazine *O,* her TV channel *OWN.* There is Oprah's infamous "book club," which single-handedly has the power to make bestsellers out of the books she chooses. The books on Oprah's book club tend to be heartwarming, another way to remember one's spirit. Here reading fiction is constituted as self-improvement, not so much of one's mind as one's soul — "part of a commitment to change people by changing how they view, and participate in, the world around them" (Parkins 148). There are the endless array of products personally approved by Oprah — shows with titles like "Oprah's Favorite Things" encourage viewers to model their own consumption on Oprah's presumably more spiritually enlightened preferences. Then there are the experts on her show who frequently have books and products of their own to hawk. All these work to position Oprah as one of what Bauman calls the "'prophets' of peak-experience, [...] those able to consume "more refined products [...] in a more sophisticated manner" (1997: 181). Oprah teaches her viewer how to consume in a more spiritual manner. The obvious paradox of Oprah's brand of spirituality then is that while it seems to emerge as a response to the excesses of consumerism, it poses a consumerist solution to that problem.[3]

Of course, what separates *Oprah* from the postmodern sacred is that *Oprah* is a non-fiction text; the texts of the postmodern sacred are fiction. The incredible success of *Oprah* has helped popularized New Age ideas and symbols, to make them familiar and more easily appropriated for fictional usage. *Oprah* has helped popularize an individualized, de-traditional approach to spirituality and religion. Oprah and her guests, however, rarely explicitly condemn "organized" religion — that would only alienate viewers. Instead, we see a New Age model of inclusion, one that sees figures like angels appropriated from Christianity, and "spirit" being made vaguely equivalent to God. As Wendy Parkins points out, the "spiritual discourse spoken by Oprah and her guests [in the 1998 season] was broadly inclusive, speaking of 'karma' and 'grace' in equal parts" (149). Of course, such a relativist, New Age perennialist outlook is bound to infuriate many Christians; even as it includes Christian motifs, it has implicitly discarded Christianity's exclusive purchase on spiritual truth.

It is easy then to see how the postmodern sacred takes the "real world" New Age ideas of people like Oprah and then transfers them into fictional texts. The postmodern sacred generally takes a suspicion of institutions as its departure point, but it is also unwilling to discard the entire symbolic tradition of the Jewish and Christian religions. Indeed, it is often keen to claim the ground of "real" spirituality for itself, against hypocritical religious dogma and religious figures who appear more intent on maintaining power than in seeking after the sacred. This is, of course, a reductive reading of religious institutions, one that often takes the excesses of "fundamentalism" or the Catholic Church as metonymic of the entire wide sweep of two thousand years of Christian history worldwide. But while many of these texts operate outside the authority of religious institutions to discern truth, they are nevertheless happy to use the symbols associated with those institutions. The postmodern sacred often takes a willful delight in the symbolic pilfering from religious traditions, taking pleasure in heretical reconfigurings.

An example of the distance between much contemporary popular culture and organized religion occurs in *The Simpsons* episode "Homer the Heretic" (4.03). In the episode, Homer has a number of dreams in which he converses with the Christian God. Like Homer, even God would prefer to be "watching football" than attending church. In fact, Reverend Lovejoy "really displeases" God. In this version of de-traditionalized spirituality, we see Homer's "heresy" of not attending church allied with bodily pleasure — sleeping in, Homer dancing in his underwear, eating waffles. Traditional Christian practice is suggested to be boring, judgmental and hypocritical, embodied by Reverend Lovejoy and Homer's irritating neighbor Ned Flanders. Homer says to God, "I'm a not a bad guy, I work hard, and I love my kids and why should I spend half my Sunday hearing about how I'm going to hell." Significantly, though, this episode also features Homer at his most spiritual — attired in monk's garb, he communes with nature in his backyard. Homer says, "So I figure I should just try to live right and worship you in my own way" (4.03) — a postmodern religious statement if ever there was. While the episode ends with the normative closure of Homer being rescued from a fire by a multi-faith fire engine crew and rejoining his church, God consoles him by saying, "Don't feel bad Homer, 9 out of 10 religions fail in their first year" and then with the open-ended statement "The meaning of life is...." This leads to an ambivalent closure to the episode at best; while Homer has rejoined the flock, it is obvious that meaning cannot be found in organized religion. This particular episode evocatively sums contemporary postmodern approaches to religion, but it is after all only one episode of a show only marginally interested in the spiritual. The question then, is how does the postmodern sacred more generally make use of these individualized and de-traditionalized New Age ideas and practices?

The Transcendental Signifier or, the New Age in Pop Culture

The French post-structuralist philosopher Jacques Derrida provides an interesting way into thinking through how New Age, Jewish and Christian ideas might function in popular culture. Derrida's thoughts about religion are tremendously complex and more usually considered in terms of Judaism and Christianity (see for instance Caputo 1997, Caputo et al. 2005 and Cixous 2004). Derrida argues that God functions as a "transcendental signified," inhabiting a position outside the usual realm of signification (1981: 19–20). He argues that while signs usually function as *both* signifier and signified,[4] the transcendental signified breaks down the chain of meaning, and no longer functions as a signifier. In such a linguistic economy, this means, as literary theorist Kevin Hart points out, that the Trinitarian Christ signals perfect meaning, the complete conflation of the sign of presence and presence itself — "since Christ is God, what He signifies is signified in and of itself" (8). This echoes the Christian theological tradition of defining God tautologically in the Jewish Bible because of his "I Am Who I Am" statement in Exodus 3:14. Religious scholar Karen Armstrong suggests that "He [God] certainly did not mean, as later philosophers would assert, that he was self-sufficient Being" (30). Rather, the statement is designed to evade the question — "Hebrew did not have such a metaphysical dimension at this stage and it would be nearly 2000 years before it acquired one [...] So when Moses asks who he is, God replies in effect: 'Never you mind who I am!'" (1999: 30). Interestingly, both these examples show how a history of readings has modified the subject in question. Even God, as Armstrong shows, has a history.

So the transcendental signified — God — is a function of language, a way of "nam[ing] the nameless" (Caputo, 2005: 37) as Derrida eloquently puts it. Significantly, too, Derrida argues that God works as a guarantor of meaning, for in the metaphysical-theological tradition people have only been able to speak imperfectly to one another. The Biblical story of the Tower of Babel, for instance, has usually been taken to illustrate the folly of aspiring to match God, but humanity's punishment as a result of that folly was that language became a source of antagonistic separation between different peoples.[5] Perfect meaning is for the biblical God and God alone.

But metaphysics and theology are haunted by the possibility — even inevitability — of their own failure. The dream of "pure" meaning might be the precondition for translation, but as Derrida shows again and again, translation does not leave the text unmodified. The text can always be shown to exceed itself, to have currents that run counter to its explicit purpose. And this is an idea that Derrida himself rigorously applies to his own corpus; for instance, Geoffrey Bennington's *Jacques Derrida* was accompanied by a "Circumfession" by Derrida, a deconstruction of an explanation of deconstructive theory.

Of course, it should be noted that God is merely one example of a transcendental signified for Derrida, however. Drawing on Derrida, Mark C. Taylor points out that

> this does not mean [...] that every sign refers directly or even indirectly to God. The point to be stressed is that some notion of the transcendental signified is required by any referential system that gives priority to the signified over the signifier. While not always explicitly named God, the transcendental functions as the purported locus of truth that is supposed to stabilize all meaningful words [1984: 105].

Derrida argues that the transcendental signified structures the entire history of Western metaphysics as a guarantor of meaning and furthermore that the distinction between signifier and signified begins to break down once one begins to question the possibility of such a "pure" meaning (1981: 19–20). While meaning — the signified — is usually privileged over the signifier, that distinction becomes collapsed by the Derridean insight that the signified is itself a signifier. For as Taylor says, "Consciousness, therefore, deals *only* with signs and never reaches the thing itself" (1984: 104). Rather than "representing" a pure Platonic idea or material object outside of signification, we find, only and ever, more signs. Most especially then, God is a mutable sign whose meanings are shaped by a history of signification.

While Derrida explores (and disrupts) the metaphysical and theological implications of the transcendental signified, in this chapter I propose to modify his concept in my reading of New Age style narratives to what I will term the transcendental *signifier*. The transcendental signifier is a recurrent trope of the postmodern sacred, a way of gesturing toward the transcendental without using the specific language of theology. Rather than referring to God or heaven, the New Age uses such transcendental signifiers as "spirit," "the afterlife," "the great whatever." Frequently de-traditional spirituality posits the notion of something "up there," unable to be conceptualized any further. This often has the feel of a sort of lay negative theology; God — or spirit, or energy, or whatever you want to call it — is unable to be explained except by recourse to what it is not, the world down here of signs and the exchange of meaning.

Negative (apophatic) theology has long been a form of Christian theological discourse. Its prominent writers have included 6th-century mystic Pseudo-Dionysius, and medieval writers Nicholas of Cusa and Meister Eckhart. The basic premise of negative theology is that the transcendent cannot be described directly by language; since the transcendent is by definition not of this earth it cannot be described within any definition of the sacred formed by earthly experience. God, therefore, can only be described negatively by what "he" is *not*. Apophatic language therefore suggests that earthly concepts are inadequate to the task of describing or producing the sacred, except negatively. Characteristic of this is fifteenth century mystic Nicholas of Cusa who argues that "the language of negation is so necessary to the theology of affirmation that without it God would not be worshiped as the infinite God but as creature; and such worship is idolatry, for it gives to an image that which belongs only to truth itself" (qtd. Boesel and Keller 5). In other words, to situate God as an embodied creature is to always-already create an idol. In the cataphatic ("positive") theological tradition, God is Being itself (*esse* in Latin, essence); in the negative tradition, God is beyond even that.

The New Age transcendental signifier therefore has a certain kind of resemblance to the God of negative theology. While traditional theology has holy texts and a history of theological interpretation with which to buttress the transcendental signified, New Age-ized language will often strip the transcendental signified to its barest,[6] leaving only the notion that there exists *something else* not of this world. So the transcendental becomes even more significant in talking about the shift toward a New Age language of spirituality than in the Judeo-Christian model, which retains certain anthropomorphic features in the Godhead, and in the Incarnation of Christ (for Christians). The New Age takes the transcendental signifier and disconnects it from the *figure* of God, who is associated with the "dead" traditional religions.[7]

The transcendental signifier works most clearly in the postmodern sacred as a means of making some kind of gesture toward the transcendent without having to tie that (fictional) ontology to any established real-world religious tradition. Gesturing to the transcendent is a characteristic textual strategy of the postmodern sacred, for it allows the pleasure of play with the transcendent without the commitment or even need for belief that an established religion would have. It fits perfectly with the postmodern sacred's vacillation between belief and unbelief, and roots in the New Age.[8] The transcendental signifier is suggestive rather than descriptive, and perhaps that is all it can ever be (although we shall see in the following chapter how the corporeality of the image functions in a different way in the postmodern sacred). More kindly, it is perhaps an admission of the human inadequacy — since we cannot definitively know what the supernatural or transcendent is, it is best not to try. And any definitive reading would run counter to the New Age idea of discarding "dogma," which places the transcendent largely in the individual's experience of it.

My argument is that the postmodern sacred largely uses the language of the New Age — "spirit" instead of God — as a means of grounding its *textual universes* outside of the bounds of traditional religion (but not as an ontological grounding of reality itself). Massimo Introvigne argues that "popular culture [...] confirms that stories our generation of non-belonging believers [...] like to tell and hear are not about secular universes, but involve notions of a Higher Power. These stories, however, more often than not, have no sovereign, omnipotent transcendent God" (n.p.). The coordinates for many of the New Age style SF/fantasy universes were arguably set by *Star Wars*, which combined portentous seriousness with pop–Buddhist ideas and an absence of formal "real world" religious institutions. *Star Wars*, of course, provides perhaps the key example of the transcendental signifier with its suggestive phrase "the Force." While it predates most of the texts I have analyzed by at least 15 years (and thus is occurring in a slightly different cultural context), the initial *Star Wars* trilogy remains one of the key touchstones for visual science fiction and fantasy. It is arguable that *Star Wars*' use of the transcendental signifier precipitates at least part of the postmodern sacred's move toward nebulous New Age conceptions of spirit. In the concept of "the Force," George Lucas clearly draws more on Eastern, or at least New Age, ideas — the Force is roughly analogous to the "chi" in Taoism. Indeed, more than one writer has read *Star Wars* as a Buddhist text (see for instance Matthew Bortolin's *The Dharma of Star Wars*). One of the many disappointments of the second trilogy is that George Lucas decided to explain "the Force" in pseudo-genetic terms, creating the less satisfying concept of "midi-chlorians" to explain the Jedis' mystical powers. It's arguable then that the power of the transcendental signifier lies in being suggestive, in not telling too much. But *Star Wars* is not alone in using New Age style transcendental signifiers — other ways of conceptualizing the transcendental signifier in the postmodern sacred include fantasy author Robert Jordan's "the Light" in his *Wheel of Time* series of novels[9], "heaven dimensions" in *Buffy*, and a kind of barely articulated divine Providence in Peter Jackson's *The Lord of the Rings* movie adaptations.

The television series *Angel* provides another useful example, for the titular hero is sent on missions relayed by his sidekicks Doyle and Cordelia from the "Powers That Be," a phrase that is both suggestive of a surplus of meaning *and* absent in actual detail. These "Powers That Be" fulfill some of the traditional roles that God has occupied, sending Angel on his quests for Good and on his road to personal redemption, yet it remains unclear if these powers have created the world, or have any power to intervene personally, and so on. Interestingly the character Cordelia ascends to a "higher plane of being" in the finale of Series 3 ("Tomorrow" 3.22), again a phrase more redolent in the present with New Age connotations than with those of the Christian tradition. One needs to note, though, that even though many texts use the language of spirit, they are not necessarily making a statement about the ontological nature of reality itself (though characteristically postmodern irony would refuse to disallow that as a possibility either). These are fantastic texts, after all, not meant to be read in a straightforward Realist fashion. Much of the relationship between the postmodern sacred and "reality" is metaphorical, what science fiction theorist Darko Suvin would call an "estranged" relationship to realistic representation. Suvin coins the term "estranged cognition" in order to describe the way that science fiction allows readers to perceive the world as new and unfamiliar. He argues that "in SF the attitude of estrangement — used by Brecht in a different way, within a still predominantly "realistic" context — has grown into the *formal framework* of the genre" (1979: 7). Suvin's theorization has been highly influential, with Marxist theorists following his lead in suggesting that SF is constitutively more progressive than other fantastic texts, for its estrangement historicizes the present more thoroughly. Carl

Freedman for instance, distinguishes SF from the "irrationalist" estrangements of fantasy and horror (262); even as he seeks to find more properly historical estrangements in the fantasy work of Samuel Delaney. Yet even the most apolitical and generic of texts can produce some estranged cognition from the real.

The postmodern sacred's use of the transcendental signifier can be seen clearly in the television series *Dead Like Me*. *Dead Like Me* is the story of George, an 18-year-old who is killed by a toilet seat dropped from the space station Mir. After her death, rather than go to heaven or indeed hell (because she's "not that interesting"), she remains on Earth and becomes a "Reaper," a harvester of souls. Though *Dead Like Me* is set largely in a realistic universe — this is no futuristic sci-fi or medieval fantasy world — it does nevertheless dramatize and embroider an elaborate post-death cosmology. Death is set in motion in this world by "gravelings," small malevolent creatures. People's deaths are almost always inevitable and fated, the details given to George's boss Rube, with a location and ETD (Estimated Time of Death).[10] While on the one hand, we see the Reapers go on living after their deaths (some seventy years or so in Rube's case), they themselves do not know what happens to people when they die. Reapers get to go on living like the rest of us, more or less, having to hold down day jobs they hate, balance relationships, and enjoy the pleasures of life like "delicious key-lime pie" ("Pilot" 1.01) and so on. So what is significant about the way *Dead Like Me* characterizes the afterlife is that the final destination where people go after their deaths is never specified — Rube says, "It's not for us to know" ("Pilot" 1.01). But it is, however, gestured to, "the great whatever" as George puts it ("Curious George" 1.03). We see manifestations of the afterlife and the recently deceased follow, but the Reapers themselves can't follow. The afterlife is individualized and varies depending upon the person who has just died — it is, among other things, a carnival, the cliffs of Dover, a Hindu goddess. The sacred, then, becomes amorphously pluralistic, able to be manifested in multiple ways, though always with the same transcendental source. This is, once again, a common New Age point that has been taken up by the postmodern sacred's fictional texts and used for its own pop-cultural pleasure.

Thus it is that the postmodern sacred is notable for the way it separates this transcendental gesturing from traditional anthropomorphized theology. The afterlife *could* be a Christian heaven or hell, but it could just as likely be a fun fair or Hindu goddess. Any kind of definitive theological reading is impossible in the world of *Dead Like Me*. Similarly with God: when George asks Rube about the existence of God, his response is a blunt "You tell me," and other figures such as angels are reconceptualized as "upper management types" ("Pilot" 1.01). On one hand, this could be seen as a failure of imagination for the postmodern sacred, an inability or unwillingness to fully conceptualize other realms of existence. On the other, gesturing to the transcendent is one way in which the postmodern sacred opposes its spirituality to the religious traditions. It suggests that *real* spirituality has got very little to do with traditional theology, indeed it largely discards the concept of God — or at the very least it is at pains to distinguish itself from the God of the Jewish, Christian and Islamic traditions.

Instead, *Dead Like Me* provides a New Agey, vaguely Eastern style philosophy. As Rube says, "Life and death have to exist in perfect harmony. Yin and Yang, call it what you want, but that balance has to be maintained" ("Pilot" 1.01). But if *Dead Like Me* draws on Eastern ideas, it appropriates them into a decidedly Western viewpoint — conspicuously absent are ideas like reincarnation. *Dead Like Me* thus ultimately proves unable to provide many answers for the questions it poses about the afterlife, and perhaps this is to be the credit of the show — that it refrains from giving us easy or familiar answers (it's not for us to know). Thus we end in the real world rather than the transcendent; the last episode, "Haunted" (2.15), ends with George affirming the pleasures of living (sort of), saying, "It's not so bad, being dead like me." Interestingly, this ending comes quite close to the religious dogma *Dead Like Me* attempts to distinguish itself from. George is "dead" in this world with something else to look forward to after, possessing a surer knowledge of the hereafter than any believer can have. It might be "not so bad" being dead like her but there is always the prospect of going somewhere else. *Dead Like Me* would surely be more radical if there was nowhere else to go, but as it is, this suggests that there remains a remarkably strong continuity between the New Age and post–Christianity.

So, while light on details, the postmodern sacred is characteristic for its suggestion that spirituality exists through what we might call a surplus of meaning. The postmodern sacred, then, frequently makes recourse to symbol. This has, of course, certain theological precedents in the Christian tradition, for as Catholic theologian Avery Dulles argues, "revelation never occurs in a purely interior experience or an unmediated encounter with the God. It is always mediated through symbol [that] suggest[s] more than it can clearly describe or define" (Dulles 131). Although Dulles is clearly describing a Christian model of divine revelation, *symbol that suggests more than it can describe* sums up rather well the postmodern sacred's use of the transcendental signifier in pop culture. In Christianity, this mediation of symbol could occur in any number of contexts; the symbol of the Cross can be found in Church art, worn as jewelry, and ritually enacted in bodily movement in churches, homes and even on sporting fields. In the postmodern sacred, however, we find that there is no transcendent revelation (or hierophany as Eliade would term it), instead we find that it is the symbol that is foregrounded, in order to grasp at a transcendent that is almost, by definition, unrepresentable.

The Alien as Transcendental Signifier

The transcendental signifier emerges in a slightly different manner in supernatural/horror texts like the hugely popular fin de siècle television series *The X-Files*, as well as its many imitators like *The 4400*, *Supernatural* and even the Superman prequel series *Smallville* (which has an *X-Files* influenced litany of weird occurrences). I shall restrict my analysis here largely to *The X-Files*, which is the most culturally significant of those texts I have mentioned. The structure of the majority of the *X-Files* series is simple. The show centers on two FBI agents, Fox Mulder and Dana Scully, working on the "X-Files," the cases the FBI has designated unsolvable by conventional explanations, and possibly involving the paranormal. Mulder is the believer, formulator of exotic theories involving such unlikely protagonists as aliens or ghosts, which are of course frequently found to be the truth. Scully, on the other hand, is the skeptic, the scientist recruited by the FBI to debunk Mulder's work on the paranormal.

The X-Files works as a text of the postmodern sacred in a number of ways. First, it exhibits a postmodern distrust of "official" meta-

Three — "Something Up There"

narratives, centering largely on the activities of the U.S. government, its Army and law-enforcement agencies. Behind that very obvious paranoia (and paranoid is surely the best way to describe the series), though, one sees in *The X-Files* a Lyotardian skepticism toward Enlightenment-derived meta-narratives of scientific rationality. The series, instead, entertains the possibility of the supernatural, with a particular interest in aliens (and the government's cover-up of their existence). A short list of the series' plotlines would include an ongoing alien abduction narrative, a man with pyrokinetic powers ("Fire" 1.12), a boy with stigmata ("Revelations" 3.11), and killer cockroaches ("War of the Coprophages" 3.12). In short, *The X-Files* lets back in what modern science has sought to banish. As Lavery et al. argue, "For many viewers, their weekly experience with the show is an unsettling, sometimes frightening experience that powerfully interrogates a consensus reality that excludes the paranormal" (12). While the series slogan, "The truth is out there," suggests on one level an unfashionable attachment to truth, the truth is ultimately unknowable on *The X-Files*; since as Lavery et al point out, episodes frequently end without full resolution or explanation (17). This is certainly in part because of the serial nature of the television series—full narrative closure must be deferred for another week or even another series in order to maintain a viewing audience — but it's worth pointing out that many dramatic episodic TV shows wrap up their plot strands weekly, only to begin anew the next week. Yet even "one-off" episodes of *The X-Files* remain as open-ended as those involving long-time plotlines (such as the alien abduction of Mulder's sister, for example). But Mulder's search to find the answers to his sister's abduction, however, only finds merely more questions. Truth on *The X-Files*, while continually posited as findable, is forever out of reach, deferred for another week. Conspiracies overwrite each other, rendering previously taken for granted knowledge suspect. That lack of narrative closure seems to bespeak both a suspicion toward epistemological certainty — we can never really truly know the entirety of the truth — as well a postmodern play with narrative itself.

While it might seem that *The X-Files* shows simply a tabloid-fueled credulous postmodern willingness to entertain the most ludicrous of beliefs, arguably the series is more subtle than its lurid plotlines might suggest. After all, the emblematic poster behind Mulder's desk says "I want to believe"— not "I believe." The series, then, is about *wanting* to believe in the supernatural, or the extraterrestrial, not being able to. But Mulder's take on the supernatural is scarcely the only position on the show (though it does seem to be the dominant one). The counterbalance to Mulder's willingness to believe is Scully's skepticism. Scully is the voice of Reason and rationalism, a medical professional, who believes that life is explainable. More often than not, the deficiencies of scientific rationalism are exposed; most of the events on *The X-Files* are only partially explainable. But it's the interplay between the two agents (and not just the sexual chemistry) that makes *The X-Files* work—a series that only featured Mulder would have been far less entertaining, since the series requires the presence of rationality in order to expose its weaknesses (but not discard it entirely). So, like the postmodern sacred generally, *The X-Files* is caught between belief and unbelief, unwilling to trust in rationalist meta-narratives, but equally unable to shed that legacy to truly believe in the supernatural.

Interestingly, in some ways, the alien has become more of an epistemologically sustainable belief than the sacred for some secularists. As Lynn Schofield Clark points out, by the 1990s some 27 percent of the American population believed that aliens had visited the earth (5). As scientists have discovered precisely how large the universe is, the idea that life has only occurred on this one planet has become questionable. Of course, this belief in alien visitation—with a particular focus on the "alien crash" that supposedly occurred in Roswell, New Mexico[11] in 1947—is fueled in some part by a recurrent fictional representation of the alien in science-fiction narratives like *ET*, *Close Encounters of the Third Kind*, and of course *The X-Files*.

Throughout its run from 1993 to 2002, *The X-Files* doled out equal doses of conspiracy theorist paranoia about the American government and supernatural spookiness in the form of aliens, monsters and so on. While New Age style narratives use a language appropriated from the New Age to gesture toward the transcendental, in *The X-Files* it is the alien which functions as the transcendental signifier—specifically the "little grey men" often associated with alien abduction narratives. Alien "encounters" in *The X-Files* are often rendered in the same way as encounters with the divine—deserted areas, a flash of white lights, mysterious occurrences, lapses in space and time. Alien encounters work as another version of Eliade's hierophany—a fragment of a barely explainable transcendent. Alien encounters are literally transcendent; they come from above, and most definitely appear as "a reality of a wholly different order from 'natural' realities" (Eliade 10). Like the divine, aliens are both mysterious and powerful, unknowable, unpredictable.

An example occurs in the episode "Little Green Men" (2.01), in which we see a flashback of the kidnapping of Mulder's sister. The room is bathed in white light, an alien appears at the doorway, and Samantha floats out of the window, never to appear again. Aliens in *The X-Files*, particularly in Mulder's search for meaning in his own life, in some ways recall what Hugh Ruppersberg calls "the alien messiah" (32), the redemptive figure in films such as *ET*, *Close Encounters of the Third Kind*, and *Cocoon*. Yet if those films largely invoke, as Ruppersberg says, "a messiah figure [...] whose numinous, supra-human qualities offer solace and inspiration to a humanity threatened by technology and the banality of modern life" (33), *The X-Files* offers no such solace. The alien in *The X-Files* may appear as transcendent and utterly Other, and as such as miraculous at times, but it is *far* from comforting. Instead, like Rudolph Otto's *mysterium tremendum*, alien abductions on *The X-Files* provoke both awe and terror.

Thus, the line between *The X-Files*' hyper-paranoid search for the extraterrestrial and American evangelicals is not as firm as one might think; both use the figure of a corrupt and secretive government, for instance. Read from another angle, *The X-Files*' tag-line, "The truth is out there," resembles nothing so much as an evangelical slogan, and Mulder's quest for truth that of a prophet. Both conspiracy theory and evangelical survivalist are simultaneously invested in modern social forms (the nation, the government, capitalism, the nuclear family and so on) and estranged from them. The government creates these conspiracies — and it's interesting to note the conspiracy theories surrounding September 11 — but at the same time provides the possibility for recovering the truth. It's hard not to think of this as a redemptive fantasy inherent in liberal democracy itself, that the State will redeem itself somehow.

Although the series does use the alien as a variation on the transcendental signifier, it should be noted that it also features New Age–styled transcendental gesturing to "spirit" as well. Generically speaking, *The X-Files* occurs somewhere at the intersection of conspiracy theories,

UFO abduction narratives and New Age spirituality, and as such has a reverence for Buddhist and particularly Native American spiritual practices. The series three episode "The Blessing Way" (3.01), for instance, sees FBI agent Fox Mulder undergo a Navajo healing ritual. Mulder floats in a bed in the middle of space, talking with his dead father and mentor. The presence of the Navajo—codemakers for the U.S. government in World War II—is of course given a conspiracy theory gloss suitable for the show's premillenial paranoia. Regardless, the episode and others like it suggest that real spiritual experience may occur *anywhere* if you choose to see it. While the episode continues the tradition of white American appropriations of Native American, it is characteristically New Age in doing so, universalizing "inner truth" even as it co-opts specific native traditions.

In the broadest sense, however, *The X-Files* is polytheistic, dramatizing countless versions of the supernatural to construct a strange, mysterious, even occasionally sacred world. The supernatural people, animals and creatures found in *The X-Files* produce an Weberian-style enchanted world—not a sentimentalized premodern Arcadia but a world brimming with capricious, even malign, inexplicable powers. Almost every encounter with the supernatural provokes a *mysterious tremendium* mixture of awe and terror, something most obvious in the transcendentally signified alien abductions. More than most texts in the postmodern sacred, and perhaps this is a function of its frequent references to the horror genre, *The X-Files* retains some of the power of the sacred to terrify. Significantly though, like many of the texts of the postmodern sacred, *The X Files* maintains skepticism toward Christianity, yet it is unwilling to entirely discard its symbolic power, or the possibility of a "real" Christian supernatural/spiritual experience. We see this most clearly in "Revelations" (3.11), an episode in which Scully must deal with her discarded Catholic faith, and ponders whether there might be something beyond the scientific rationalism through which she explains the world.

Fragments

Interestingly, although the postmodern sacred is often notable for its suspicion, even hostility, toward traditional religious institutions, it nevertheless draws on those same traditions for its symbolic power. The question, then, is how to recycle religious motifs without an epistemological grounding that would tie the postmodern sacred to those suspect institutions. As I argued in my first chapter, one of the ways in which the postmodern sacred can be understood is through its use of the characteristically postmodern textual strategy of pastiche. The postmodern sacred borrows liberally from many different traditions—Buddhist, Christian, Taoist, Native American, Celtic and Jewish—though perhaps because of the general suspicion with which the West holds Islam, it is far less likely to embrace elements of Islam. All of these traditions have similar textual elements available for symbolic appropriation—holy books and histories of interpretation, religious symbols and paraphernalia, rituals and ritualized bodily movements. Perhaps unsurprisingly given their origin in a post–Christian West, the texts using religious signifiers in a detraditionalized fashion, such as *Buffy*, have mostly used Christian signifiers. Similarly, fantasy epics like *The Lord of the Rings* have used Christianity creatively in their parallel universes, from metaphoric Christ figures (Aragorn, Frodo, C.S. Lewis's Aslan) to sacramentals such as Elvish lembas bread. The Taoist Ursula LeGuin's writing remains a notable and significant exception within the genre, with her Earthsea series infused with Taoist concerns about the ethics and responsibility of (magical) behavior.

Interestingly, the third *Star Trek* incarnation, *Star Trek: Deep Space Nine*, provides an indicator of the cultural shift involved in the postmodern sacred. Rather than the roving spaceships of the other four series (*Star Trek*, *Star Trek: Next Generation*, *Star Trek Voyager*,[12] *Star Enterprise*), *DS9* is set on a space station near the planet of Bajor. The series begins with the Federation taking control of an old Cardassian space station at the request of the Bajoran provisional government. Bajor had been occupied by the Cardassians for the previous 50 years, and the Bajoran people fought a guerrilla war. As such, *DS9* is partly set in an estranged postcolonialist context. While earlier versions of *Star Trek* largely provide an atheist, rationalist viewpoint, *Deep Space Nine* is the spiritual exception in the *Star Trek* mega-text.[13]

In the first episode, "Emissary" (1.01), Deep Space Nine Commander Benjamin Sisko discovers a wormhole to an undiscovered quadrant of space, the Gamma quadrant. Inside the wormhole, Sisko encounters a race of aliens who seem to exist outside of space and time. These aliens occupy a central place in the Bajoran religion, who call them "The Prophets," and the wormhole itself "the Celestial Temple." Over the course of the series, the Prophets are suggested to have sent "orbs" to communicate with the Bajoran people, and to intervene in their destinies. Indeed, in "Destiny" (3.15), their prophecies come true. Because of his encounter in the wormhole, Sisko becomes an unwilling religious figure for the Bajorans, who dub him "The Emissary." Sisko finds it difficult to surrender (shades of New Age language already) to his role as the Emissary, preferring the atheist rationality of Star Fleet, although over the course of the series he learns to adjust to his religious role.

Like many of the fictitious religions in the postmodern sacred, the Bajoran faith's chief real-world referent is Buddhism, with Buddhist style robes, references to meditation and chanting. But if Buddhism seems the chief referent, references to Christianity nevertheless abound (say in the Catholicism-recalling *realpolitik* that occurs behind the scenes in the election of the Bajoran spiritual leader). While the series is limited by the necessity of conforming to an identifiably "*Star Trek*" style, it nevertheless suggests an interesting sea-change within science fiction — direct atheism is to be avoided, and an ambivalent relationship to the sacred, refracted largely through the New Age, is to be attempted.[14] Peter Linford suggests that in *Deep Space Nine* "religion is significant only to the extent it impacts on the [individual] believer" (99). In this, *Deep Space Nine* follows a New Age model of individualized spirituality, disconnection from history and wider cultures. Ultimately, "the position *DS9* finally holds is that where religion exists, then so be it. Where it is absent, so much the better" (99).

Slavoj Žižek makes the point regarding *Star Wars: Revenge of the Sith*, that given *Star Wars*' version of the New Age (and a certain kind of pop–Buddhism), it is unsurprising that the metamorphosis of Anakin into Darth Vader is tinged with a Christology (2006: 101). Žižek says, "Since the ideological universe of Star Wars is the New Age pagan universe, it is quite logical that the central figure of Evil should echo Christ — within the pagan horizon, the Event of Christ is the ultimate scandal" (2006: 101). While it is true that the postmodern sacred quite often associates aspects of Christianity into its visions of evil (say in the use of King James Bible–style language by vampires in Season 1 of *Buffy*, or perhaps the monotheism of the Cylons in *Battlestar Galactica*), it needs to be noted that this use of Christ as a figure for Evil is only one of a number of New Age-ized tropes in the postmodern sacred. The postmodern sacred is as likely to make use of Christ figures in its characterization of heroes; to turn to *Buffy* again, say in the titular heroine's quite literal "leap of faith" to her death at the conclusion of Season 5 ("The Gift" 5.22). Yet as Jana Reiss rightly points out in her *What Would Buffy Do*, that Christ-coding redeems only Buffy herself; ultimately "on *Buffy* the redemption process starts—and ends—with the individual, an approach that has more in common with Buddhism than Christianity" (119). While it is true that the more New Age-ized postmodern sacred remains skeptical toward the institutions of Christianity, and even delights in the heretical speculation of texts such as the *Da Vinci Code*, one must not mistake that anti-institutional impulse as specifically or solely *anti*–Christian. One must instead recognize that the postmodern sacred remains highly indebted toward Christianity as its primary symbolic source, even as it looks elsewhere for an ontological foundation for its textual universes. It is thus best understood as *post*–Christian; even when it defines itself against religious institutions it remains fixated on such typically Christian themes of sacrifice and redemption, as well as Christian symbols like the Cross or holy water.

Avery Dulles's insight about symbol, however, need not be solely applicable to a Christian tradition, for the idea that symbol suggests more than it can describe is quite clearly characteristic of the postmodern sacred. Those symbols, however, are freely appropriated from various spiritual traditions, often without any real contextualization. Meaning, then, resides in the play of signification, or recognizing spiritual signifiers without holding to their religious traditions of origin. Indeed, the postmodern sacred can often manifest the paradoxical relationship of relying on a religious tradition for its symbolic power—say in the evocative Christ-symbolism scene of the usually mocking *Buffy the Vampire Slayer* in which Spike drapes himself across a cross, asking Buffy, "Can we rest now?" while his flesh steams ("Beneath You" 7.02).

Jacques Derrida's argument about trace texts seems particularly apt when considering the postmodern turn toward pastiche. He argues that, rather than signify to a "real world" outside the text, texts contain traces "that [continue] to signal not in the direction of another presence, or another form of presence, but in the direction of an entirely other text" (1982: 65). While Realist texts appeal first and foremost to a verisimilitude with the "real," Derrida argues that texts work as palimpsests of other texts. This argument seems most compelling in considering texts of an unreal nature, those that do not attempt to reproduce some version of the generally accepted real. This might also explain the often derivative nature of these texts, for they can have a stronger relationship with other texts of the same genre than they do with an estranged real-world referent. The texts of the postmodern sacred are even more indebted to their textual predecessors; they exist as the result of the textual sedimentation of signs (and indeed the history of interpretation *of* those signs). For example, one could choose to foreground any number of trace texts in the fantasy genre — children's literature, medieval romances, pastorals, historical bodice-rippers — while some scholars have found resonances with Thomas Aquinas's theology, among others. Even though one could argue that the genre attempts to present a version of the medieval, it is arguable that this comes first and foremost through the textual sedimentation of medieval literature through the aforementioned literary genres, as well as the inescapable influence of figures like Tolkien.

Perhaps it is fitting then that the postmodern sacred should emerge as so culturally vital in an age that, as Fredric Jameson argues, has forgotten how to think historically. This inability to think historically is undoubtedly bound up in the inability to conceive of a real world outside of the text, and this is manifested in not only the un-noted simulation of other texts, but also in the constant and explicit intertextuality of many postmodern texts. The postmodern sacred's invocation of religious signifiers, then, is hardly exceptional. Indeed, while postmodern textuality may often be taken as a play on genre, and on the pleasure of recontextualizing signs into new contexts, the postmodern sacred may also be taken as a play with belief — specifically the belief that those appropriated symbols imply. Symbols in this circumstance may then be taken as metonymic of the belief of the communities of the traditions that the postmodern sacred cannot quite allow itself to believe in, since the death of God narrative remains as important in the postmodern as the death of belief in the scientific meta-narratives that were supposed to replace him. As Mark C. Taylor poignantly says, "Postmodernism opens with the sense of *irrevocable* loss and *incurable* fault. This is inflicted by the overwhelming awareness of death — a death that 'begins' with the death of God and 'ends' with the death of our selves" (1984: 6).

If as I have argued, the postmodern sacred refuses to make any epistemological claims about the nature of "reality," then the question arises, what precisely is the point of both transcendental gesturing and the pastiche of religious signifiers? It is too easy, as many religious scholars have done, to claim popular culture as a new site of resurgent belief in religion, and highly simplistic to map textual consumption onto a real-world belief (say, Christianity with *Lord of the Rings*). Yet it is just as simplistic to entirely dismiss the rise of such texts in the context of a postmodern turn away from modernist atheism. The postmodern sacred needs instead to be understood as the play of belief, as a movement between belief and unbelief.

The transcendental provides an ontological *framework* from which texts pastiche together religious signifiers from different and even contradictory traditions. These religious fragments are moments that are subsumed within the transcendental gesture. Even though they do, usually, come from religious traditions, they do not possess the same ontological value in the postmodern sacred; they are used instead to gesture to a transcendent distinguished from the God of organized religion. The question, then arises, what happens in postmodern texts when a corporeal God *does* appear?

CHAPTER FOUR

Of Gods and Monsters: Metaphor and the Postmodern Sacred

"God doesn't want you ... but I still do."
Darla to Angel, *Angel*, "Dear Boy" 2.05

"We separate angel and monster to our peril."
Ingebretson, 2001: xiv

In this chapter I shall look at how the postmodern sacred presents the "real" textual presence of gods and monsters. While it frequently uses the transcendental signifier, the postmodern sacred also dramatizes the existence of "real," corporeal Gods, monsters, angels and demons. Gods walk on the screens and pages of numerous contemporary fantastic texts. *Xena: Warrior Princess* showed a host of Greek and Roman Gods, *Buffy* has Glory, an evil "hell–God," and the two *Stargate* series have a complicated array of phoney Gods and transcendent beings. The movie *Constantine* features a more Christian figuring of a transcendent unseen God, a very real Devil, and a duplicitous archangel Gabriel, while the TV series *Supernatural* portrays angels, demons and even Lucifer himself.

A Comic God: God on Futurama

An interesting example of the corporeal God occurs in the *Futurama* episode "Godfellas" (3.20). "Godfellas" sees the robot Bender, adrift in

Four — Of Gods and Monsters

space, become God to a tiny race of aliens called Shrimpkins, who have become lodged on his stomach.[1] Because robots in *Futurama* require alcohol to function, Bender gives his one commandment to his faithful servant Malachi — "God needs booze." The Shrimpkins build a brewery which maims many of Bender's followers, while pestilence kills many of the rest. Bender is moved to tears by their plight, but his teardrop is the size of a river to the Shrimpkins, which washes away Malachi's son. Bender saves the child — "This looks like a job ... for God!" — which results in the rest of the Shrimpkins praying for miracles of their own. One village prays for wealth, so Bender flips down a coin which accidentally crushes them to death. Farmers pray for sunlight, so Bender gives them light which sets their fields on fire. He blows the fire out, which also blows the people away into space. A breakaway "heathen" group on Bender's backside ceases believing in him, so the faithful Malachi begs Bender to intervene. By this point, however, Bender has decided to leave matters in the hands of the Shrimpkins — "Every time I intervene, I only make things worse. You're better off solving your own problems." Nonintervention, though, ends with an apocalyptic war between the two groups. Bender floats on in space, where he meets the *real* God, who appears as a giant, flickering constellation of stars. God commiserates with Bender about his struggles with divinity — "you were doing well until everyone died" — and proposes a surprisingly funny and sophisticated theory about divinity:

> GOD: Being God isn't easy. If you do too much, people get dependent on you. And if you do nothing, they lose hope. You have to use a light touch, like a safe cracker or pick-pocket.
> BENDER: Or a guy who burns down a bar for the insurance money.
> GOD: Yes, if you make it look like an electrical thing. When you do things right, people won't be sure you've done anything at all.

Though God sends Bender back to earth in what Leela calls "by a fair margin the least likely thing that's ever happened," the episode ends firmly with an affirmation of human agency. As Bender says, "You can't count on God for jack. He pretty much said so himself."[2]

While this episode renders the notion of a God active in human events decidedly suspect, it nevertheless suggests that miraculous is the true province of the divine. The episode concludes with God repeating, to the camera, "When you do things right, people won't be sure you've done anything at all." God's intervention into the mundane (in the form of the unlikely event of returning Bender to Earth) works clearly as a (textual) hierophany, a brief intrusion of the sacred into the profane. Moreover, God's repeated affirmation of divine inscrutability suggests that the sacred can *only* ever occur erratically; to do otherwise would interfere with free will. Most subversively, it affirms agnosticism as a legitimately spiritual position (since "people won't be sure" of the existence of God).

Like many other postmodern texts, the episode suggests that institutional churches are of little practical use. Fry visits the "First Amalgamated Church" (a combination of the Jewish, Muslim and Buddhist faiths) and asks the priest "Is there anything religion can do to help find my friend?" The priest replies, "Well, we could join together in prayer." Fry asks, again, pointedly, "Uh huh ... but is there anything useful we could do?" Not only are churches of little use on a day-to-day basis, but the episode suggests that *real* spiritual experience is to be found outside of church, anyway. Bender finds God alone in an unoccupied part of space, just as saints in the Christian tradition found God alone in the desert. Like other postmodern texts featuring corporeal Gods, *Futurama* at once affirms the possibility of God and distances itself with more than a dose of irony.

"Godfellas" thus dramatizes a number of interesting points about the sacred. First, it has the postmodern sacred's characteristic skepticism toward organized religion and dogmatic truth, as well as a fair helping of heretical humor. Bender's attempts to be a good God for the Shrimpkins are a comedy of errors that only end in disaster. The genocidal sectarianism of the Shrimpkins might be somewhat of an atheist cliché (atheists often cite religious wars like the Crusades as evidence against religion on the whole, rather than separating between violent, dogmatic interpretations of religion and the traditions themselves), but it is nevertheless a pertinent one in these days of the much touted "Clash of Civilizations" popularized by Samuel Huntington and the neocons.

Of course, it would be a mistake to read *Futurama* utterly seriously — indeed to do so is to miss the point. The show is, after all, a science fiction comedy. *Futurama* is a postmodern text par excellence, redolent with irony, pastiche and lightning quick references to other pop-culture texts.[3] While *Futurama*, like all science fiction texts, has an estranged relationship to the real, the series frequently moves between a satirical comment on the real and a playful exploration of the possibilities of its fictional universe. "Godfellas," one suspects, lies somewhere in between the two, a disavowed comment on real-world spirituality that begs not to be taken seriously.

Stargate

The science-fiction series *Stargate SG-1* takes the motif of the corporeal God from another angle. Whereas *Futurama*'s God appears as a flickering constellation, many of *Stargate*'s "Gods" appear as human, albeit with deep, synthetically altered voices.[4] *Stargate* provides an interesting mix between the transcendental signified and a rationalist, Realist demystification of "primitive" religion. The series dramatizes Arthur C. Clarke's Third Law, that "any sufficiently advanced technology is indistinguishable from magic," taking the premise to its logical conclusion — that any sufficiently advanced technology would be indistinguishable from divinity. This occurs largely in the form of an alien species called the Goa'uld, a parasitic race that take control over their human hosts, who remain unable to speak or use their bodies in any way (though the original personality remains hidden deep in the unconscious). The Goa'uld use such advanced technology that they are able to pose as Gods to their pre-modern worshipers, enslaving much of the galaxy and of course threatening the Earth on a regular basis. Besides the usual SF props of interstellar spaceships (shaped like pyramids in this case), personal shields and laser guns, the technology of the Goa'uld also gives them the superhuman seeming abilities of life spans of several thousand years, and the ability to die and then be brought back to life using an alien device called a "sarcophagus," which revives the dead and increases the life of the living, albeit at the cost of rendering them evil. While this means resurrection is no longer constituted as miraculous within the textual universe, there is nevertheless something uncanny (if slightly predictable, given their status as villains) about the Goa'uld returning from death so often. And finally, the personae of the Goa'ud are taken for the most part from Egyptian mythology, although Hindu, Chinese and Babylonian Gods have also been used.

Stargate also poses another alien race called the Asgard, who have themselves taken their personae from Norse mythology — the "good aliens" to be opposed to the diverse, racially Othered Goa'uld. Although they are initially contacted in the form of holographic simulations of Norse Gods like Thor, the Asgard themselves appear as the familiar "little gray men" of alien abduction narratives. Being both powerful and benevolent, the Asgard in some ways fit what Hugh Ruppersberg calls "the alien messiah" (32) model. Colonel O'Neill's first visit to the Asgard home world is rendered in blurry white, a definite numinous experience. And the Asgard do save Earth more than a few times over the course of the ten series. Yet the Asgard prove to be as fallible as the Goa'uld, unable to save themselves from their Replicator enemies without help from the SG-1team. It is arguable that the redemption offered by the alien messiah struggles to fit the constraints of episodic television, which must continually affirm human capability instead.

Besides advancing a dubious politics of race[5] and a largely benevolent American imperialist agenda (it was, interestingly, filmed with the approval of the U.S. Army and guest-starred a four-star general), *Stargate* at once affirms the real presence of super natural beings from many of Earth's religious (mostly dead) traditions, and works to demystify those apparent divinities, pointing out the fallibility and mortality of both the Goa'uld and the Asgard. On the one hand, it is a play with belief, namely, that the various religions were in fact literally true, albeit in disguised ways. In this sense, *Stargate* seems an attempt to wed myth to post–Enlightenment rationalism, recalling some of the more bizarre New Age alien-based versions of spirituality of the *Chariots of the Gods* ilk. But unsurprisingly, *Stargate*, on the whole, comes down on the side of an Enlightenment-based scientific rationality and works to problematize belief, although given its American context it takes pains to separate its critique from directly attacking the Jewish and Christian God.[6]

The episode "Absolute Power" (4.17), however, is a notable exception, featuring a mystic boy whose attire and demeanor clearly reference Tibetan Buddhism, with his supernatural wisdom, an ability to transform into pure white light, and a habit of speaking in cryptic metaphors. Similarly, "Meridian" (5.21) sees Daniel Jackson, one of the key characters of the show, die but "ascend" to a higher level of being. This event begins the series' pre-occupation with a race called "The Ancients," the race of

Four — Of Gods and Monsters

aliens that originally built the Stargate system, who had themselves discarded their physical form and become pure energy. Builders of the lost city of Atlantis (which becomes the setting for a *Stargate* spin-off), the Ancients developed technology far more advanced beyond the Goa'uld, who were mere scavengers after the Ancients disappeared. When Jackson eventually reappears, he has both supernatural powers and incredible knowledge, but the Ancients it seems, live by a code of nonintervention in the free will of "lower" beings. Needless to say, eventually the heroes of SG-1 find this ethic impossible to understand, and Daniel himself is sent back to the human plane after intervening in the Earth war with the Goa'uld Anubis.

In an interesting combination of pop spirituality and scientific rationality, ascension in *Stargate* is suggested to be both a matter of evolution and of meditation into the right psychological state. In a *Stargate Atlantis* episode entitled "The Tao of Rodney" (3.15), Dr. Rodney McKay, the supreme scientific rationalist on Atlantis, is caught in an accident with an Ancient machine that hastens his evolution, to the point where his choices are death or ascension. He says:

the universe may seem mystical to those without understanding, when in truth anything and everything can be quantified. Look, all that hocus-pocus is just a way of getting the brain into the proper electrochemical state to allow the final physical evolution, at which point the matter which makes up this body will turn into pure energy.

McKay attempts to give a rational explanation for what is otherwise suggested to be a mystical experience, measuring his brain's synaptic levels to see that he reaches the right state for ascension. However, McKay struggles to "let go" enough to make the spiritual transformation that Daniel Jackson does in "Meridian." The more sympathetically inclined Dr Weir argues with McKay, in which she makes the characteristically New Age distinction between spirituality and religion:

> WEIR: I know, spirituality to you is a load of mumbo-jumbo, but it does help people find peace with themselves.
>
> MCKAY: But you have to believe.
>
> WEIR: I'm not talking about religion. I'm talking about shedding yourself of guilt, of anger, of ill-feeling, of anything that makes you feel shame. And then you can focus all of your energy on ascending.

On the point of death though, McKay finds himself floating in a "big empty space," where he "momentarily thought of how difficult it is to rid oneself of ego, and that existence without the individuality of consciousness would be pointless." In that space, of course, McKay thinks of a way to return his body to its usual, non-evolved self, choosing to live rather than ascend. Both Weir and McKay's descriptions clearly evoke a version of "Eastern" spirituality, suggesting spiritual progress to be about "letting go" of negative emotions. The episode sees a number of characters make New Age style comments—Weir suggests Rodney is struggling to accept the problem "can't be solved with science," military commander Shepherd advises Rodney "release his burden" and helps him meditate, while the stoic soldier Ronan tries "not to let things I can't change bother me." So, while *Stargate* infrequently evokes "real" mystical experience (as opposed to the advanced technology which it usually uses), when it does so, it does so clearly outside of the bounds of traditional Christian theology. "Real" spiritual experience thus remains only possible within the terms of the amorphous transcendental signified "Spirit" that characterizes New Age movements.

So, while the transcendental signifier tends to be the postmodern sacred's attempt at an ultimate truth claim for its universes, the corporeal God is a much less grandiose claim, for the corporeal God is almost always merely *one* of a number of supernatural entities. While the New Age-ized postmodern sacred sees almost *any* spiritual tradition as possessing some kind of truth (or of expressing the same eternal truth in a different fashion), it nevertheless retains the typical postmodern inability to hold firmly to any meta-narrative. It remains profoundly ambivalent as to the possibility of belief, playing with the corporeality of Gods but unable to truly concede their existence. Anthromorphic Gods are very much considered part of the past (and its attendant patriarchal, homophobic and racist baggage), the New Age vocabulary of Spirit much less so.

The postmodern sacred marks, then, not just the collapse of the separation between sacred and profane but the return of the supernatural to the (post)modern. Theorists of the Gothic have noted that the genre works in part as a return of the repressed, which is suggestive in both psychoanalytic and textual terms. Mark Edmundson says, "Gothic is the art of haunting, and in two senses. Gothic shows time and again that life, even at its most ostensibly innocent, is possessed, that the present is in thrall to the past. All are guilty. All must, in time, pay up" (5). It's easy to see how classic Gothic like Horace Walpole's *Castle of Otranto* or Stoker's *Dracula* might betray a fear of the return of the aristocracy, or the French Revolutionary Reign of Terror, but it is just as easy to see the Gothic return of the aspects of the supernatural that the Enlightenment was said to have banished as "superstition." The postmodern sacred, however, takes that Gothic return and applies it not just to monsters, but to the monotheistic God, to angels and to "pagan" (that is, non–Abrahamic) Gods as well. In doing so, it betrays an insight that perhaps Gods and monsters are not so far apart after all.

Monsters

Monsters occur throughout the postmodern sacred; they are the counter balance to the supernatural "good" of these texts. These monsters are almost always taken from myths and legends— werewolves, vampires, fairies, dragons and so on — although some, like the Gravelings of *Dead Like Me*, are original and specific to their texts. Literary scholar Edward J. Ingebretson begins his work *At Stake* with the insight that angels and monsters are more closely related than has typically been thought. He says:

> Fear and dread, of course, are traditional markers of divinity. In this monsters are more like angels than not. On the other hand, angels, in the terror they inspire (see Titian's *Annunciation*, for example), are more akin to monsters than not. Indeed, a characteristic of all angelic visitations is that they are terrifying. Scripture tells us that ritual salutation of the angel is "Be not afraid!" The regularity of this greeting suggests that a bracing fear should mark the angel's visit, since it betokens mystery as well as grace; since the angel challenges as well as comforts [Ingebretson, 2001: xiii].

Ingebretson's point is a well-made one, and suggests that any analysis of the sacred will need to take account of the comingling between religious awe and the awful that discourses of the spiritual should provide. The sentimentalizing of angels as "guardian angels" clearly sees the sacred stripped of its potential for terror. As Mark Edmundson bitingly suggests, contemporary depictions of angels are the "spiritual equivalents of smiley faces" (80). While the postmodern sacred is rife with examples of these sorts of easily bestowed "facile transcendence," it is arguable, too, that the postmodern sacred is also an attempt at the sublime — that is, an attempt at presenting the unpresentable. I take this conception of the sublime from Lyotard's reworking of Kant where he says, "[the sublime] takes place [...] when the imagination fails to present an object which might, if only in principle, come to match a concept" (Lyotard, 1984b: 78).

The postmodern sacred, then, depends on both images of the transcendental *and* the monstrous, while there are indeed differences between the two; they are nevertheless necessarily dependent upon one another. Queer theorist Judith Halberstam points out that "monsters have to be everything that the human is not and, in producing the negative of human, make way for the invention of the human as white, male, middle class, and heterosexual" (22). This invention of the human clearly applies to the postmodern sacred's heroes, whose heroism often lies in their affirmation of the normative (and concurrent banishing of the non-normative abject embodied in the monsters they fight). And it's not overstating the case to suggest that often the superhuman in the form of the hero is merely that same construction of the human writ large. Think of Superman, whose affirmation of "truth, justice and the American way" is a celebratory version of straight, white, middle-class masculinity tied to discourses of criminality and the nation-state.

The television series *Dark Angel* ties together both senses of the monstrous that Ingebretson describes. The title refers not only to the black hair of the heroine Max Guevera, and to her Latino ethnicity, but to the dual status of the character. Max is both monster — she is the product of genetic manipulation by a secret government organization called Manticore, bred and trained to be a supersoldier — and angel, as she works in traditional super-hero mode to correct the injustices of an post-apocalyptic near-future. This is similar to the genetically mutated super-heroes of *X-Men*, although *Dark Angel* ties the monstrous to the conspiracy theories familiar from *The X-Files*.

The show at once plays with racist fears of miscegenation (not uncoincidentally, Max is part cat, and goes into "heat," literalizing the stereotype of the animalized, over-sexed Latina) as well as suggesting that traditional models of the human (white, male) have become insuffi-

Four — Of Gods and Monsters

cient. And of course, one can see in the dual figure of Max the simultaneous fear and desire that the "kick-ass" post-feminist heroine inspired for many straight male viewers, the masochistic interplay between the sexually coded "hotness" and the fear of being dominated by the supernaturally strong heroine. While Max is physically strong and psychologically capable, the straight white men of *Dark Angel* are either ineffectual — the rich, wheel-chair user Logan and the uptight Normal — or evil — the Bad Father head of Manticore, Colonel Lydecker.

The Buffy spin-off *Angel* shows the vacillation between monster and angel in even starker relief than *Dark Angel*, with its central conceit of the character Angel, the vampire with a soul. Angel is cursed by gypsies with a soul, which he can lose upon experiencing a moment of perfect happiness, in which case he transforms into the soul-less Angelus, a violent and brutal killer. Angel works as a private investigator to "help the helpless," trying to atone for the crimes (sins) he committed as Angelus. *Angel* is quite clearly a narrative of redemption. While the series usually has a clear demarcation between the personas of Angel and Angelus (signaled visually by Angelus's smoking and tight leather pants), it nevertheless maintains a continuous tension between the two, contriving on numerous occasions to resuscitate Angelus. Angel must remain constantly vigilant, guarding against the desires that trigger his transformation into Angelus — namely, sexual desire, which effects his initial change in *Buffy* when he and Buffy sleep together. This fraught, guilt-stricken relationship to sexual desire, needless to say, is remarkably Augustinian, where "spontaneous sexual desire [exists] as the proof and penalty for original sin" (Pagels, 1989: 112). In naming the distinct personalities, and maintaining a tension between the two, *Angel* foregrounds the dual nature of the monster and the angel, even as it points out the artificiality of that separation.

In her wonderful book *Our Vampires, Ourselves* Nina Auerbach argues compellingly that vampires embody the particular fears of their immediate milieus into which they are published. She points out that that "since vampires are immortal, they are free to change incessantly" (5). Auerbach traces the cultural anxieties which vampires embody — from the "dangerously close friends" (6) of pre–Dracula English writers like Byron (11) to the Reagan-esque vampire of American films in the 1980s affected/infected by the AIDS epidemic. Vampires offer a dizzying array of cultural fears, from Marx's famous image of the capitalism-as-vampire, to more predictable fears of racial miscegenation, the "monstrous" working class, phallic women and effeminate men and so on. While it is beyond the remit of this book to fully explore the capacity of monsters to personify cultural fears, they are of course highly significant for the study of popular culture.

Queer theorist Judith Halberstam's *Skin Shows* is an important work on the study of monstrosity. Halberstam suggests that, given their multi-significations, for critics to attempt to pin monsters to one specific meaning (say, Dracula as capitalist) is a reductive and flawed critical enterprise, one that the texts themselves refuse (84). She says, "What we should resist at all costs, therefore, is the impulse to make the monster stabilize otherness. What the monster does [...] is to call into question the project of interpretation that seeks to fix meaning in the body of the monster" (84). Implicit in Halberstam's work is a warning that the attentive critic should not, in their haste to ascribe metaphorical readings, ignore the corporeality of monsters; that is, the affective response of the reader/viewer to the literal presence of creatures who do not, *can not*, exist in the real world (and in Realist texts of the same). *Skin Shows*, while problematically shifting its historical perspective from nineteenth century Gothic novels to late twentieth century splatter films with nary a point in between, is nevertheless highly useful in thinking through contemporary approaches to the monstrous. As Halberstam points out, late twentieth-century films like *Silence of the Lambs*

> reproduce the terms, conditions and technologies of nineteenth-century horror but tend to shift the position of monstrosity within those narratives. The monster, eventually, is no longer totalizing. The monstrous body that once represented everything is now represented as potentially meaning anything—it may be the outcast, the outlaw, the parasite, the pervert, the embodiment of uncontrollable sexual and violent urges, the foreigner, the misfit [27].

Implicit in Halberstam's statement here is a Jamesonian acknowledgement of pastiche. Postmodern horror might pastiche older signifiers of monstrosity but the meanings of such monstrosity have shifted significantly. Postmodern monstrosity here is figured as an excess of meaning, a movement from one signifier to another to another (there *is* nothing outside of the text).

Four — Of Gods and Monsters

Halberstam approvingly quotes Oscar Wilde's "Those who go beneath the surface do so at their own peril" (178), which is indicative of her own argument that postmodern horror is a genre of surfaces, a play of signs, whether they be textual or corporeal. The monstrous is very much a monstrosity of technology, for as Halberstam says,

> the appeal of the Gothic text [...] lies in its uncanny power to reveal the mechanisms of monster production. Like the bolt through the neck of Frankenstein's monster in the modern horror film, the technology of monstrosity is written upon the body. And the artificiality of the monster denaturalizes in turn the humanness of its enemies [106].

Those Gothic technologies end up scrambling the binaries of a misogynist and heterosexist world — between self and other, male and female, straight and queer, white and black, human and inhuman. Halberstam argues that both the heroes (Stretch) and the monsters (Buffalo Bill, Leatherface) of postmodern horror films fashion posthuman bodies for themselves, suturing new technologies onto the old. Halberstam's project, then, is a similar one. She says that "by refusing to make the human into a refuge from monstrosity, this book imagines a posthuman monstrosity that is partial, compromised, messy and queer" (188). One wonders, however, that even given the potential of an affective response to such queer posthumanity, whether a still dominant humanism will largely reinscribe those bodies as monstrous. The question, of course, hinges on whether the normative closure of many Gothic texts simply re-instates the "normal" or whether the Gothic code scrambling that Halberstam describes so vividly has problematized the normative beyond the hope of rehabilitation. Here I find myself perhaps more pessimistic than Halberstam, for though it is true that part of the pleasure of the Gothic is a partly (pre-dominantly?) disavowed affective response to a monstrosity of Otherness, just as surely part of the pleasure is the inevitable demise of the Other — the Other being violently put back in its place. While Halberstam's reading is a sophisticated work arguing for subversive acts of reading by women, queers and people of color, she also understates the ideological conservatism that Gothic texts can provoke.

Nevertheless, Halberstam's work is an imaginative and intriguing reflection on the Gothic and the categories of human and monstrous. *Skin Shows* suggests that, first and foremost, one should resist the easy moralizing that Gothic texts can provoke, the apparently straightforward relationship between monstrosity and the immoral. Monstrosity is, all too frequently, the visible sign of a subject guilty *even prior to committing a crime*. Although many of the texts I have analyzed are not specifically Gothic, that insight is nevertheless widely applicable, given that the postmodern sacred is always constructing monsters for its heroes to fight. The Gothic always arrives as a moment of utter terror in the postmodern sacred text, be it the demonic imagery of Mordor in *Lord of the Rings*, or the intermingled awe and terror at the appearance of the alien in *The X-Files*. Any analysis of unreal texts must account for the generic mixing between Gothic, horror, science fiction and fantasy, and for the ability of the divine to scramble codes of its own.

While I have argued there is a strong link between Gods (and other sacred creatures like angels) and monsters, arguably Gods are less diverse in the meanings they carry. While Gothic monsters contain our cultural anxieties writ large, Gods can sometimes be the precise opposite — containing our most idealized qualities. Gods do indeed function as "meaning-making machines" as Halberstam terms it (22), but they are usually meanings of a very different kind — as images of goodness, desirability and cultural privilege. These privileges almost inevitably produce the ideal (angelic, pure) subject as the same straight white male subject that Halberstam argues is inversely produced by the Gothic — or produce a passive, desexualized and idealized white female subject (as personified in the Virgin Mary). Thus the conventional image of Jesus, for instance, betrays a racial bias at the heart of Christian representation. While historians have argued that by today's standards Jesus would be considered a person of color, the Western pictorial tradition has historically portrayed Jesus as a white man.

It is not surprising, then, that Gods and angels are perhaps less likely to inspire the constant shift of meanings than monsters. Gender, sexuality, race and class are less fluid than in the Gothic, where multiple versions of these can exist in the same text; indeed the Gothic in its incoherence threatens to destabilize all meaning by simultaneously telling *too much and not enough* (Halberstam 23). Gods and angels do, however, shift over time, if more slowly than monsters; indeed postmodern texts often take great glee in their revision. For instance, God has been envisioned as a woman in *Dogma* (played by Alanis Morissette) and as a black man in the woeful Jim Carrey "comedy" *Bruce Almighty* (played by Morgan Freeman). And, as my previous chapter has argued, most significant of all has been the New Age precipitated shift away from the figure of God into an amorphous, non-corporeal conceptualization of "spirit."

Angels, too, have seen a shift in their representations. While traditionally they have been the subject of both awe and dread, they have more recently often been considerably domesticated (Edmundson 80). Indeed, while it is true that angels have been largely inherited from Christianity, today's angels have been disconnected from that context and now, more often than not, are consumed in a detraditionalized and deinstitutionalized fashion. Angels are frequently used as signifiers of the transcendent — for instance, in their sentimentalization as "guardian angels"— without that necessarily implying the existence of a sovereign God, or Christ, and so on.

One text that explicitly restores the dread to angels is Tony Kushner's *Angels in America*. While Christian conservatives have been at pains to insist on the utter irreconcilability of Christianity and homosexuality, Kushner foregrounds the homoerotic trace of Judaism and Christianity.[7] Angels appear as the harbinger of doom in Kushner, as well as hope for the queer community after the decimation of the AIDS epidemic in the 1980s. Interestingly, in imbuing angels with the dual sense of awe and dread, Kushner's text is the exception; far more common is the sentimental and comforting image of the angel in such pop-culture texts as *Touched By An Angel*. Thus Kushner's work is a kind of deconstructive reading of the Bible — simultaneously faithful *and* heretical. As a/theologian Mark C. Taylor says, "An a/theology that draws on deconstructive philosophy will invert established meaning and subvert everything once deemed holy. It will be utterly transgressive" (1984: 6).

Similarly, Ingebretson's reading of the Matthew Shepard case inverts the economy of the sacred and the profane. In a well-publicized case, Matthew Shepard, a gay freshman student at the University of Wyoming, was tied to a fence and struck 18 times in the head with a pistol, and left for dead. Shepard spent 5 days in a coma and then died. Ingebretson shows how easily the profane queer "monster" Matthew Shepard can be transcribed into an angelic, Christ-inflected martyr. Ingebretson says of Shepard: "To read the perverse implications of this body is to read against the grain of sentimental Christianity, which tosses the *monstrum* out, leaving only the bathos of a simpering Jesus, my best friend. Theologically Jesus who is The Christ is a hybrid — a bodied and bloodied Christ. In both its aspect of body and blood the image circulates a mixture of taboo, religiousness [...] monstrousness, as well as legal criminality" (281). In a monstrous semiotic economy, sacred and profane quickly turn into their opposites.

It's not surprising then, that the separation between Gods and monsters in the postmodern sacred begins to fall apart. The postmodern sacred returns to the supernatural in a fundamentally polytheistic way — the simultaneous return of the God of fundamentalisms, the transcendental signified of New Age and pop–Buddhism, the rediscovery of Gnosticism, the comingling between monstrous and angelic. While fundamentalists are at pains to distinguish themselves from the rest (and of course manifest a number of important differences), they are nevertheless part of the same cultural moment, a moment in which the postmodern distrust of Enlightenment meta-narratives has produced a vast number of post- and anti-rationalist offspring. Perhaps it is unsurprising then that we see sometimes a peculiarly literal approach to the text shared by both supernatural fictional texts and the fundamentalists that generally oppose such "witchcraft."

On the one hand, this often seems to confirm the lack of belief in anthromorphized Gods, since, as Darko Suvin points out, elements of religion only become available for textual appropriation once belief in them has in some measure died — the transformation from religion into "myth," of course, already implies the loss of belief *in* the myth. It's unsurprising that the living beliefs of the Jewish, Christian and Muslim traditions have a certain kind of ambivalence toward representation since as Baudrillard points out, there is the sense that the simulacrum nature of representation will in some way dissolve the possibility of God (1994: 4). Jews and Christians maintain the impossibility of truly representing God, and the Muslim tradition adds the law against showing the Prophet. Of course, Western tradition has nevertheless represented God — one usually thinks of the patriarchal figure with white beard and booming voice — but as often as not, the fantastic texts that make up the postmodern sacred have tended to prefer the polytheistic pantheons of pagan mythologies such as the Greek, Norse, Celtic and so on.

Four — Of Gods and Monsters

While the postmodern sacred will occasionally explicitly draw on "pagan" traditions such as the Greek or Norse myths, it is more generally polytheistic in the sense that it relativizes religious traditions; its perennialized outlook maintains that each tradition contains its own truths. In this kind of syncretic movement, monotheisms remain powerful symbolic traditions; however, their claims to exclusive purchase on the transcendental truth are to be minimized and largely ignored (except of course as a reminder of the problematic history of organized religion that postmodern spirituality opposes). Arguably then, we are not dealing with simply a *return* to pre–Christian polytheism, we are dealing with a post–Christian polytheistic pop culture, one that feels free to pastiche from many different religious and mythical traditions. Of course, Judaism is haunted by the ghost of polytheism, since God's "Thou shalt have no other gods before me" commandment clearly presumes the existence of other gods.[8] Christianity, too, can be said to in some ways be polytheistic, given the centrality of the doctrine of the Trinity to the Christian tradition. However, what separates the two from postmodern polytheism is an ostensible commitment to the monism of the one true God.

So, in the light of Enlightenment skepticism, the point is then that a corporeal God would require rather less belief than a transcendent one whose actions can appear second-hand. To represent a corporeal God or Goddess then, as the postmodern sacred so frequently does, is to attempt a text that in some ways mimics the holy texts of religious tradition, because it shows a more direct encounter between character and the sacred, unmediated by such texts as the Bible. It mimics the encounter of belief, but belief itself is always-already foreclosed by the generic expectation produced by reading and viewing fictional texts (and unreal texts most of all). Largely, the texts of the postmodern sacred are explicitly and unproblematically read as unreal. Thus the postmodern sacred's representation of Gods is a play with the *possibility* of the corporeality of the transcendent, not an affirmation of itself. One notable exception however is the infamous "All descriptions of artwork, architecture, documents and secret rituals in this novel are accurate" introduction to Dan Brown's *Da Vinci Code*, which undoubtedly gave the book a veneer of non-fiction, thus shifting the boundaries of generic expectation unstably for its readership, which I will turn to in Chapter Six.

CHAPTER FIVE

Buffy and Xena: Polytheisms On-Screen

The television series *Xena: Warrior Princess* provides an interesting version of the postmodern. A spin-off of *Hercules: The Legendary Adventures*, *Xena* ran between 1995 and 2001, and like *Hercules* was ostensibly set in ancient ur–Greece, "in a time of myths and legends" (that is, before history proper commenced). Both shows, however, balanced their mythic settings with a knowing postmodern referentiality. In this, *Xena* is squarely a 1990s text, an exuberant, kitschy refiguring of myth and history. While the setting could, in other hands, lend itself to a portentous, humorless mythic rendering (for instance, the dire sword-and-sandals epics *Troy* and *Alexander*), *Xena* maintains an ironic distance to its subject material. While some postmodern texts produce their hyper-reality through the absolute fidelity toward reproducing the real (and this most particularly in nostalgic texts), *Xena* abandons the search for authenticity and instead creates an ahistorical play with signifiers. As Joanne Morreale points out, "*Xena* may be regarded as a pastiche in the way it weaves a tapestry of images and themes from different cultures, mythological and Biblical traditions, and historical time periods" (82). *Xena* is myth, religion and history refracted through a postmodernism more versed in B Grade movies than it is in classics. And as David Adcock argues, it is clearly a Baudrillardian simulation of mythic "Greece," a copy without an original.

In "Athenian City Academy of the Performing Arts" (1.13), what seems to be in part a standard sitcom "clip show" is playfully reworked.[1] In the episode, Xena's companion Gabrielle enters a storytelling contest, and

Five — Buffy and Xena

it is this metaleptic device (as Jean Genet terms it) that frames the episode. The episode begins with a moonlit fight scene from a previous *Xena* episode, but the footage is stopped and "rewound" when an audience member interrupts Gabrielle to point out that she'd said the action had occurred during the day. The scene then recommences, this time set in daytime. When other storytellers in the episode tell stories, the footage for their story is drawn from old epic movies—and then critiqued as "lacking in character development." The climax of the episode features a story by Homer, whose story is merely an extended clip from Kirk Douglas's *Spartacus* movie. The episode is a play with the overt fictionality of *Xena*, explicitly drawing on its own generic history in using other Greek-style texts.

The fictionality of the text is also foregrounded in the episode "The Xena Scrolls" (2.10). The majority of the episode is set in the 1940s. The actors play descendants of their usual characters. Mell (Xena) and Janice (Gabrielle) are archaeologists who uncover the "Xena Scrolls," which tell of Xena's exploits (that is, the series' episodes). It is suggested that, rather than being fictional myths, the episodes are in fact real history. This is of course a claim not to be taken seriously, given the overt textuality of *Xena*'s pastiche of various, often contemporary, sources. The episode concludes by shifting further into the future to a scene in which a writer (played by Ted Raimi, who more usually plays Xena's erstwhile companion Joxer) uses the Xena scrolls to pitch an idea for the series to a producer named Robert J. Tapert. Robert J. Tapert is, of course, *Xena*'s real-life producer, and the episode ends with the *Xena* opening credits rolling. The episode thus weaves together the fictional elements of the Xenaverse with a play with it being "really" history, *and* the real-world knowledge of its status as a produced commodity.

The explicit unreality of *Xena* is produced in other ways as well. In "Girls Just Wanna Have Fun" (2.04), Gabrielle wanders into a nightclub-style dance, complete with hip-hop music in the soundtrack. The music on *Xena* more usually tends toward the combination of classical film scores and Celtic and vaguely "exotic" (that is, Eastern or African) sounding instruments—the Bulgarian gaida and kava, the dhol and tabla percussion of Indian bhangra music—an amorphous blend meant to signify "pre-modernness." This musical blend is postmodern in itself, an unobtrusive eclecticism that repeats in other texts of the postmodern sacred (the early series of *Buffy*, *Dead Like Me*). The theme for *Xena* is a reworking of the Bulgarian folk song "Kaval Sviri" and combines a gaida (a Bulgarian bagpipe) with the more usual film instruments of horns, strings and timpani percussion. In "Girls Just Want To Have Fun" however, the music for the dance scene is unambiguously postmodern and intentionally anachronistic, with the rapping and hip-hop drum loop setting the song clearly in the present. *Xena* is an unstable, shifting text, constantly rupturing and then being sutured back together.

So if *Xena* is a strikingly, almost paradigmatically, postmodern text, the religious content of the series is equally striking. Like *Stargate* and *Constantine*, *Xena* provides a literal, corporeality to its spirituality, with Xena interacting with Greek and Norse Gods as well as personages from the Jewish, Christian, Taoist and Hindu traditions. In addition, theologian David Fillingim argues that there is, too, an indigenous coded religion in several episodes featuring a group called The Horde ("The Price" season 2 episode 44 and "Daughter of Pomira" season 4 episode 79). All of this indicates an eclectic, pluralistic approach to religion.

The Gods on *Xena* are the very real Gods of Greek myth, who both reside in transcendental realms (Mount Olympus and the underworld) and interact with humans. In keeping with their characterization in Greek myths, the Gods on *Xena* are capricious, even malicious at times. Hades, God of the underworld, appears in a number of episodes ("Death In Chains," and "Mortal Beloved"). In "Mortal Beloved" (1.16), Xena travels to the underworld, where Hades' rule has been usurped by a serial killer named Atyminius, who has stolen Hades' helmet, the source of his power. The episode replays all the classic tropes of Greek myths, from the journey with the boat keeper Charon on the river Styx, to Tartarus and the Elysian fields. In "Death In Chains" (1.09), Celesta, Death personified, is imprisoned by King Sisyphus. While this might initially seem positive, the episode suggests that the absence of death only prolongs the pain of the sick and dying. It is only with the intervention of Xena who frees Celesta that the necessary balance between life and death can be restored (shades of New Age Taoism perhaps?). Other divine appearances include Aphrodite and Cupid in "For Him the Bell Tolls" (2.16). Ares loses his divinity in "Ten Little Warlords" (2.08), causing ordinary people to become aggressive, and Xena is forced to help him regain his stolen powers. So *Xena* provides another example of the corporeal God in the postmodern sacred, and of literal heaven and hells.

Yet this representation does not, of course, necessarily indicate an affirmation of the Greek gods. Much of the arc of the series has Xena doing penance from her earlier misdeeds as a warlike chieftain, guided by Ares, the God of war, who often attempts to lure Xena toward her dark side. As Fillingim rightly points out, though she certainly accepts their existence, Xena maintains a skeptical distance to the Gods, refraining from worshiping any of the Greek pantheon. Indeed, they frequently appear as antagonists. In "Ulysses" (2.19) Xena helps the epic hero Ulysses (the Latin name for Odysseus) return home to his kingdom Ithaca. The sea god Poseidon warns Xena not to help Ulysses in his quest, to which she replies, "Poseidon, if you've heard about my dealings with Ares, you'll know that I'm not afraid of the gods." Poseidon attempts to lure Ulysses to his death using the Sirens' song, but Xena proves impermeable to their charm. Later in Ithaca, Ulysses is greeted by his friend Metacles in Ithaca who exclaims, "Thank the gods you're here!" Xena remarks coolly, "The gods have nothing to do with it"—a comment one suspects functions not just about Poseidon's actions in this episode but as a broader theological statement from the pragmatic hero.

Xena is keenly aware of the role that the gods have in perpetuating violence and injustice in this mythic world, both in themselves and in their influence of humans. Worship of the gods very often appears to impede human self-determination on the show, with the negative effects of religious fanaticism shown frequently. In "Dreamworker" (1.03) for instance, Gabrielle is kidnapped by followers of the God of dreams, Morpheus. They force her to undergo a series of tests, intending to sacrifice her when she kills. She ultimately evades this fate using wisdom given to her by Xena about the necessity of avoiding violence. But though it is done in Morpheus's name, this human sacrifice is suggested to be a recent perversion of his true worship, and the episode ends with a new head priest pursuing a peaceful worship of the God: "From now on, the only thing we'll sacrifice is corn."

But of course though *Xena* shows the gods, as we have been making clear throughout, representation and belief are not connected in any straightforward kind of way. There are today still a small number of modern Greeks who worship the ancient Gods,[2] but given the postmodern production and consumption of *Xena* primarily in Anglophone countries, it is doubtful that series is in any way responsive to that small minority of Greeks (both in Greece and the diaspora) — or indeed to any notion of fidelity to those traditional stories. These corporeal Gods and Goddesses are hardly supposedly to be believed in as really-existing-deities outside of the text, and yet onscreen they incarnate a certain kind of camp post-rationalist enchantment.

Things get perhaps more serious when it comes to representations of Jewish and Christian stories — there are real constituencies among viewers to offend there. Like most of the other texts of the postmodern sacred, *Xena* neither entirely discards the Judeo-Christian legacy nor holds faithfully to it. In "The Giant Killer" (2.03), Xena helps David kill the giant Goliath, rewriting the biblical story. Goliath is refigured as an old friend of Xena's, a giant hired to work for the Philistines. Goliath is given a sympathetic back-story — 10 years previous, he and Xena had fought side by side, in a battle in which Goliath had saved Xena's life only to have his wife and children killed. Ignoring a warning from Xena, Goliath works for the Philistine leader Dagon to find the information that would help him avenge his family's deaths, a path which leads him to conflict with Xena and the Israelites. This of course leads to his eventual death at David's hand, but it is hardly the triumphant Israelite victory more usually told. Goliath is pitiable, foolish in seeking revenge, but not evil. Xena regrets Goliath's death, calling him "a great warrior, a loving husband and my friend."

Xena rewrites the Jewish and Christian religions in "The Giant Killer" along with its characterizations. Rather than assert the singularity of biblical God, David says that he is "greater than Zeus, Ares, *all the lesser Gods* put together" (italics added). While there is certainly some evidence of tacit henotheism in the Hebrew Bible, this is a far from orthodox take in the present day after several thousand years of accumulated metaphysical monotheist baggage. Some hints of Hebrew spirituality are included: David reads a Psalm, and during the climactic scene, while a heavenly choir sings on the soundtrack, there are a few strategic shots of clouds that might suggest the existence of a transcendent God. Given the polytheistic context of *Xena*, this introduction of a Jewish story only serves to relativize the Biblical monotheisms, displacing its purchase on spiritual truth and rendering the Bible as just another myth among the Greek and Roman myths more usually told on *Xena*. As David Adcock suggests, "*Xena* appropriates 'authentic' cultural tropes, mythemes and icons, but in the recontextualized fabric, the entire 'original' is called into question" (n.pag.). *Xena* as a simulation exposes the simulacral nature of not only its popular culture and pagan sources, but the Jewish and Christian traditions as well.

Of course, the Jewish story on offer in *Xena* has itself been glossed through the dominant readings of Christianity. It is always-already "Judeo-Christian" rather than strictly Jewish. Here we should remember Lyotard's point that "Judeo-Christian" sublates Judaism into Christianity, working the content of the Hebrew Bible/Tanakh through Christianity's interpretative history and remaking Judaism in Christianity's own image.

There are other veiled references to Christianity in the series, too. In its third season, *Xena* begins a long story arc involving the God "Dahak," a derivation of the Persian god Zahhak. Dahak recalls both Christian and pagan worship at the same time—Dahak is termed "the one true God" by his adherents. Gabrielle becomes supernaturally pregnant by a worshipper of the God. While Xena is convinced that the child is evil, Gabrielle is not so sure. The birth recalls both Hebrew and Christian narratives—the baby is born in a stable like Jesus, and rather than kill the child as Xena suggests, Gabrielle secretly puts the child in a basket and floats her down a river (definite shades of Moses). Her child, Hope, grows at a supernatural rate and is a young woman the next time they meet. But Hope, of course, is evil, and it is only when she murders Xena's son Solan that Gabrielle realizes her daughter's true nature. So, the arc recalls both pagan worship and an inverted Christian coding. In some ways, this recalls Žižek argument regarding *Star Wars*, where he says that "since the ideological universe of *Star Wars* is the New Age pagan universe, it is quite logical that the central figure of Evil should echo Christ" (2006:101). However, *Xena*'s relationship to Christianity is more ambivalent than that of *Star Wars*.

In its final two seasons, *Xena* begins its most obvious Christian plot trajectory. Xena herself gives birth to the immaculately conceived Eve, who it is suggested will bring about a change that will end the time of the Greek Gods. The pagan polytheism of *Xena* is thus suggested to give way to a (Christian-coded) monotheism ("Motherhood" 6.01). Ivar Kvistad argues that the concluding seasons of *Xena* suggest that because of

> the structural logic of the series' representation of epochal succession, the Judeo-Christian tradition becomes the rightful successor and antidote to the pagan world [and that] construct it as the superior religious and moral paradigm among its competitors [n.pag.].

Kvistad goes so far as to suggest that *Xena*'s Christian turn fits easily into a neoconservative framework. Kvistad makes an interesting point; however it is difficult to definitively position the series into a Christian (let alone Jewish) framework. *Xena*'s blank irony is hardly affirmative of any one strand of its texts. The presence of such Christian figures as the archangel Michael appears as just another trope in *Xena*'s stylized, hyperreal versions of religion. Christianity thus becomes as simulated as the Greek myths it is supposed to have superseded.

Importantly, too, *Xena* enters into the supplementary relationship between the New Age and Christianity. If its concluding season suggests that it tipped more strongly toward Christianity, its earlier seasons problematize that reading, relativizing and rewriting the "Judeo-Christian" tradition. Screening for 6 seasons, *Xena* contains enough ambivalences and ironies to encompass a multiplicity of readings. As a pastiched simulation, it creates incomplete and fragmentary readings, which is, I suspect, part of its appeal.

Then there are the decidedly un-neoconservative takes on gender and sexuality. As it gleefully rewrites myth, *Xena* shows its postmodern positions ethically too. Xena herself is most definitely a post-feminist heroine — a strong, fighting action hero with a spectacularized, often sexualized body. While this is not an unproblematic development for some feminist writers, it is nevertheless interesting and preferable to classically passive heroines waiting to be saved by men and heterosexual romance. Morreale, for instance, suggests that *Xena*'s textual excess itself may be regarded as camp, giving the series a feminist potential for a critical estrangement on gender. And of course, the homoerotic relationship between Xena and her companion Gabrielle gathered the series a devoted lesbian following, something the series clearly played to but never tipped into a definitive textual reading of the two as a couple. While of course same-sex love was a feature of the ancient world, *Xena* hardly features the many queer-coded characters one might expect to find in a more faithful representation of the mythic Greek milieu.[3] Instead, it walks the line between subtext and text dictated by the generally homophobic norms of contemporary TV and film. *Xena* thus very definitely disguises its postmodern ethics toward gender and sexuality beneath its pre-modern setting. As Kvistad makes clear, the Sapphic relationship between Xena and Gabrielle is as important to the series as its religious underpinning. The female action hero and lesbian subtext sits ill at ease with an American neoconservative religious reading.

Echoing that ambivalence, there are a number of nostalgic tendencies at work in *Xena*. There is a muted pastoralism, a virtue of its real-world filming in New Zealand/Aotearoa (later to be the site for Peter Jackson's *The Lord of the Rings* film trilogy). Then, there are the lost heroic narratives of postmodernism, which have become problematized by shattering of meta-narratives. Every episode begins with the voice-over, "In a time of ancient Gods, warlords and kings, a land in turmoil cried out for a hero." In postmodernism, which begins as Taylor says "with a sense of *irrevocable* loss and *incurable* fault," (1984: 6), there is very definitely the sense that real-world heroes are difficult to find. But if an unproblematic hero has been lost, then it is a traumatic loss which the postmodern sacred returns to, again and again. The postmodern condition serves to qualify heroism — for instance, in the way that doctors are sued by their patients, or the suspicion directed toward altruism (what's in it for *them*?). Even given some temporary revivals of real-life heroes (the firefighters of New York in September 11), it still remains difficult to imagine heroes like *Xena* in a Realist setting. So the estranged setting of *Xena* in the distant, mythic, past, is perhaps the only solution to the postmodern nostalgia for heroic figures.

But the chief nostalgia at work in *Xena* is that of cinema, for itself as a "lost object" as Baudrillard puts it (47). As episodes like "Athenian City Academy of the Performing Arts" (1.13) show, *Xena* foregrounds its own inauthenticity and textuality. So this strain of nostalgia is hardly mournful. *Xena* is very definitely in the "end of history" celebratory mode of postmodernism dominant in the 1990s. In contrast to *Harry Potter*, *Xena* is postmodern nostalgia at its most *in* authentic, an intentionally inaccurate rendering of Greek myths that has discarded fidelity for eclecticism, textual play and revision, and which treats the monotheistic and pantheistic as equally camp. In this, *Xena* is perhaps more indicative of the 90s than any other text in the postmodern sacred.

Buffy the Vampire Slayer

Nostalgia can be a multifaceted thing. While as Susan Stewart argues, it is always marked by loss, it can be celebratory or depressed. It may be pro or anti postmodernism, but in either case, it remains profoundly postmodern in perspective. In general, nostalgic texts like *Harry Potter* and *Xena* have a tendency to elide the ethically unpalatable aspects of the past, preferring to revel instead in aesthetics. The willfully unfaithful reading of myth on *Xena* makes the series a very obviously pre–September 11 text. On *Buffy the Vampire Slayer* however, we see a television series that straddles 9/11, and that makes an immense difference in tone in its later seasons. *Buffy*, the jarringly titled Joss Whedon created cult series, offers up a cornucopia of nostalgia, most frequently a nostalgia for the lost referent of film. Indeed, Whedon has gone on record stating he envisioned the series as a "cull-from-every-genre-all-the-time thing" (qtd. Albright 65). Over its 144 episodes, the series often seems awash in postmodern irony and self-reflexivity, painfully aware of its own textuality, but also at key moments providing an anti-postmodern nostalgia for real experience (see Chapter Two for more on *Buffy* and the transcendental signified). As such it provides the perfect example for the two dueling nostalgic tendencies I have described in this chapter.

The premise of the series, for those unaware, is that Buffy Summers, a high school student, is a supernaturally gifted killer ("a Slayer") of vampires and other supernatural entities like demons. She, along with Giles, her "Watcher" from a Council in England dedicated to fighting evil, and some close friends, fights to save mankind from various supernatural beings out to do us harm. As the title suggests, the series plays off a contrast between the horror and the teen lifestyle of Buffy and her friends in the fictional small Californian town of Sunnydale. *Buffy* is a television series largely about vampires, especially in its earliest seasons, however the series also makes use of many other film and mythological creatures and references. Its chief referent is clearly the horror genre,[4] yet it also takes in other fantastic elements, weaving in fairy tales and science fiction motifs into its own invented mythology. Richard S. Albright rightly points out that Buffy "rejoices in its postmodern refusal to be pinned down to a single generic formula" (65).

While the dialogue frequently reworks the language of game-shows[5] and advertisements, the series' postmodern referentiality goes deeper than dialogue. As well as its pop-culture references, *Buffy* liberally weaves in references to fairy tales and classic literature. Hansel and Gretel appear as demonic entities goading the Sunnydale adults into a literal witch hunt in "Gingerbread" (3.10), in a clear metaphor for contemporary hysteria about child abuse. In "Go Fish," (2.20), the Sunnydale swim team become monsters reminiscent of *The Creature from the Black Lagoon*, a reference the series is only too quick to knowingly point out.[6] *Buffy* reimagines Dr. Jekyll and Mister Hyde in "Beauty and the Beasts" (3.04) as an allegory for domestic abuse. Adam, the "Big Bad" (i.e., the main evil antagonist) of Season Four, is a version of Frankenstein's monster, an amalgam of demon and human parts.

In "Buffy Vs Dracula" (5.01), we see the series' mythology square up, finally, to the vampire genre's most famous text. When Buffy meets Dracula, she says, "Get out," as if to purge the series of the one referent it has hitherto circled but never named.

> BUFFY: So let me get this straight, you're Dracula. *The* guy, the Count.
> DRACULA: I am.
> BUFFY: And you're sure this isn't just a fanboy thing? Cause I've fought more than a few pimply, overweight vamps who called themselves Lestat ["Buffy Vs Dracula" 5.01].

While the episode replays a number of classic vampire tropes that the series has otherwise eschewed — Dracula turns into mist, bats — it maintains its sense of irony toward its subject matter. Xander asks Dracula sarcastically, "Where'd you get your accent, *Sesame Street*?" yet the excitement of the characters after their first meeting with the Count is clearly that of fans meeting an idol (and very much a fanboy and fangirl thing). While *Buffy* itself is a meta-riff on the horror genre, this episode, which comes after four seasons, folds the series back on itself, playing with the genre's source materials part mockingly and part seriously.

Interestingly, *Buffy* only features Dracula once, as though the incorporation of the Dracula mythology into the series renders anything more than a superficial self-referential encounter redundant. Yet *Buffy*'s nostalgic tendency is hardly limited to pastiching the horror genre; the dialogue frequently makes quick-witted references to other shows and movies, not to mention popular culture ephemera like game shows and ads. In "Once More With Feeling" (6.07), the series' infamous musical episode, the referent shifts to Broadway musicals as a demon's spell compels people to break out into song and elaborate dance numbers. Indeed, Anya complains that her number is a "retro pastiche, it's never going to be breakaway pop hit."[7] "Superstar" (4.07) features an alternate Sunnydale in which the geek Jonathan has transformed himself into a suave James Bond style character, complete with suit and bow-tie — a published author, accomplished musician, consultant for the U.S. Army and so on. The Bond references occur too in the soundtrack, which clearly allude to John Barry's famous scores. "Dirty Girls" (7.18) features an original series *Star Trek* sequence in which Faith fights a Vulcan.

The series is well known for its lightning quick dialogue, in particular for the creative ways it makes use of pop culture references. For instance, in "The Wish" (3.09), Cordelia refers to the alternative universe she now inhabits as "Bizarre-o World," one of many references the series makes to the Superman comics. In the same episode, Xander refers to his and Willow's feelings of guilt (for having been caught cheating) as "Guiltapalooza." The reference is here is to Lollapalooza, a massive music festival tour that featured many different acts, yet *Buffy* characteristically twists the reference into a new phrase of its own, playing on the audience's presumed knowledge of the festival in order to create a new phrase. This kind of language usage, dubbed "Slayer Slang," has attracted the notice of a number of scholars.[8] Richard S. Albright suggests that "correspondences between the Buffyverse and our world are hyperrealized through a sharing of imaginary works between both worlds" (64). In other words, the popular culture references in *Buffy* work to ground the fictional universe in our postmodern referentiality. Albright argues, for instance, for the villains of season six, the Evil Trio of Andrew, Jonathon and Warren, "the boundary between fantasy and reality is permeable and they seem motivated to make their lives imitate art, to live in the imaginary worlds that supply so much of their dialogue" (64). The Trio argue over such geek topics as SF and comics (*Star Wars, Star Trek: The Next Generation, Superman* and *Spiderman*), and who makes the best Bond ("Life Serial" 6.05).

So referentiality on *Buffy* then becomes a matter of explicit discussion as well as textual incorporation. Postmodern pastiche, after all, can function in a number of different ways—for instance, the seamless unacknowledged retreads of the sort that Jameson talks about with regard to *Body Heat, Chinatown* and so on. Then, there is the self-referentiality of genre, in which a text points self-consciously toward its own generic features. Finally, there is explicit referentiality, in which texts either self-consciously recreate scenes from other texts (visual quoting, if you will), or have characters discuss other texts. *Buffy*, unsurprisingly, does all of these at times. The "Once More with Feeling" episode both signals unspecifically to Hollywood musicals of the 1940s and 50s, as well as having its characters explicitly discuss the conventions of the genre (Giles: "That would explain the huge backing orchestra I couldn't see and the synchronized dancing from the room service chaps").

But if *Buffy* is, as critic David Lavery has termed it, "a religion in narrative," then it is one marked by a profound ambivalence toward the power and attachment to narrative. On the one hand, as all of these examples suggest, there is a loving, if irreverent tribute to the show's source materials. Every possible permutation of narrative culture is put through Whedon's postmodern blender, from French farce to Medea, as he put it in one interview (Longworth 211, qtd. Lavery). On the other hand, the postmodern referentiality in *Buffy*, while often a matter of glib banter, is also occasionally interrogated more deeply than perhaps one would expect from a fantastic television series airing on a major network. The remarkable episode "Storyteller" (7.16) is a case in point where the series rises above its generic limitations. Andrew, after fleeing Sunnydale at the end of Season Six, has returned and murders his friend Jonathan at the bidding of his (dead) friend/crush Warren in "Lessons" (7.01). He has now joined Buffy and her team, part prisoner, part guest. The episode begins with an elaborate Masterpiece Theater style set and Andrew's mock poetic narration, and features multiple textual frames—the glossy TV look of Andrew's pop-culture fantasies, the grainy video-camera look of the documentary Andrew is making about Buffy, the "real world" shots of the characters in the show's usual style. Andrew's narration provides a direct self-referential textuality to the episode. In the climactic scene, Buffy has taken Andrew to the Sunnydale High school basement where Andrew murdered Jonathan and threatens him with a knife:

ANDREW: So this is my redemption at last, buy back my bruised soul with the blood of my heart but [falters] not enough to kill.

BUFFY: Stop! Stop telling stories. Life isn't a story [...] you always do this, you make everything into a story so no-one's responsible for anything because they're just following a script.

ANDREW: Please don't kill me. Warren said Jonathan would be OK. I trusted him, and I lost my friend.

BUFFY: You didn't lose him. You murdered him.

ANDREW: I know, but you don't need to kill me. You said we could all get through this.

BUFFY: I made it up. I'm making it all up. What kind of hero does that make me?

ANDREW: No, you're doing great. Really. Kudos.

BUFFY: Yeah? Well, I don't like having to give a bunch of speeches about how we're all gonna live, because we won't. This isn't some story where good triumphs because good triumphs. Good people are going to die! Girls. Maybe me. Probably you. Probably right now.

Of course, Buffy doesn't actually kill Andrew (she is, after all, a hero).[9] The episode ends with Andrew speaking directly into the camera, in the toilet, saying, "Here's the thing. I killed my best friend. There's a big fight coming, and I don't know what's going to happen. I don't even think I'm going to live through it. That's, uh, probably the way it should be. I guess I'm..." and then he turns the camera off. The episode proves remarkable for its strained relationship toward narrative, at once affirming the pleasures of textuality, and then swiftly undercutting itself. Andrew's storytelling *is* pleasurable, and his postmodern referencing is hardly dissimilar to any other character on the show. The episode's apparent confirmation of "reality" — Andrew admitting he really did kill Jonathon, and that cannot be easily moralized away into a redemption narrative — is not merely a trite, easy affirmation, rather it is an examination of the consequences of the postmodern turn. But even as it seems to raise a critique of the power of narrative to conceal reality, *Buffy* is painfully aware of its own textuality, its own unreality — and indeed the unreality that the postmodern hyperreal has produced of its own world — and self-aware enough to realize how much pleasure its audience takes from its aesthetic.

Even Christianity is often folded within the aestheticized irony.

"Note to self: religion freaky." And when she's asked if there's any proof of the existence of God she replies, "Nothing solid." As critic Greg Erikson points out, "Within the show itself, although ethical decisions and even religious rituals are presented seriously, the presence of traditional Christian symbols, churches, and divinity is generally lightly mocked" (1). Jana Weiss in *What Would Buffy Do* suggests that *Buffy* may be at times considered Christian form if not content, with Buffy's self-sacrificing suicidal swan dive a kind of Christ-like moment ("She saved the world a lot," as her tombstone goes). Yet at the same time, as Weiss points out, the show draws on an eclectic blend of religious traditions and ethical principles and is unable to be contained within any one tradition.

Buffy *and the Enchanted World*

The founding mythos of *Buffy* is a kind of reversal of the Christian Edenic narrative. In an early episode, Giles states portentously that

> this world is older than any of you know. Contrary to popular mythology, it did not begin as a paradise. For untold eons, demons walked the earth. They made it their home, their ... their Hell. But in time they lost their purchase on this reality. The way was made for mortal enemies, for man. All that remains of the old ones are vestiges, certain magics, certain creatures ["The Harvest" 1.02].

The world of *Buffy* is, like *The X Files* before it, an enchanted world full of all manner of supernatural elements. There are vampires, werewolves, witches, a plethora of invented demons evil and benign and even a nebulous spirit claiming to be the very first form of evil. Unlike *The X-Files* however, *Buffy* for the most part does not have a Todorovian epistemological uncertainty — it is indeed marvelous, with never-real. But where for Todorov and Rosemary Jackson the marvelous comforts with its long-past historical viewpoint, *Buffy*'s setting in the present in a vaguely recognizable (if idealized) California town does not comfort in quite the same way. Indeed, the series was overtaken by real-life controversy, when an episode that featured a teen shooter was shelved in the weeks after the Columbine massacre in 1999. Even the supernatural dimensions of the episode (Buffy gained the ability to read thoughts) were not sufficiently unreal for the network to remain untroubled.

This capacity for the show to unsettle is made abundantly clear in the one truly Realist episode of Buffy's seven seasons. In "Normal Again" (6.17), the entire foundation of the series is undermined. Buffy is poisoned by the Trio and flicks back between realities, between the familiar "reality" of her life as a Slayer in Sunnydale, and her life as a patient in a mental hospital. It is suggested that all of Buffy's adventures onscreen are the result of psychosis, that her friends, sister and supernatural powers are simply figments of her imagination — a Realist interpretation of the text if ever there was one. The doctor tells Buffy that she needs to kill her friends, but this proves too difficult, and eventually, she chooses Sunnydale over the mental institution. The conclusion of the episode is deeply ambivalent; it ends not in Sunnydale and the resumption of "real" life, but in the mental hospital, with the doctor telling Buffy's mother that "we've lost her" and Buffy staring blankly in her catatonia. While this could easily fall into the clichéd "it was all just a dream" explanation for fantastic texts, *Buffy* is more nuanced a text than that. It's important to note that the episode occurs toward the end of the sixth season; there are another 27 episodes after this one. So clearly this episode is not a mere Realist denouement that retrospectively rewrites the series as a psychotic delusion. But "Normal Again" does however offer the one plausibly Realist explanation for the series, and it is characteristic of the text that it neither ends firmly on one side or another — neither reality nor fantasy. We end, predictably, back in Sunnydale, but more uncertainly than when we began.

Buffy, as a nostalgic postmodern text, knows the pleasures of its viewers lie in playing with unreality, with both belief and unbelief. The serial form of episodic TV usually means an equilibrium is disturbed and then recovered, but *Buffy* persistently challenges that. Instead of the Realist closure that "Normal Again" promises (and indeed many fans speculated that the final episode would revisit the mental institution), the series ends with Buffy and her friends looking out on a destroyed Sunnydale. Willow asks Buffy, "What are we going to do now, Buffy?" and Buffy answers wordlessly with an inscrutable smile ("Chosen" 7.22). This ending too is open-ended, leaving the viewer to answer the question instead. This is one text that does not "always [opt] for the real" (1994:21) as Baudrillard puts it, but neither can it so easily banish the weight of skepticism, even for itself in an explicitly fantastic text.

One final reference to sum up this discussion of Buffy's postmodernist sensibility. In "I Only Have Eyes for You" (2.19), 50s school nostalgia a la *Happy Days* returns in the form of phantom lovers, who are doomed to replay their deaths through possessing human proxies. As the title suggests, the old Flamingos doo-wop song features prominently in the episode, as do a number of flashbacks to the period. We see a number of standard tropes of '50s nostalgia — the fashion, the language ("He's dreamy"), a high school yearbook. Of course, *Buffy* is hardly alone in re-visiting the period, for as Fredric Jameson reminds us, the 1950s remain the privileged referent for American nostalgia (1991: 19). Metaphorically, though, the episode works as reminder of the haunting the past (and most especially the 1950s onward for Americans) works on the contemporary.[10] However ambivalent we may be toward postmodern referentiality, and even as we seek to find real experiences outside of the textual, like the lovers on *Buffy* we seem nevertheless doomed to repeat the past again and again, trapped eternally in a nostalgia mode. If the earliest seasons of *Buffy* seem to exhibit a more celebratory mode of postmodern nostalgia, the sixth and seventh seasons mark a post–September 11 shift toward an ostensibly anti-postmodern postmodernism. The loss of nostalgia remains a constant, but this is more bitter than sweet, and the search for a pure authentic experience remains as elusive as ever.

Buddhism and the Afterlife

In doing so, *Buffy* plays out the underside of postmodern simulation, the desire for "real" experience. This occurs most dramatically in the Series 6 arc. At the end of Series 5, Buffy dives dramatically into a dimensional portal, closing it off, saving the world, and dying in the process. Convinced, however, that Buffy is in a "hell dimension," her friends work a spell to bring her back ("Bargaining" 6.01 and 6.02). Of course, this being television, nothing is ever simple, so that hell dimension turns out to have been heaven. The heaven described resembles not so much a Christian heaven as a Buddhist state of nirvana, a world free of hurt and pain. By contrast, this world is "hard ... and bright ... and violent" ("After Life" 6.03), an excess of sensation too much for Buffy to cope with. "Hard and bright and violent" seems a succinct way of describing some of the negative experiences of postmodern simulation.

Not unexpectedly then, she comes back from heaven withdrawn, unable to feel *anything*. "Give me something to sing about," she sings in "Once More with Feeling." Paradoxically, this world is too much, *and* too little, for Buffy. In between working shifts at a burger joint, Buffy starts having rough, BDSM sex with the vampire Spike, just to feel something. Their first sexual encounter in "Smashed" (6.09) begins with the pair fighting, then having sex, as a building collapses around them. Much like Taylor's tattooed and pierced anti-postmoderns, Buffy attempts to recover her lost sense of self by recovering her body through rough sex. Tellingly, Jana Reiss suggests that Buffy's "misery, her profound despair, makes it impossible for her to crack jokes" (45) in the sixth season — this turn toward the body coincides with her inability to trade in postmodern referentiality. But this does *not* mean that *Buffy* has suddenly exited postmodernism for "the real," rather, it has shifted gears into a postmodernist nostalgia of a different sort.

Ignoring for the moment the theological implications of Buffy's falling from heaven (which I have already dealt with in Chapter Two), the arc illuminates a peculiarly postmodern approach to the body: disconnected from itself, yet unable to break out of the circularity of postmodern simulation and self-referentiality — the knowingness of singing "Give me something to sing about," while the seeming outside of rough sex becomes just another move in the postmodern commodification of the body. Once again, "what is promoted as 'genuine culture' always turns out to be 'simulacra of genuine culture'" (Taylor, 1997: 204), and this is as true for bodily experiences as it is for culture (and most especially bodily experiences being simulated on-screen).

It's no accident that the storyline coincides with the most regularly shown job Buffy has on the series (she works part time as a school counselor in Series 7, but this is infrequently shown); indeed a number of episodes played viscerally on the fast-food angle before agitation from sponsors forced the producers to abandon the storyline. Fast food, as we know, combines modern forms of discipline with postmodern forms of simulation. George Ritzer argues that employees' ability to interact with customers in such jobs has become so heavily scripted — the ubiquitous

"Have a nice day!"—that human interaction itself has become a form of simulation in postmodern capitalism. Such interactions are produced by the combination of explicit surveillance (on the part of managers, supervisors and so on) as well as internalized discipline. Thus postmodern forms of capitalism are often highly reliant on modern rationalist forms of organization, surveillance and discipline. For Buffy, working in such an environment, where she is told she is "one of the lifers," is clearly motivation for her to use violent sex to get "out" of herself (not to mention her job). The arc swings between the two extremes of postmodern extratextual "reality" and simulation, and while the violent sex might at first glance seem ill at ease with *Buffy*'s playful postmodern referentiality, it instead condenses a dynamic at the heart of the postmodern condition. It's arguable that the graphic sex and violence emerge as a response to the anaestheticizing effects of postmodern simulation, a way to reclaim the material from the symbolic.

Having said that, the series codes Buffy's searching for transcendent experience (non-experience) as a kind of sin. Buffy has persistently coded fighting as a metaphor for sex, and vice versa; for instance, Faith, the other Slayer, has sex with Xander after an unresolved, unsatisfying fight in "The Zeppo" (3.13)—"a fight like that and no kill ... I'm about ready to pop." The rough sex of the Buffy/Spike relationship is coded as a self-destructive flirtation with the dark side that she must repent from, well before his attempted rape in "Seeing Red" (6.19) which numerous writers have seen as punishment. When Buffy breaks down sobbing in Tara's arms, when she admits her relationship with Spike, it's a kind of penitential confession.

Does that, then, mean that "realism" to us has become only reduced to the most visceral experiences of life? Do we need sex and violence to be this "real" and graphic precisely because our lives are so fake, or is it the opposite, *Buffy* as simulation, textual copies without originals? Or possibly, and this is particularly evident in the post–September 11 discourse on the "real," it may be *both*. Yet as Bauman points out, the search for "peak experience" is itself a significant strain of contemporary capitalism, simultaneously "spiritual" and profane. Yet in its sacralization of sex, like *The Da Vinci Code*, this arc on *Buffy* demonstrates a profound ambivalence around (particularly female) sexuality and the ability of bodies to deliver beyond the material.

CHAPTER SIX

Whither Leonardo da Vinci? New Age Gnosticism

Selling over 60 million copies, Dan Brown's *The Da Vinci Code* has been a pop-culture phenomenon, spawning a cottage industry of imitators and interpreters. In this chapter, I shall argue that the success of *The Da Vinci Code* can be at least partly attributed to a dual textual move — a rejection of institutional religion (in the form of the Catholic Church), and an affirmation of individual spiritual experience in the form of a Gnostic "feminine" spirituality. *The Da Vinci Code* thus has a relation to the various New Age movements discussed in Chapter Two, which posit a similarly individualized spiritual experience, albeit with a twist toward early Christian Gnostic traditions rather than Buddhism or Hinduism. "New Agers are inclined to go back to the past" (42), as Paul Heelas puts it. Archeology, not futurism, is the dominant New Age motif.

Interestingly, though it's a work of fiction, The *Da Vinci Code* featured a much discussed disclaimer to the book — "All descriptions of artwork, architecture, documents and secret rituals in this novel are accurate." Much of the discussion of the book has centered around this ambiguous statement and the likelihood of the novel's (and later film) rereading of real-world religious traditions and institutions being accurate. *Time* magazine declared 2006 "the summer of Mary Magdalene" in response to the novel's success. *The Da Vinci Code* has had enough of a cultural impact that a number of Catholic and Anglican priests have felt it necessary to dispute the rendering of Christianity in the book.[1] Despite the implausibility of *The Da Vinci Code*'s plot, Dan Brown's novel produced a distinct frisson among many of his readers.

Six — Whither Leonardo da Vinci

What is most notable about *The Da Vinci Code* is its explicit references to the hitherto largely unknown Gnostic gospels. Though fragments of some esoterica had floated around Europe for the previous century or so, it wasn't until the discovery of thirteen codices containing fifty Gnostic texts in Nag Hammadi, Egypt, in 1945 that Gnosticism really re-emerged. The find contained the Gospel of Thomas, the Gospel of Philip, and many other significant texts. Over the next thirty years, the collection was translated into English, and has slowly permeated into the public consciousness ever since. As such, it was probably a matter of time before some enterprising writer made mileage from the Nag Hammadi Gospels, and though a few attempts were hazarded before, ultimately it was American thriller writer Dan Brown whose version really made a cultural impact.

The novel rereads Jesus' life radically, if not entirely originally, given its oft-noted similarity to the nonfiction book *Holy Blood, Holy Grail*, rearranging the chaste Christian narrative to include a purported marriage between Jesus and Mary Magdalene and the birth of their children. Brown weaves references to the Gnostics into a conspiracy theory of a hidden Christianity with the Holy Grail, Leonardo da Vinci, the Knights Templar and other secret organizations. The character Leigh Teabing reads from the Gnostic Gospel of Philip to support the idea of the marriage between Mary Magdalene and Jesus, "And the companion of Jesus Christ is Mary Magdalene. Christ loved her more than all the other disciples and used to kiss her often on the mouth" (331). Teabing states:

> "These are photocopies of the Nag Hammadi and Dead Sea scrolls, which I mentioned earlier ... the earliest Christian records. Troublingly, they do not match up with the Gospels in the Bible." Flipping toward the middle of the book, Teabing pointed to a passage. "The *Gospel of Philip* is always a good place to start."
> Sophie read the passage:
> And the companion of the Savior is Mary Magdalene. Christ loved her more than all the disciples and used to kiss her often on her mouth. The rest of the disciples were offended by it and expressed disapproval. They said to him, "Why do you love her more than all of us?" [401].

Sophie then objects that the passage says nothing about marriage, but Teabing corrects her: "'*Au contraire.*' Teabing smiled, pointing to the first line. 'As any Aramaic scholar will tell you, the word *companion*, in those days, literally meant *spouse*.'"

In a preposterously unlikely storyline, Jesus and Mary Magdalene's children's bloodline turns out to be the Holy Grail, and our heroine Sophie Neuve. But as thrillers go, this is a particularly metaphysically resonant secret to build a chase around, neatly tying together Gnosticism, the Matter of Britain, Leonardo da Vinci's artwork, the Knights Templar and assorted others into a marvelously incoherent conspiracy theory. Everything is grist for Brown's story, a pastiche of spiritual signifiers as pulpy as any of the other texts I have discussed.

But it is Brown's Gnosticism that is *The Da Vinci Code*'s most interesting, and striking, religious characteristic. In her groundbreaking work on Gnosticism, Elaine Pagels argues that Gnosticism may be largely distinguished from orthodox Christianity by its positions on "organization of authority, the participation of women, martyrdom [and] a fundamental religious perspective that remained antithetical to the claims of the institutional church" (1979: 121). Gnosticism, as Pagels describes it, is an individual practice akin in some ways to contemporary New Age spirituality, anti-institutional, prone to seeing spiritual wisdom as a personal, rather than collective experience (*gnosis*, after all, comes from the Greek word for knowledge)—a clear contrast to the Christian notion of divine revelation as mediated through the Church and the clergy.

It is the very marginal status of Gnosticism that makes it appealing to New Agers. Heelas adds that for New Agers, "what matters is the 'arcane,' the 'esoteric,' the 'hidden wisdom,' the inner or secret tradition,' the 'ageless wisdom'" (27). Just as other mystic Abrahamic traditions like Kaballah[2] and Sufi have been embraced in some part by New Agers, Gnosticism's historic disappearance gives these deuterocanonical ancient texts a mystique they may not have otherwise possessed. But even more than that, Gnosticism is explicitly secretive, with Gnostic teachers offering to teach Jesus' "secret" teachings (Pagels 14). Indeed, its very name (*gnosis*, knowledge) signals Gnosticism's general interest in pedagogical instruction, a transmission of knowledge from teacher to initiate. Arguably, though *The Da Vinci Code* explicitly references Gnosticism, it remains as much in dialogue with contemporary New Age and pagan movements. Slavoj Žižek quite rightly, if negatively, links individualistic contemporary pagan spiritualities with Gnosticism, saying, "Against the pagan and/or Gnostic Wisdom which celebrates the (re)discovery of one's true Self—the return to it, the realization of its potentials or whatsoever — Christianity calls upon us to re-invent ourselves" (2001: 148). To quote Heelas once again, New Age spirituality suggests that "the same wisdom can be found at the heart of all religious traditions" (29), something undoubtedly raised in *The Da Vinci Code* by symbologist Robert Langdon's references to numerous religious traditions — Egyptian, Greek, Mithraic and so on. *The Da Vinci Code* reads the disparate Gnostic traditions through the perennialist New Age lens, a sentimentalized, cleaned-up version of sometimes bracingly foreign traditions. But as Elaine Pagels and Karen King point out, Gnosticism (an after-the-fact term devised in the 18th century) cannot be easily said to be only *one* tradition — to do so is to implicitly adopt the perspective of the "orthodox" declaring all departures to be "heresy" (xviii–xxii). Brown therefore lends the contradictory traditions of Gnosticism a false coherence.

Furthermore, theologian Nancy Calvert-Koyzis points out a number of basic inaccuracies in *The Da Vinci Code*'s take on the Gnostic gospels. First, she points out that the *Gospel of Philip* found at Nag Hammadi was, in fact, written in Coptic, and likely to have been transcribed from Greek rather than Aramaic. Further, she points out that while "companion" can refer to marriages, it also referred to spiritual relationships, and that the *Gospel of Philip* only uses the Coptic word for "wife" when describing marriages. She argues persuasively that *The Da Vinci Code* makes use of a dubious, untenable reading of the Gnostic texts in its truth-claim of an originary, suppressed Gnostic Christianity. *The Da Vinci Code* suggests that *The Gospel of Philip* and *The Gospel of Mary* were written earlier than the canonical Gospels (400). Yet Calvert-Koyzis points out that *The Gospel of Mary* was written in the first or second half of the second century C.E. Nevertheless, it is worthwhile examining what kinds of thematic resonances the Brown text has with early Christian Gnostic ideas.

In an interesting textual sleight of hand, the historical fact of the disappearance of the Gnostic gospels, codified in the formation of the canonical Bible, is conflated with an elaborate theory in which the misogynistic Church suppressed Gnostic ideas of a sacred feminine, rewrote Mary Magdalene's place in Christianity, and excised from history the existence of a divine bloodline, though nevertheless enshrined in the myth of the Holy Grail. Juxtaposed against the stifling institutional religion in *The Da Vinci Code* is a sacred sexuality, which is advocated throughout the book, in such forms as a secret society orgy and the gender "balanced" androgynous face of the Mona Lisa. Robert Langdon states succinctly in the novel that "the power of the female and her ability to produce life was once very sacred, but it posed a threat to the rise of the predominantly male Church, and so the sacred feminine was demonized and called unclean" (322). Similarly, the addition of a relationship between Jesus and Mary Magdalene foregrounds a sexuality often overlooked in the Bible and repressed in Christian traditions.[3] This is in some measure in keeping with Gnostic writings, as in the Gospel of Philip, which suggests that "the virgin birth [and] bodily resurrection [are] naïve misunderstandings" (Pagels 1979: xv).

The notion of a "sacred feminine principle" in *The Da Vinci Code* is a vague kind of replaying of some tropes of feminist pagan New Age spirituality. Adding a veneer of gender equality and sex positivity to spirituality is arguably a populist move in a culture that has often (for good reason) opposed Christianity — especially the Catholic Church — to sexual pleasure, especially given the many criticisms of the heteronormative patriarchal nature of the Church. Of course, *The Da Vinci Code* is nevertheless hardly a feminist text, given its reliance on a narrative of heroic men throughout history, and use of such phallic imagery of women as "chalices" waiting to be filled. Indeed, the "sacred sex" rituals described positively in the book hardly feel particular empowering for the women involved, with Langdon effusing over the male orgasm's ability to produce "a moment of clarity during which God could be glimpsed" (504).

Sacred sex represents something of a traumatic, Freudian primal scene for the main female character, Sophie. In a key moment, she remembers witnessing a sex ceremony involving her grandfather as a child:

> "*The woman whom you behold is love!*" The women called, raising their orbs again.
> The men responded, "*She has her dwelling in eternity!*"
> [...]
> On a low, ornate altar in the center of the circle lay a man. He was naked, positioned on his back, and wearing a black mask. Sophie instantly recognized his body and the birthmark on his shoulder. She almost cried out. *Grand-pere!* [509].

Writing in a psychoanalytic mode, Žižek suggests that witnessing this scene effectively blocks Sophie's sexuality (this despite it occurring in her 20s, rather than childhood). "The sexual life of Christ and Mary Magdalene is the excess which inverts (covers up) the fact that the sexual life of Sophie, the heroine, Christ's last descendant, is non-existent: *she is like a contemporary Mary, virginal, pure, asexual*" (2008: 67). The intrusion of Brown's hyperbolic ancient sexuality into the modern day is, like the sacred itself, a secret whose traumatic effects linger long afterward.

The sexual excess is everywhere — not merely for the modern initiates of the Knights Templar like Sophie's grandfather, it is imagined for the ancient Israelites: "Men seeking spiritual wholeness came to the Temple to visit priestesses— or *hierodules*— with whom they made love and experienced the divine through physical union" (505). The Hebrew Bible certainly documents prostitution in the Temple (1 Kings 15:13, 2 Kings 23:7), though it is generally in the mode of brief lapses by the Israelites into the behavior of their pagan neighbors rather than really appearing as ingrained native practice (does another conspiracy lurk behind the formation of the Jewish canon?).

Indeed, what is left out of *The Da Vinci Code*'s invocation of the sacred feminine is the thread of Gnosticism that is not merely antisexuality, but antimatter.[4] Asceticism among the early Christians was certainly a fairly prevalent practice. A look at the Gnostic idea of the "hidden God" is illuminating in showing the antisex attitudes of some Gnostics. In Gnostic texts The Apocryphon of John, On the Origin of the World and The Hypostasis of the Archons, a demi-urge caretaker figure called Yaldaboath appears instead of the God of Hebrew and Christian Bibles. As religious scholar E. Aydeet Fischer-Mueller puts it, "for Gnostic ascetics, the fiery Yaldaboath is a symbol for sexuality and procreation, and an obstacle on their path to light and life" (85). This stems from a great disdain for sexuality, for as Guy Gedaliahu Stroumsa suggests in his study of primarily Manichean Gnosticism, in "Gnostic Mythology [...] evil stemmed from a series of sexual sins" (33).

Similarly, the apparent value for the "feminine" attributed to Gnosticism in *The Da Vinci Code* is a far more ambivalent phenomenon. In On the Origin of the World, for instance, it's stated that "the woman followed earth. And marriage followed woman. Birth followed marriage. Dissolution followed birth." Other translations suggest "death" instead of dissolution; in either case, there is a distinct association between femaleness and materiality as fallen in the Christian, traditionally misogynistic sense. Fischer-Mueller argues that Yaldaboath is a highly feminized figure in these Gnostic texts. The God of the material world is set aside for the pursuit of Sophia (Wisdom), a feminine element to be sure, but one decidedly unattached to female corporeality. So ironically, some Gnostic teachings position the Jewish God Yahweh as female, sexual, and fallen as a result—all of the things Dan Brown has attributed to orthodox Christianity in the name of Gnosticism. An orgiastic sexuality therefore cannot be considered remotely unequivocally Gnostic.

Nevertheless, as critic Kirsty Maddux argues, *The Da Vinci Code* "celebrates the female body specifically as a spiritual route to God only for men. Men need women's sexuality in order to see God" (241). Maddux suggests that *The Da Vinci Code* confines women's participation in the religious to the private sphere, situating it in a biologically determinist celebration of female embodiment divorced from any social revaluation of sex/gender roles. *Our Bodies, Ourselves* it is not.

So, it is clear that *The Da Vinci Code*'s interest in Gnosticism—indeed, any symbolism—is merely surface deep. The text is instead a mere miming of spiritual signifiers inherited from the New Age as much as the Gnostic Christianity to which the text refers. Sexuality as the path to the sacred is a common idea in the New Age. As any scan of a bookstore's self-improvement will show, references to the Kama Sutra, tantra, and other Eastern mystic sex traditions abound—with other variants adding Judaism, Christianity and so on. For example, in a typical formulation of the sacred sex thesis (Oprah-approved) New Age guru Deepak Chopra has written that

> true intimacy is union between flesh and flesh, between subtle body and subtle body, between soul and soul. Sexual energy is sacred energy. When we have restored the sexual experience to the realm of the sacred, our world will be chaste and divine, holy and healed [n.pag.].

This New Age "sacred sexuality," far more than any form of ancient Christianity, is the true referent to *The Da Vinci Code*'s vision of sexuality, albeit married to the conspiracy theory content of orgies and secret societies. The line between self-improvement pop-psychology and New Age spirituality has long been a blurry one, with sexuality emerging as one clear path to the goal of "self-fulfillment" common to both. The "sacred sex" of *The Da Vinci Code* merely capitalizes on this popular genre of New Age writings.

This slippage between Gnosticism and a pagan New Age is suggestive of more of a postmodernist practice of pastiche, given that the Gnosticism of *The Da Vinci Code* is a minute fragment of the Nag Hammadi texts disconnected from their context, rather than any espousal of real-world belief or truth. In contrast to traditional Christianity, the Gnosticism Brown draws on have not been hegemonic beliefs. Rather than simply reject traditional Christianity, *The Da Vinci Code* incorporates it and heretically re-signifies it, in the process displacing its exclusive purchase on religious truth — or rather, demonstrating its existing displacement. That Christianity has in some ways already been displaced from its cultural singularity is evident; Gianni Vattimo for instance suggests that "charity will eventually replace truth [...] Are we expected to believe that when the Pope meets up with the Dalai Lama he worries that the Dalai Lama will end up in hell because he is not Catholic?" (45). The creative use of numerous religions and myths as well as the Gnostic revisioning of the Christian canon in *The Da Vinci Code* is undoubtedly a symptom of this kind of spiritual relativism.

Similarly, the portrayal of the Catholic Church (and in particular the secretive organization Opus Dei) in *The Da Vinci Code* maintains a similar duovocality toward Gnosticism and the New Age. The portrayal of the Church certainly recalls in some fashion anti-authoritarian Gnosticism, where orthodox Christians are characterized as outright malevolent at times. In the recently discovered second century Gospel of Judas, for instance, the writer accuses other Christians of "human sacrifice, false worship and other despicable heresy" (Pagels and King xvii) in order to voice their disgust with the martyrdoms of the early Christian Church.

However, this turn more obviously takes its cues from New Age distinctions between "spiritual" and "religious." The Catholic Church is, of course, the secretive, rigid, arcane, antimodern institution par excellence — perhaps *the* prime referent for New Age–influenced texts. The secretive Opus Dei order is Catholicism intensified in Brown's novel, with the Bishop Aringarosa referring to Vatican II's modernizing reforms as a "fiasco" (242). The practices of Opus Dei are themselves grotesque in the novel, with "vows of chastity, tithing, and atonement for sins through self-flagellation and the *cilice*" (47). The order's asceticism (literal and symbolic) are opposed to the excessive sexuality of the Priory of Sion's orgiastic rituals (though not to Sophie herself, if you follow Žižek's reading of her frigidity). In a bowdlerized Freudianism, the Church's history is explained by its sexual repression, its inability to cope with the sacred feminine which is then displaced into aesthetic masochistic rituals. This repressed Church apparently needs to "let go" New Age style. "The Self must be liberated; 'de-identification' must be effected; the person must drop 'ego-attachments' or 'games'" (Heelas 20). To put it bluntly, for Brown it seems the Church simply needed to get laid a lot more over its history.

While there is indeed a correct quotation from the Gospel of Philip, and the revelation of the highly politicized creation of the canonical Bible may be new to some readers, the quick slide into tracing the divine bloodline means Brown's use of Gnosticism is ultimately fanciful. The vaguely Gnostic reading of Christianity, like its anti-institutional posturing and the references to da Vinci's artworks, is merely there to provide theological and cultural spice to an otherwise unremarkable thriller. But for all the mystification produced by its disclaimer and apparent scholarliness, it is somewhat naïve to read *The Da Vinci Code* as simply a Realist rendering of either Gnosticism or Christian orthodoxy. It is, after all, a work of fiction, one that incorporates multiple threads from detective thrillers, romance, conspiracy theories and speculative readings of artworks. The "secret" ultimately revealed, about a divine bloodline, a secret organization, and a Renaissance artist leaving clues in his artwork is a tad on the fanciful side — to suggest therefore that it is being read in a strictly Realist fashion is implausible.

While *The Da Vinci Code* is not *truly* supposed to be believed in, by drawing on Gnostic and New Age versions of spirituality it opens up a reading position of the text on "the border that joins and separates belief and unbelief" (Taylor, 1984: 5). It might instead be considered a mild form of Russian structuralist Tzvetan Todorov's fantastic, where the reader may be confused as to whether phenomenon described by the text is real or not. Which practices in *The Da Vinci Code* are real? Which histories? The descriptions of artwork, architecture, documents and rituals may be real in the denotative sense, though not in the connotative sense implied by Langdon's improbable narration.

Six— Whither Leonardo da Vinci

The anxiety provoked by *The Da Vinci Code* among some Christians is arguably that this liminal position will spill into a real-world belief or practice, and it is for this reason that the Catholic Church in particular has spoken out against the text. The danger posed by *The Da Vinci Code* is therefore that of what British historian of evangelical Christians David Bebbington calls "conversism" (3), the belief that lives have been or should be changed by the faith being practiced. Christianity, which maintains a conversion narrative so strong that born Christians can be "born again" into the Christian faith, is peculiarly vulnerable to competing narratives because its truth-claims are based on claims to exclusion purchase on religious truth rather than ethnic identification. The idea, therefore, that Christianity is founded upon a lie, and that the Gnostic Gospels tell a more historically accurate story than those of the canonical Gospels, is unsurprisingly anxiety causing in some quarters — especially with the novel's brief capture of the general public's attention. Yet such an anxiety is over-stated, for like its disclaimer, the spirituality in *The Da Vinci Code* promises much more than it actually delivers.

CHAPTER SEVEN

Christ Figures and the Messianic in *The Lord of the Rings*

J.R.R. Tolkien's *The Lord of the Rings* series presents an interesting paradox as a text. A favorite among the 1960s counter-culture for its anti-industrial pastoral nostalgia, the series is tremendously Christian without ever explicitly mentioning Christ once. David Gooderham has argued that the fantasy fiction genre has since the 1860s lacked "explicit reference to [real-world] religious institutions, practices and beliefs [...] almost entirely" (156). He argues that the religious is overtly disavowed in the fantasy text, for the endeavor of "unreal" secondary world building is premised on its differentiation from our own. Real-world religion is, however, still present in the fantasy text, albeit displaced from the literal into the metaphorical. Gooderham argues that fantasy functions as a metaphorical mode, so religion is "transpose[d] into the landscape, beings and activities of the secondary worlds of the fantasies" (156). It is the very act of world-building itself which is religious. Tolkien himself in "On Fairy Stories" notes that "fantasy is made out of the Primary World, but a good craftsman loves his material, and has a knowledge and feeling for clay, stone and wood which only the art of making can give." For *Lord of the Rings*, this means that the series is profoundly Christian, and as Tolkien was himself Catholic, a profoundly Catholic text in particular. I have elsewhere argued that the work exhibits the Catholic idea of sacramentality in such relics as Galadriel's phial and the nourishing Elvish lembas bread,[1] which demonstrate Tolkien's love of the "potency of words and the wonder of things."

But unlike Tolkien's colleague and friend C.S. Lewis's *Narnia* series, *The Lord of the Rings* refuses allegorical interpretation. As Jarod Lobdell notes, there is only a brief reference to God ("the One") and to gods ("Valar") in *The Lord of the Rings* proper, although the posthumous publication of the series' mythos *The Silmarillion* "made perfectly clear what had been seen in a glass darkly [...] in *Lord of the Rings*. Tolkien's Middle Earth is part of a Christian universe" (50). And yet, this does not mean that the action of the series is necessarily Christian in any straight-forward fashion. Ralph Woods has rightly suggested that *The Lord of the Rings* is set in a "prebiblical period of history — a time where there were no Chosen People, no incarnation, no religion at all — from a viewpoint that is distinctly Christian" (209). Instead, *The Lord of the Rings* contains only the *traces* of religion, with multiple and necessarily incomplete Christ figures. The three notable Christ figures are Gandalf, Frodo and Aragorn, who each foreground a different aspect of Christ's character. Frodo recalls aspects of the humble sacrificial Christ, Gandalf the resurrected Christ, while Aragorn is the triumphant returned Christ Warrior-King.

Gandalf

I shall start this study of Christ figures in *The Lord of the Rings* with the most decidedly minor of these — Gandalf. In his return from death in the mines of Moria, and subsequent transformation from Grey to White, Gandalf recalls the resurrected Christ. As Alison Milbank notes, Gandalf's robes become dazzlingly white, which "echoes that of Jesus in Luke 9:29 and Mark 9:3, when he appears in glory to three chosen disciples on a mountain" (51). When he first returns in a white haze of light, Gandalf is not recognized by Legolas and Aragorn and instead mistaken for Saruman. The White Wizard approaches" says Legolas, and he and Aragorn attack Gandalf to no avail. He states, ""I've been sent back.. until my task is done" though declines to note by *whom* he has been returned to life.

"Forgive me, I mistook you for Saruman."
"I am Saruman, or rather Saruman as he should have been."

This interestingly recalls Jesus' return in Luke and the longer ending of Mark,[2] where Jesus returns from the dead[3] to meet two disciples "but their eyes were holden that they should not recognize him" (Luke 24:16). They then have an extended conversation about Jesus' death, and it's only when he breaks bread with them and blesses it that "their eyes were opened, and they knew him, and he vanished out of their sight" (24:31). In the movement from forced ignorance ("their eyes were holden") to knowledge ("their eyes were opened"), the narrative elucidates a carefully choreographed revelation sequence. Peter Jackson's film, too, carefully controls the knowledge of actors and audience alike, flooding the screen with a beatific white light, while dubbing Saruman's voice (played by Christopher Lee) over that of Gandalf.

If we read Gandalf as Christ, then we must also see Saruman as a kind of Lucifer figure. Unlike Sauron, who is mostly a disembodied elemental Evil, Saruman has fallen from good. Theologian Alison Milbank argues that evil in Tolkien's work is in Augustinian terms, as the deprivation of good. She quotes Augustine's *Enchridion*:

> Nothing, then, can be evil except something which is good [...] it is not because he is a man that he is evil, or because he is wicked that he is good but that he is good because he is a man, and evil because he is wicked [79].

The resurrected Gandalf, after all, is Saruman as he "should" have been — innately good because he is a man — while the actual Saruman turns to evil because of his weakness and his pessimism.

Gandalf's confrontation with Saruman comes at an interesting time in the first book. Gandalf's disappearance from the Fellowship is ostensibly to gather information about the One Ring, yet of course he already suspects the Ring's purpose and capabilities. His consultation with Saruman thematically makes more sense in part to allow Frodo the space for a bildungsroman from which to grow from the innocence and spiritual immaturity of the Shire to full maturity, and in part for Gandalf himself to be tempted by Saruman with the inevitability of defeat. This recalls Christ's tempting by the Devil in the desert, pre-resurrection (as this indeed occurs for Gandalf, too), wherein Satan tempts Christ to use his powers to survive (by turning stones into bread), test God's protection of him, and with the power to rule the world. "All this I will give you," he said, "if you will bow down and worship me" (Matthew 4:9). In a similar vein, Saruman attempts in *The Fellowship of the Ring* to persuade Gandalf to give up and join him with Sauron: "You did not seriously think a hobbit could contend with the will of Sauron? Against the power of Mordor there can be no victory. We must join with him, Gandalf. We must join him. It would be wise, my friend."

Saruman is indeed correct that Sauron's victory is overwhelmingly likely, for Sauron offers the greater power. Kristin Thompson has quite rightly noted that the fight between Gandalf and Saruman largely takes its cue from kung-fu movies, a deft melding of Eastern and Western religious elements into this temptation sequence.

Aragorn

The most obviously apocalyptic coding of a Christ figure is Aragorn, the long-lost King of Gondor (946). Gandalf to Aragorn: Sauron "fears what you might become." The third book of the series is called *The Return of the King*, and it is this aspect that marks Aragorn as a Christ figure — specifically Christ as he appears at the end of time, post-apocalypse. This is a King who is returning, after all, not appearing for the first time. Faramir says to him, "I would not have you appearing like a beggar at the door" (843), clearly reminiscent of Christ's "thief in the night" warning about his return. One can therefore read the stewards of Gondor, Boromir and Faramir's family, as representative of the Church on earth, who can never properly replace Jesus, as Faramir replays this conversation between his father and Boromir: "How many hundreds of years needs it to make a steward a king, if the King returns not?" he asked. "Few years, maybe, in other places of less royalty," my father answered. "In Gondor ten thousand years would not suffice" (655).

Boromir's betrayal of Frodo, of lusting after the power of the Ring himself (390), bespeaks a failure to recognize a power more legitimate than his own stewardship. One could easily see this as a rebuke of the Catholic Church's own stewardship, in particular that of the Pope, a warning not to seek to usurp Jesus' place as absent head of the Church. Jared Lobdell argues that: "It may be noted here, also, that Aragorn may be taken as a Christ figure to the extent that in him the Adamite unity of Prophet, Priest and King seems to hold, as it holds in the new creation in Christ, before being separated in His successors in our world — Peter, James and John" (52).

Peter Jackson's film adaptations bring Aragorn's romance with Arwen from Tolkien's footnotes to occupying the front stage, with the marriage of the two capping Aragorn's restoration to his throne. This maneuver of Jackson's, which is thematically satisfying to be sure, conflates the nation with the bedroom, providing a kind of heterosexual symmetry of sovereignty (a King and Queen, to rule). As the returned Christ, therefore, Aragorn is rewarded with the church-bride, with Viggo Mortensen having grown a fitting Christ-like beard to complete the look. Needless to say, this is a masculinist metaphysics of nation and church of the kind long critiqued by feminist and queer theologians. But in Tolkien's world, even the return of the king is a joyous occasion that presages a greater melancholy in the Age of Men — a far cry from a post-apocalyptic heaven-on-earth.

Frodo: The One They Have Pierced

Frodo functions as a Christ figure in his redemptive sacrifice in carrying the Ring. Heroic epics, and indeed much modern fantasy, have tended to have larger-than-life heroes, but it is the very ordinariness of Frodo that enables him to succeed in his task. Frodo and his hobbit friends illustrate the Christian dictum "the first shall be last, and the last shall be first," meaning that these humble characters are the most worthy in a Christian setting to be exalted.

When Frodo accepts the challenge to destroy the Ring, Tolkien describes this as a moment of another order of reality imposing itself upon this one. "At last with an effort he spoke and wondered to hear his own words, as if some other will was using his small voice. 'I will take the ring, though I know not the way,' he says." Elrond replies, "It is a heavy burden, so heavy that none could lay it on another. I do not lay it on you. But if you take it freely, I will say that your choice is right." We can, if we wish, see this as a moment of Eliadian hierophany in Tolkien's text, or divine Providence. Or of course, we can locate this as a moment of self-estrangement, for as Freud well knew, no person can ever be said to fully know themselves. Consciousness never totally coincides with the subject's unconscious, though moments of such unknowing provide glimpses of what is usually hidden. In any case, Frodo's surprise at his own words and actions, offers an opportunity to locate alterity within the text, whether it been as divine or (another aspect of) self. Or perhaps we can see this "other will" as an intuition *of* the divine through the self.

This sacrifice is played out on Frodo's body. His designation of Ring-Bearer thus refers to much more than his possession of the One Ring. His body bears the spiritual evil that the Ring represents—the temptation toward power as a means of control—literally weighs him down, so much so that Sam resorts to carrying him at times. As the Ring-Bearer, Frodo is largely protected from the seductions of the One Ring, wanting only to return to the idyllic pastoral banality of everyday life in the Shire. Yet hobbits are not of themselves necessarily immune to the Ring's pull, with the hobbit-like creature Smeagol seduced by the Ring, and indeed Bilbo being corrupted by exposure to it over nearly a century. One can conclude therefore that Frodo is chosen for this role in a certain sense, Messianically suitable for the task of bearing the evil of the world.

Indeed one of the more striking aspects of the series is the repeated penetration of Frodo's body, echoing the penetration of Christ's body on the cross by nails and a Roman centurion's spear.[4] As John 19: 36–37 tells the crucifixion story:

> Because the Jewish leaders did not want the bodies left on the crosses during the Sabbath, they asked Pilate to have the legs broken and the bodies taken down. The soldiers therefore came and broke the legs of the first man who had been crucified with Jesus, and then those of the other. But when they came to Jesus and found that he was already dead, they did not break his legs. Instead, one of the soldiers pierced Jesus' side with a spear, bringing a sudden flow of blood and water. [...] These things happened so that the scripture would be fulfilled: "Not one of his bones will be broken," and, as another scripture says, "They will look on the one they have pierced" [NIV].

Like Christ's, Frodo's is a penetrated body. In the Peter Jackson-directed films, his body is penetrated three times. In *Fellowship of the Ring*, Frodo is stabbed by one of a sword of one of the Nazgul. His body quickly wastes away, requiring Elvish healing. While being stabbed in an action movie is of course far from a Christ coding in itself, the scene occurs at Weathertop, an ancient fort. Immediately before his stabbing, the camera intriguingly pans to a statue resembling that of a medieval saint or indeed Christ himself. We then see a close-up of Frodo's body being penetrated by the sword.

Later in *Fellowship*, Frodo is stabbed again, this time by the cave troll. Unlike the first time, he is miraculously unscathed by this penetration, for he was wearing his uncle Bilbo's magical elf-forged mithril shirt. This is a Christ-body of another kind, the untouchable spiritual body of Christ — "death no longer has mastery over him" as St. Paul puts it in Romans 6:9. Frodo's body becomes penetrated but not wounded, a body-without-organs in a certain sense. In the film, we briefly see Sam touching the mithril, as if to confirm that Frodo is alive — a caress which obliquely recalls Renaissance artist Michelangelo Merisi da Caravaggio's famous painting *The Incredulity of Saint Thomas*, in which the apostle Thomas touches the resurrected Christ's side wound in disbelief. Indeed, Sam plays the role of the faithful apostle throughout the story. By the end of the journey to Mount Doom, Sam is literally carrying Frodo, who has become so burdened by the Ring that he cannot walk — "I can't carry it [the One Ring] for you ... but I can carry you!"

Sam is clearly not the only apostle figure. While the Fellowship as a whole can be considered to recall Christ and his apostles, Boromir in particular plays the Judas figure. Boromir states that, "yes there is weakness, there is frailty, but there is courage too in Men," but is himself overcome with his own weakness when he attempts to seize the Ring for himself. Boromir desires to use the Ring to protect Sauron, but his inability to comprehend the evil of the Ring leads him himself to evil, breaking the Fellowship of the Ring. Having pledged to support Frodo, Boromir betrays him.

After his failure to take the Ring, he attempts to make amends for his betrayal by buying hobbits time in a futile last stand against a horde of Orcs. Like Judas, Boromir dies for his betrayal. This fits neither of the two deaths ascribed to Judas in the New Testament exactly, though it does recall both in some senses. In Matthew, Judas is described as committing suicide in despair — a moment too bleak for redemption (and indeed suicide remains a mortal sin in Tolkien's Catholicism). Boromir's death certainly has the element of willful self-destruction, and though he repents as in Matthew, his doomed heroic last stand retains a redemptive element that Judas's hanging himself lacks. In the Peter Jackson films, we see Boromir's chest full of arrows, a gruesome death that more obviously recalls Acts 1:18, in which Judas "acquired a field with the reward of his wickedness; and falling headlong, he burst open in the middle and all his bowels gushed out'" (NSRV). The Acts story, however, has an element of divine judgment of Judas which is absent from Boromir's self-willed death. There is certainly space within Tolkien's pre–Christian world for divine judgment — a more malevolent alterity to that which Frodo encounters — but it is decidedly missing from Boromir's death. Instead, Boromir just as easily resembles the heroes of Greek tragedy brought low by his own hubris and violation of the divine order. As such, he does not require the *deus ex machina* of Acts, for it is his own actions which cause his downfall and ultimate death.

But in the end, Frodo proves to be no better than Boromir. After the Garden of Gethsemane moment in which Frodo and Sam have a conversation in a garden in Minas Tirith ("I don't think I'll be coming back"), when it comes to the very pit of Mount Doom, Frodo ultimately makes the same choice as Boromir and Isildur before him — "why shouldn't I have it?" Less a moment of Christ-on-the-Cross dejection than a profound betrayal of his own mission and the Fellowship that had supported, the Ring has corrupted even the most humble and self-effacing of hobbits. It's only the fortuitous attack of Gollum, and the fight that ensues that leads to the Ring's destruction. In the end, it is Gollum who is sacrificed along with sin (the Ring), not Frodo. This sacrifice defeats Sauron, a kind of Satan figure rather different from that of Saruman, and his Hellish abode of Mordor, but it is not by Frodo's Christ-like sacrifice so much as a kind of grace occasioned by Gollum's Pyrrhic victory. Ralph Woods argues that it is the Christian quality of mercy, exhibited first by Bilbo to Gollum ("The pity of Bilbo may rule the fate of many," *Lord of the Rings,* 58) that determines the fate of Middle Earth. For his part in this drama, Frodo is rewarded by moving from Middle Earth to a kind of heaven with the elves and Gandalf, though this is greeted with more of a resigned melancholy than Christian joy. Early in the *Fellowship of the Ring,* Frodo and Sam see wood elves on a similar journey, leaving Middle Earth, never to return and Sam says, "I don't know why, it makes me sad." Closure that it is, the elves' leaving Middle Earth is a source of profound melancholy, leaving the world disenchanted and ruled by imminently fallible men.

Conclusion

Tolkien's Christ figures, thus considered, are unstable and partial. Though Middle Earth is indeed saved from Sauron, none of these Christ figures delivers any true form of messianic redemption. If we follow Woods in seeing *The Lord of the Rings* as a pre–Christian epic, then this incomplete pre-figuring of the Christian drama makes a certain sense, leading the reader to intuit the role of Christ in the real world as the completion. This would recall Tolkien's friend C.S. Lewis's Christ figure Aslan, who says, of the real world: "there I have another name. You must learn to know me by that name. This was the very reason why you were brought to Narnia, that by knowing me here for a little, you may know me better there" (270).

While this is certainly plausible, and likely to be shared by those who tend to theories of author intentionality or follow the Christian faith, it is also to see these pre–Christian, fragmented Christ as emblematic of our own postmodern Christ, after the death of God. John D. Caputo has persuasively argued that God is a weak force, one which does not, cannot redeem, cannot provide salvation. "God is a hope, not a magician [...] It is because God is a weak force that Auschwitz was possible, that all the Auschwitzes, all the ethnic cleansings that have stained human history" (94). Like Frodo, the postmodern Christ can only get to the scene of salvation, to Mount Doom, he cannot redeem the great burden of history by himself. From there, well, it is up to grace.

CHAPTER EIGHT

The Cultural Logic of Postmodern Christianity: The Christian Right and Popular Culture

The influence of so-called "fundamentalist" Christianity in American political life has been strong ever since the (fake) born-again Ronald Reagan avowed his faith publicly, romping into office over the (real) born-again Jimmy Carter in 1980. The infamous Jerry Falwell once declared that President Reagan and his vice-president George H. Bush were "God's instrument in rebuilding America" (Taylor 2007: 273). Yet, as Christopher Haley and Creston Davis have argued, "the Christian Right is intimately connected with what is often characterized as its exact opposite: (neo)liberalism and its supplement, multiculturalism" (66). There are no fundamentalists without permissive liberals to rail against, just as the tolerance discourse discussed by Brown requires the imagined presence of *in*tolerant Others to work against. Indeed, as Žižek points out, this may often taken on the terms of a disguised class warfare when upper and middle class liberal defenses of multicultural tolerance and women's rights become constituted as the "counterposition" to their alleged opposites in the lower classes (2008b:224). At the same time, evangelical Protestantism has inspired neoliberal neoconservative politicians from Reagan to George W. Bush to policies "whose compassion [are] more a matter of word than deed" (Taylor, 2004: 309) that have disproportionately affected the poor and working classes. Yet as Haley and Davis make clear, the shortcomings of both evangelical and New Age positions lie in their eschewing of the economic solution for the consumptive. Economic analysis disappears in favor of the so-called "Culture War" between Right and Left, Christian fundamentalist and multiculturalist. Both take for granted that the world can be transformed via cultural practices, while ignoring the possibility of economic *justice*.

As Taylor has argued, outside of the United States and Europe, "conservative or even fundamentalist religion often becomes a strategy to fight global capitalism and all it represents. In the United States, by contrast, conservative religion is commonly used to promote the spread of global capitalism" (2004: 30). Indeed, "what [American] moral conservatives fail to perceive is how [...] in fighting the dissolute liberal permissive culture, they are fighting the necessary ideological consequences of the unbridled capitalist economy that they themselves fully and passionately support" (Žižek 2008b: 229). Some mega-churches combine the church with the Starbuck's-style postmodern non-spaces of coffee shop and bookshop. Evangelicals take the American cult of counseling and self-help experts to its logical conclusion in making God the ultimate prescriptive counselor, finding "biblically correct positions on every issue, from gay marriage to income tax rates" (Goldberg 2006: 5). Ironically the characteristic movements of evangelicalism (in particular, the arms-raised, eyes-closed motion during Christian rock songs parodied quite accurately by Mandy Moore in the movie *Saved!*) are remarkably close to the expressive individualism of the New Age. While an explicit affirmation in an evangelical context of, say, New Age–glossed Buddhism would be likely to cause an uproar, perhaps even an accusation of Satanism, the two are nevertheless linked in their inattention to the economic and their relentless fixation on the individual.

Indeed, having largely removed the mediating influence of Church dogma and theology, evangelical texts are as equally reliant on consumerist multicultural, New Age ideas of the primacy of unverifiable self-experience as the traditions they claim to be faithful to. Even New Age–style lip service to diversity and tolerance-speak (as Wendy Brown calls it) can appear at times. The appeal of many of these texts, therefore, is that they dramatize a conflict that is internal to postmodern global capitalism, yet ultimately it has no way to break out of the evangelical-/neo-liberal deadlock. Both ethoses are symptoms of a neoliberalism that foregrounds culture rather than economics and is largely unable to think its way past this binarism.

The Postmodern Evangelical

As I argued in my first chapter, the profane/sacred split is erased in numerous ways in postmodernity. There exists a considerable industry devoted to distributing various forms of religious kitsch, for the sacred has become well and truly commodified in postmodernity. This can be manifested in such commodified relics as dashboard Jesus and the rosary, or the union of church and marketplace in the form of churches with coffee and gift shops. And the sacred has been just as surely mediatized, most especially in evangelical circles with televangelists, large-screen TVs at worship services and "satellite campuses" that watch part of the main service on a closed-circuit television broadcast. And there is, of course, a large body of religious pop culture directed at the faithful such as *The Passion of the Christ*, or the immensely successful *Left Behind* series of novels. Though *Passion of the Christ* and *Left Behind* come from different Christian backgrounds (Catholic and Protestant, respectively), hidden among these texts is an unacknowledged correspondence with the New Age. *Left Behind*, a series of novels written by Tim La Haye and Jerry Jenkins, is a literalization of a certain kind of American dispensationalist reading of the apocalypse, yet is just as clearly reliant on secular genres like the thriller and the disaster movie as it is on an evangelical theological and literary tradition (Gribben 2004: 86). *Left Behind*, which has thus far yielded 12 books and a number of increasingly high-budgeted movies since the first novel was released in 1995, dramatizes the coming apocalypse, the appearance of the Antichrist (interestingly identified with the UN, and not with the Catholic Church as is traditional in evangelical Rapture theology). In contrast to the fantastic postmodern sacred, *Left Behind* clearly alludes to a truth referent outside the text — under a certain kind of evangelical reading of the Bible, this is an imaginative version of what *really* will happen. Yet despite its apparent truth-value, *Left Behind* is as reliant on fantastic and horror tropes as *Buffy*. However, these are far from self-reflective, and the fictionality of *Left Behind* is disavowed as its nature is as religious simulacrum and supplement.

It is important to recognize therefore that much of the postmodern swing toward the sacred has been in the form of fundamentalisms that are inextricably linked to the postmodern. The Christian Right in the United States, like the New Age, can be traced to the impact of the 1960s (Taylor 2007: 254). Though some conservative religious figures have denounced both postmodernism and the New Age, they are *nevertheless* postmodern in televangelism or organizing online, presenting simulacra of religious worship onscreen. Zygmunt Bauman (1997), for instance, finds fundamentalism to be a characteristically postmodern phenomenon, arguing that it takes the (undeniably New Age-ized) cult of counseling and self-help experts to its logical conclusion in making God the ultimate prescriptive counselor. He argues that the "allure of fundamentalism stems from its promise to emancipate the converted from the agonies of choice. Here one finds, finally, the indubitably *supreme* authority" (1997). Popular evangelicals like Rick Warren preach a gospel that "more closely resembles the feel-good messages of New Agers than the demanding challenges of earlier evangelicals" (Taylor 2008: 291). They often seem to emerge out of a postmodern nostalgia for "authenticity"—one of the main rhetorical strategies of the fundamentalisms of the Book (Jewish, Christian, Muslim) is a nostalgic discourse on modernity as a process of loss, stripping people of their true religion, making society a pit of sin, and so on and so forth. While this is undeniably an anti-postmodern discourse, the very terms of it have been set from within postmodern culture, and as such are hardly that dissimilar from other postmodern nostalgic yearnings. So fundamentalism thus both exposes the inadequacies of postmodern culture (by pointing out the flaw in "egalitarian" consumerism) and is itself implicated in it. Ironically, by creating their own temples of consumption, fundamentalists and evangelicals produce a form of individualized spirituality not too dissimilar to the New Age that some denounce.

Where fundamentalisms depart from other forms of the postmodern sacred, then, is in content, for they are generally not kindly disposed toward the New Age. Paul Heelas and Linda Woodhead argue that in strongly hierarchical and conservative congregations, "even when the language of 'spirituality' and 'spiritual growth' is adopted, it is used to speak of a life in which the individual listens and conforms to God-given rules and roles rather than to his or her inner feelings, convictions, instincts and judgments" (61). Indeed, even as they create post-rational texts of their own, evangelicals remain ambivalent about the supernatural per se — for they *do* aim to produce some kind of a truth value with their texts.

Even though they arise out of postmodernity, they are produced with a specifically religious audience in mind (as distinguished from the presumed-secular audience of other supernatural texts) and frequently exhibit a disdain or even hatred of the ethical and textual positions of the postmodern (the much vaunted "culture wars"). And yet though it has an explicit pedagogical purpose, *Left Behind*'s readers become caught up in the pleasure of the text (as Roland Barthes called it) — potentially displacing the eschatological truth-claim in part or in full. In her study of the series in *Rapture Culture*, literature scholar Amy Johnson Frykholm dedicates a chapter toward interviewing "marginal" readers of the text who do not share the evangelical values of Jenkins and LaHaye and instead use the text for their own sense of "escape." Another literary scholar, Glenn W. Shuck, however, suggests that *Left Behind* provides not merely escape but evangelical acceptance and accommodation to the (post) modern world (26).

Though the content of *Left Behind* is largely similar in narrative to that of the 19th dispensationalist evangelicalism from John Nelson Darby and Cyrus Scofield, the emphasis is different for their modern-day heirs. Noting the cultural continuity between fundamentalist forms of Christianity with extraordinarily oppressive forms of capitalist domination, theologian Elisabeth Schüssler Fiorenza suggests that "fundamentalist media-apocalypsism misuses Rev[elations] because it does not either proclaim the apocalyptic promise of justice and salvation to the poor and to the oppressed or challenge the complacency and security of the relatively well-to-do" (1). Fiorenza asks, "What does the story of rapture and tribulation mean if it is no longer an antiworldly and antimodern formula?" (36). One answer is that when fundamentalists and evangelicals engage in pop culture of their own like the *Left Behind* series, they are similarly engaged in aiming at the transcendent through simulacra. Similarly, the irrational is folded into the realm of the rational, the apocalyptic into the familiar formulas of evangelical self-expression. We can see some contrasts then, with the more well known fantastic texts of the postmodern sacred, though it remains difficult to make ultimate separations.

Passion of the Christ

The Mel Gibson–directed 2004 movie *The Passion of the Christ* illuminates the paradoxes at work in evangelical and fundamentalist production and consumption of popular culture. The controversial movie gathered accusations of anti–Semitism even before its release (later confirmed by Gibson's 2006 drunken tirade about Jews being "responsible for all the wars of the world). Nevertheless, the film, shot in Aramaic, became the most successful non–English language movie of all time, making over $370 million in the United States alone.

Despite Gibson's Catholic heritage (and traditional Catholic/Protestant tensions), the movie was embraced by American Protestant evangelicals who saw the film in their droves. As Peter Maresco points out, the film was primarily marketed through American Catholic and evangelical Protestant churches, with whole churches buying out cinemas (para 18). An extreme example occurred in Plano, Texas, where one Arch Bonemma purchased all six thousand seats at the local 27-screen megaplex, distributing tickets to members of his church and seminary (Maresco para 24). This rapprochement between ultraconservative Catholicism and evangelical Protestants was one of the more interesting elements of the film's reception, with prominent evangelicals like Billy Graham and James Dobson endorsing the film as a valuable tool for evangelizing. Biblical scholar Richard Walsh confessed that "even though the movie is obviously Catholic, it recalls for me the evangelical Baptist religion of my youth" (2005: 2).

Thematically, *The Passion* has an extraordinary focus on the death of Christ, covering only the last 12 hours of Christ's life and famously featuring a graphic extended scourging scene in which Christ is brutally tortured. Walsh (2008) argues that *The Passion of the Christ* may be considered to fit squarely within the horror genre, with its graphic violence, demonic possession and strangely Gothic androgynous Satan (far from an orthodox interpretation of the Devil). Further, as Walsh points out, *Passion*'s gloss on Christ revives elements of Gibson's early work in *Braveheart:* "the soulful, meaningful looks toward the followers; the close-ups of the anguish of heroes and disciples; and the slow-motion torture" (5). Rather than constituting a "pure" experience of Christianity (or Catholicism specifically), *The Passion of the Christ* is a profoundly simulated

Eight — The Cultural Logic of Postmodern Christianity

religious experience, as much a postmodern action-hero Jesus as Neo in *The Matrix*.

Walsh suggests, however, that the film has a different ontological use value than secular horror and fantastic films — it is *supposed* to be real, to unite film with a particular historical referent. Indeed, the very success of the film depended on its perceived veracity, since "for evangelicals to embrace *Passion*, the filmmakers and marketers first had to convince the faithful of its accuracy" (Tramell 23). Pope John Paul II was reported to have exclaimed, "It was as it was." Despite this, most historians would agree that Gibson's passion spectacle is historically inaccurate — Jesus is crucified through the palms in accordance with Catholic pictorial history (not the likely wrists), and he is not stripped and humiliated publicly as victims of Roman crucifixion were. As Walsh points out, this plays out Roland Barthes' contention in *Mythologies* that "what the public wants is the image of passion, not the passion itself" (18). Walsh argues that the film places authenticity instead in its bloody images of Christ's beaten body. "For Gibson, suffering is a hierophany, the excess of blood an intelligible spectacle. No wonder, then, that Gibson contemplated offering the movie without subtitles. His spectacle of suffering needs no words" (2005: 4). Christ's bleeding body offers all the truth one apparently needs.

This is a curiously literal version of Catholicism, similar in some ways to the comic book Catholicism of *Constantine* discussed in Chapter Two. Yet Derrida in "Above All No Journalists!" (2001) would argue that this has its roots in the very mechanics of the Catholic Eucharist. He suggests that

> during a Christian mass, by contrast, the thing itself, the event takes place in front of the camera: communion, the coming of real presence, the Eucharist in a certain sense, even the miracle (miracles are produced on American television) — the thing actually takes place "live" *as* a religious event, *as* a sacred event [58].

Derrida argues that Christianity more than the other religions, and Catholicism as much as American evangelicism, is mediatized, integrates media as a fundamentally religious technology. Derrida suggests that though it began with Europe, the mediatized religion has reached its maturation in the United States. Though Protestant-Catholic divisions in the United States have often historically been tense (there still remains only the one Catholic president, John F. Kennedy), the influence of media and the culture wars has drawn the more conservative elements of evangelical and Catholicism together in the United States. It's fitting therefore that it would be Mel Gibson, a conservative American Catholic, who produced a film embraced most strongly by evangelicals.

If suffering, therefore, is the key to the evangelical-friendly *Passion of the Christ*, what is missing from the narrative? Salvation. The *Passion of the Christ* has only a brief resurrection scene; the vast majority focuses on the drama on the Cross. With Christ's redemptive power largely sidelined, this bleak worldview oddly echoes New Age individualism in an inverted form (though not supplemented by the New Age's idea of "everything is connected"). Christ's death remains the thematic center precisely because it *is* individual, because the contemporary understandings of atonement that motivate Gibson's movie understand Christ's death to be a kind of ransom exchange, one life for another, a salvation that can be purchased.

This is not, of course, the only way to understand atonement — theologian Adam Kotsko has recently argued persuasively that a "social-relational" facet of Christ's Incarnation and death motivates major patristic, liberation and feminist understandings of atonement. As he puts it, "Remaining faithful to the tradition necessarily entails breaking with the individualistic ways in which it has been interpreted in the modern era" (6). Despite being perhaps the most successful explicitly Christian movie of the last quarter century, it is this challenge which Gibson's movie singularly fails to rise to.

Twilight

Stephenie Meyer's recent *Twilight* series gives us an interesting example of the problematics of distinguishing between popular culture produced for religious and non-religious audiences. Produced for a secular audience, the Mormon Meyer's work is clearly strongly infused with conservative religious beliefs about gender and sexuality, yet at the same time, the sexual desires of her mostly teenage female readers have been foregrounded in the marketing and reception of the series. *Twilight* includes the usual post-rational urban fantasy monsters of vampires and werewolves, but it is in the service of romance, relationships and sexuality. In the following section, I will show the religious sources of *Twilight*'s gender and sexual mores, as well its resemblance to abstinence-only education.

In the *Twilight* series, the heroine Bella Swan moves to a small Oregon town. There she meets the compellingly exotic Edward, who (of course) turns out to be a vampire. The two fall into a kind of chaste love. Other vampires show up to complicate the lives of the nascent couple. In the second book, *New Moon*, Edward abandons Bella because he fears he is endangering her life. She then becomes depressed until her deepening friendship with Jacob Black, a local werewolf, soothes her heartache. Inevitably, he too falls in love with Bella. Because of a miscommunication, Edward believes Bella has committed suicide, so he decides to do the same in Italy by antagonizing a group of old, powerful vampires. Bella rushes to his side to rescue him. Eventually, Bella realizes she loves Jacob too; however, she finally marries Edward in the final book, *Breaking Dawn*. Bella becomes pregnant on their honeymoon. The supernatural child grows at a greatly increased rate, slowly killing her mother. Edward rips open Bella's stomach to deliver the baby, then make her a vampire to save her life. Jacob "imprints"—a procedure where a werewolf becomes bonded to their soul mate for life—on the new born infant.

The gender narrative of the *Twilight* "saga" appears at first telling to be fairly retrogressive. As Anna Silver puts it, "The novels' gender ideology is ultimately and unapologetically patriarchal" (122). Edward is an overly courtly, possessive boyfriend whose behavior verges on stalking—he begins watching Bella sleep without her knowledge in a fit of jealousy (Meyer 2005: 303). Born in 1901, Edward is "a relic and model of Edwardian, if not Victorian, masculinity" (Silver 130), with his Byronic bipolar swings between solicitous and angry and withdrawn reinforced by Meyer's literary references to primarily 19th century novels like *Jane Eyre* and *Wuthering Heights*. In the face of all this grand passion, Bella, on the other hand, is a clumsy teenage girl who cooks for her father and is rescued from one dangerous situation to another by Edward and then later Jacob. Her most compelling trait appears to be her utter passivity, her calm acceptance of Edward's monstrosity and controlling behavior.

These conservative gender roles unsurprisingly extend to the characterization of sexuality in the books. Bella and Edward spend the first three books waiting until their marriage to have sex, and then when they do Bella becomes pregnant and has a violent, almost fatal pregnancy. This horrific story appears to hyperbolically stage the messages of abstinence-only sex education heavily promoted by evangelicals, which pathologize sex in order to demand that "true love waits" for marriage. In practice, this occurs primarily through the policing of girls' desires (there may remain a certain anecdotal "boys will be boys" lassitude to male desire), though the narrative is applied to both sexes equally. Abstinence-only education educators use such historically misogynist imagery as a sexually-active girl as a "sponge" for boys' "dirt."

Yet if *Twilight* appears in some ways to resemble evangelical abstinence-only tracts, the series teems with repressed, even aberrant, desires. Vampirism as Nina Auerbach has argued is a supple metaphor, able to take on numerous kinds of cultural anxieties, yet here as elsewhere the most persistent association is with sexuality. Edward likens the desire to drink blood to vegetarianism, saying that "I'd compare it to living on tofu and soy milk; we call ourselves vegetarians, our little inside joke. It doesn't completely satiate the hunger — or rather thirst. But it keeps us strong enough to resist. Most of the time" (188).

For both, sex — figured in *Twilight* by the classic trope of vampirism-as-penetration — represents a surrender to a shattering, sublime abyss. Edward's desire for Bella *is* the desire to kill her, to devour her. Continuing the consumption metaphors, he compares his desire to drink her blood to an alcoholic offered one-hundred-year old brandy, to an addict offered heroin. "It would be more ... prudent for you not to be my friend," he [Edward] explained. "But I'm tired of staying away from you, Bella" (84). Bella and Edward's desires are fueled, rather than thwarted, by their denial, and this is an attitude mirrored by the series' many fans. As feminist Christine Seifart points out, "The paradox is that the more Meyer sexualizes abstinence, the more we want Bella and Edward to actually have sex. This paradox becomes extra-convoluted when we find out, in a moment that for some is titillating, for others creepy, that sex could literally equal death for Bella" (n.pag.).

Deferral, as Derrida has argued, "refers to the (active and passive) movement consists in deferring by means of delay, delegation, reprieve, referral, postponement, reserving. In this sense, différance is not preceded by the originary and indivisible unity of a present possibility that I could reserve, like an expenditure that I would put off calculatedly or for reasons of economy" (1981: 7). Kevin Hart argues that Derrida's early work (notably in *Of Grammatology*) pinpoints the link between the biblically-derived Fall from innocence to experience/guilt and the fall from speech to writing (16). Derrida's deconstruction, therefore, was an attempt to refuse the narrative of the Fall of the metaphysics of presence, instead seeing that often bemoaned fall as always-already *within* presence, always the condition of language and meaning itself. Instead, Derrida brings to light the repressed content, the excluded margins, of those texts he subjected to close reading. To return to *Twilight*, therefore, the series conjures female desire, the repressed content of evangelical abstinence-only education programs, as unmistakably central. Ironically, *Twilight* does this in such a way that aims at the sublime of différance— a desire marked by difference, the difference between human and supernatural — and deferral. Instead of thwarting desire as abstinence-only education largely aims for, it gestures to its nature as infinitely renewing.

Yet if this seductive model of desire explains the first three novels' success, given the evangelical fear of sexuality it should also be little wonder that the ultimate consumption of the Bella/Edward relationship in the final novel, *Breaking Dawn*, is catastrophic, even traumatic. The incompatiblity of romance with safety has been set up from the start, as Edward says, "I want you to be safe. And yet I want to be with you. The two desires are impossible to reconcile" (339). Rather than simply renounce their desire, the pair stand near to the abyss, desiring it. Bella's desire for Edward is a desire for oblivion, as much the inhuman movement of Freud's death drive toward self-annihilation as a grand romantic passion — she likes her *eros* thoroughly entangled with *thanatos*. And though Bella herself remains untouched, the Native American Emily Young receives prominent facial scars as the result of her werewolf fiancée Sam becoming angry with her, "phasing" into werewolf form and attacking. Male violence remains a constant threat in the novels and is intimately and explicitly eroticized.

But though there is a clearly patriarchal bias to the text, the series pathologizes pre-marital sexuality *tout court* as necessarily and only ever dangerous and harmful. As Silver puts it, "Premarital sex in *Twilight* is risky, life-threatening, and brutal for everyone involved, both men and women" (129), with it clearly dangerous for Edward's brother Jasper, his sister Rosalie and her pre-vampire fiancé. In the face of this, even the sanctifying sacrament of marriage in *Twilight* proves no match for the horror a carnal love produces, with the newlywed's first coupling leaving Bella covered in bruises and pregnant. In fact, Bella's pregnancy fits into a broader pattern of antiabortion activism among evangelicals, in which longstanding exemptions for the health of pregnant women in the United States have been steadily attacked at both State and Federal levels. In what Silver rightly calls "the novel's most undisguised political claim" (130), Bella tells the reader in *Breaking Dawn*, "I wanted [my baby] like I wanted air to breathe. Not a choice — a necessity" (132). Bella's use of antiabortion language here — "not a choice" — is a direct attack on the idea of "choice" that motivates pro-abortion activism, while she describes her own unwillingness to abort as "faith" (190). The pregnant Bella allegorically becomes an Everymother facing a dangerous pregnancy who, improbably, manages to survive her pregnancy. Except of course, she does not — the supernatural deus ex machina of her vampiric conversion by Edward explicitly means her death and then rebirth as undead (real pregnant mothers are unlikely to be so lucky). Vampirism shifts, finally, in referent from sexuality to Christianity, with Bella's rebirth rewarded with eternal (after)life. It is only at this point, having become a mother, that Meyer imagines Bella inhabiting any power, if a "purely defensive" (590) protective maternal power.

Given all of these antinomies between desire, power and safety, it is no surprise therefore that the reception of the series by its fans has been decidedly more ambivalent than that of its reviews, with the Girardian triangle between Edward, Bella and Jacob the chief focus of the marketing of the films. "Team Edward" and "Team Jacob" have been names adopted by teen girl fans to designate the proper object of Bella's desire, and hence, their own. Trailers, posters and merchandise of the second film, *New Moon*, made prominent usage of a shirtless Taylor Lautner (Jacob). The model of homosocial bonding between the two male characters over their shared object of desire is thus inverted by the series fans, who bond over their shared object of desire and their distinction from the other.

Eight — The Cultural Logic of Postmodern Christianity

We might, following Derrida, choose to refuse Meyer's narrative of the "fall" from innocence to experience. Sexuality and desire are neither necessarily horrific, nor necessarily entwined with the death drive. Similarly, Bella's passivity is not, in this context, a virtue of the kind Meyer imagines. While passivity of a certain sort can be seen in both Christian and non–Christian stories of nonviolent resistance, it is just as likely to be mobilized in justifying abuse. In their harrowing book *Proverbs of Ashes*, feminist theologians Rita Nakashima Brock and Rebecca Ann Parker recount numerous stories of domestic abuse against women justified by male abusers and male priests alike with words in praise of the holiness of the heteronormative family and platitudes about bearing crosses. The nostalgic narrative of wholeness conjured by Edward's total devotion in practice is likely to be experienced as abusive, not courtly and romantic, and it is this ugly reality lurking behind *Twilight*'s idealized teen romance which cannot be easily redeemed.

To a feminist, *Twilight* might appear more potentially disturbing in terms of its use of religious ideas than some of the other texts I have discussed, but it remains engaged in the same pursuit of the sacred—a diffused, estranged mediatized form of religion articulated through its primary romantic relationship. The fact that it requires such an elaborate fantasy to imagine the relationship forms of 19th-century religious communities suggests precisely how remote those ideas are for many readers—far enough away to be idealized and fantasized as almost transcendental. Yet given the political climate of the United States, the achievement of its more explicit anti-choice natalist fantasies is not so far-fetched after all. And it is this which should concern us, for it is one thing to long for death, it is quite another to get it.

CHAPTER NINE

The Islamic Other and SFF Responses to 9/11

The postmodern sacred's restatement of the singularity of heroes, and the heroic narrative is one, arguably its chief, response to the crisis of the meta-narrative in postmodernity. Those texts like *Harry Potter* and the first *Matrix* that were produced before 2001 might seem to intuit a shift toward a post–September 11 restatement of the meta-narrative. However, as we shall see, a number of texts of the postmodern sacred have made explicit responses to September 11 and the increasingly authoritarian policies of the West. These texts, in particular, the new version of *Battlestar Galactica* and seasons 9 and 10 of *Stargate SG-1* present critiques of the politics of fear being utilized by politicians, affirm the democratic rights of the general public, and present and critique fundamentalist versions of spiritual experience.

I have mentioned on a number of occasions the SF television series *Stargate SG-1*. Although it retains common elements throughout, the final two *Stargate* seasons can be considered quite distinct from the previous eight. This is partly due to significant changes in the cast — star Richard Dean Anderson leaves at the end of series 8, replaced by Ben Browder, former star of canceled SF series *Farscape* (though thankfully not in the same role as Anderson, soap opera style). Fellow *Farscape* alumni Claudia Black joins SG-1 as the alien Vala, while a new general (General Landry) takes control of the base. Perhaps unsurprisingly then, the series shifts emphasis thematically. In the first eight series, the plucky Earth adventurers from the United States military step through wormholes[1] built by super-powerful aliens thousands of years before and do battle with a parasitic alien race called the Goa'uld. However, at the end of the eighth series, the Goa'uld are largely defeated by SG-1 and their allies and are replaced by another nemesis—an enemy called the Ori. The Ori are beings who have "ascended" to a higher plane of existence, like the Ancients who built the Stargate system. However, unlike the Ancients, who pursue an ethics of nonaction and regard the pain of life as necessary for each being's path toward enlightenment, the Ori demand worship from humans. We find out that the Ori in fact derive power from the strength of their worshipers, and that while they promise their followers ascension they do not in fact deliver it. Series 9 and 10 see the Ori spread from their universe of origin into the Milky Way, where they begin conquering and converting people by force, exterminating en masse those who do not convert to their faith.

The shift in the series in the series, then, is an interesting one. The Goa'uld were a multi-racial group of power-hungry feudal rulers, who by virtue of their advanced technology were able to pose convincingly as Gods. The task of SG-1 was usually scientific de-mystification, to expose the Goa'uld as frauds. The Ori, on the other hand, do legitimately possess mystical powers, and bestow some of these on their followers. The issue is thus not about whether the Ori are Gods—or at least supernatural beings—so much as about fundamentalist interpretations that produce invasions and mass murders, as well as the Ori's falsehoods and blatant self-interest in demanding the faith of their human subjects. Indeed, it is arguable that where the Goa'uld provoke a fear of the racialized Other, the Ori are more about a fear of the rise of the fundamentalist Christian Right as much as Muslim fundamentalism. The followers of the Ori are almost uniformly white; indeed the makeup on the Priors is an exaggerated whiteness. Significantly too, the "quotes" from their holy texts recall firstly the Jewish and Christian Bibles. In "A Line in the Sand" (10.12), Tobin, a follower of the Ori, tries to prevent a Prior from destroying a village. The episode hinges on a theological argument between the two in which the Prior re-interprets the holy text in order to justify mass murder:

> PRIOR: They have been touched by evil. There is no salvation for them.
> TOBIN: But we eliminated all of the unbelievers.
> PRIOR: Not all of them.

TOBIN: I thought the village had capitulated, if you'll allow me

PRIOR: Markon walked away from the Ori to satisfy his hunger, but no matter how much he ate he did not feel full. Realising his mistake, he ran back to the Ori, but they denied his pleas and struck down the village that welcomed him back.

TOBIN: Forgive me Prior, but I was reviewing that very passage just this morning. Markon prayed for forgiveness, and took the first step.

PRIOR: And the hands of the Ori enveloped all those who welcomed him back. The village was destroyed. All those who stand by and accept transgressions must be punished.

TOBIN: That is not the implication of the text, Prior. The Ori granted forgiveness when Markon realised his mistake, and blessed the village with their light for showing him the way back to the path.

PRIOR: You dare question my judgement?

TOBIN: No, it's just not how I was taught.

PRIOR: There are many words but *only one truth* ["Line in the Sand" 10.12, italics added].

The arc of series 9 and 10 is an estranged critique of rigid fundamentalist codes of belief and, as the exchange shows, absolutist interpretative strategies. However, the series is at pains to affirm the right of individuals to their own private beliefs. Dr. Jackson says to Adrea, the leader of the Ori army, "There's a difference between devotion and blind submission; you can't expect to win the faith of your followers through fear and intimidation [...] Give people a choice" ("Counter Strike" 10.07).

So, given that the series has previously affirmed individual spiritual experience in the form of the "ascended" race of Ancients, there is hardly an unmitigated dismissal of spiritual experience at work here. Rather, the series provokes an implicit contrast between the Ancients and the Ori. Like Bender's God in *Futurama* (whom "you can't count on for jack"), the Ancients are unwilling to intervene directly in the affairs of humans—although they do offer some cryptic help and advice along the way. Dr. Jackson says of the Ancients, "They're not going to help us. We're in this alone" ("The Pegasus Project" 10.03). While the characters find this frustrating, the point is that the struggle of life toward enlightenment, toward "ascension," is one that only the individual can take. *Stargate* thus affirms human action, for even if supernatural beings exist, it is up to us to change the world (or universe, as may be). In comparison, the Ori offer their followers a shortcut toward enlightenment, granting their Priors supernatural powers; yet in the end, their promise of ascension after death is false.

What is interesting is that the majority of the series 9 and 10 arcs present a fairly disguised critique of the Bush administration — it is the alien Ori who are the religious fundamentalists; our heroes SG-1 are after all the best representatives of the American military. In effect then, we have a battle in which *both* sides are coded as American, albeit Americans of very different kinds (shades of the bitter "red state/blue state" division between Republican and Democrat in the 2004 U.S. election). In "The Road Not Taken" (10.13) the series' critique of the Bush administration becomes most pointed. In the episode, the explicit subject of the critique becomes the American government itself, when Colonel Samantha Carter, one of the show's main characters, is sucked into a parallel universe when experimenting with an alien device.[2] In that universe, the Stargate program has become public knowledge, causing riots, widespread panic and strife among the nations (compared to the SG-1universe where a multinational group makes up the team on the spin-off series *Stargate Atlantis*). In this alternative universe, General Landry has become the U.S president and has implemented a number of highly authoritarian policies — a unilateral "foreign" policy in the universe (compared to the regular multilateral alliance between SG-1's various alien allies), martial law, a suspension of the usual democratic rights of the American public. After saving the planet from Ori attack, Carter asks Landry about a protestor who has interrupted her congratulation party:

> LANDRY: Not everyone is happy about some of the compromises we've had to make.
> CARTER: Compromises like martial law.
> LANDRY: Believe me, Colonel, I have no desire to go down in history as the man who destroyed civil liberties in America. But I think you'll agree that compared to other presidents I have faced some pretty unique challenges ["The Road Not Taken" 10.13].

It's highly significant that General Landry is the new president — the point is *not* that these policies are the result of a power-hungry leader, rather the result of good people letting fear control their actions (and in turn marshaling fear to justify their own policies). "The Road Not Taken" suggests that the fear engendered by September 11 (or the Ori attacks) is understandable, but that the rights of American citizens should not be surrendered in exchange for security. As the series generally affirms a benevolent, collaborative American imperialism, the critique is most definitely a centrist liberal one (as distinct from a radical critique which might question the foundations of military intervention). Of course, such is to be expected from an American show designed for a mass market; one should scarcely expect entertainment to do the work of activist politics.

Still, the episode is extremely pointed in making its critique of post–September 11 anti-terror legislation. Carter argues with General Hammond, the former commander of the Stargate program in the "real" *Stargate* universe, suggesting that fear mongering authoritarian policies may be as motivated by political aspirations as much as concern for the safety of the nation:

> CARTER: Why be hasty, especially when those 302s are so handy in putting down your political enemies?
>
> HAMMOND: Now I understand you're coming to see certain things about this world that you don't like. To tell the truth, we don't much like it either. But you weren't here for the riots; you didn't see American citizens shooting each other over food, water and gasoline. Hank Landry brought us back from the brink of chaos.
>
> CARTER: That was three years ago.
>
> HAMMOND: The threat is still out there!
>
> CARTER: that's the problem. It always will be.

Such a conversation clearly poses a critique of the post September 11 "war on terror" by America and its allies. As a number of writers have pointed out, the war on terror poses an expanding definition of threat (Afghanistan, Iraq, the prospects of war on Iran or North Korea), especially taking into consideration the doctrine of preemptive strikes, which has arisen to justify war. And as Wendy Brown argues, postmodern empire (to use Hardt and Negri's term) is illegitimate in terms of notions of democracy and legal sovereignty and "can be justified only through fear, by declaring a perpetual state of emergency that allows conventional democratic principles to be overridden [...] it is above all parasitic on the fear incited by the spectre of terrorism" (10). Although antagonistic, the new forms of global empire and terrorism remain in some way complicit with another, and it is this interdependence which is tackled further in the new adaptation of SF series *Battlestar Galactica*.

Responses to September 11 in the Postmodern Sacred 2: Battlestar Galactica

The new version of *Battlestar Galactica*, presents a similar approach to *Stargate SG-1* to the post–September 11 world, albeit with some interesting contrasts. The series' premise is relatively simple. Humans created a robot race called the Cylons, who eventually rebelled and overthrew their masters. This new series is set 40 years after the original, an intervening period during which no contact between human and Cylon occurred, and the Cylons "evolved" to take on human form. These human-appearing Cylons have multiple copies; indeed, some are sleeper agents, unaware themselves that they are not human. The miniseries which commences this new saga begins with the Cylons resuming hostilities by decimating the 12 human colonies with unprovoked nuclear attacks. The remaining 50,000 members of the human race flee into space, where they are followed by the Cylon fleet.

With the miniseries beginning on 2004, this new *Battlestar Galactica* clearly emerges as a response to 9/11, the Iraq war and the post–September 11 "war on terror." Beginning, lest we forget, with a catastrophic attack on Caprican home-world, *Battlestar Galactica* is clearly post-traumatic. The human race is battling for its very survival, dispossessed from its homes, besieged by enemies both inside and out. If that seems hardly to equate with the continued American world-wide hegemony, it nevertheless arguably resonates emotionally with a post–September 11 American sense of defenselessness. *Battlestar Galactica* begins from a post 9/11 sense of "Fortress America" and as such addresses Islam more than most of the other texts in the postmodern sacred (if not always particularly positively, given that it is usually an estranged comment on Islamic terrorism).

Like in "The Road Not Taken" *Stargate* episode, *Battlestar Galactica* walks the fine line between security and democracy — a typical post 9/11 conceptualization in which democracy is deemed to be in some ways antithetical to protection from terrorism. Indeed, with martial law and the suspension of elections[3] it's as if September 11 has suspended the normal workings of democracy. Democracy on *Galactica* is held to be slightly suspicious, the necessary evil with which the benevolent leadership of President Roslin and Commander Adama must engage. Perhaps unsurprisingly, the election of Doctor Baltar at the end of season two ends disastrously, with his decision to abandon the mythic search for Earth and settle on a dank, remote planet ending predictably in the enslavement of the human race by the Cylons. As such, *Battlestar Galactica* illuminates a palpable contemporary American ambivalence toward democracy — as Žižek points out, for the neoconservatives, the problem is the "overdoing" of democracy, both at home and abroad (2004: 58).

Similarly, post–September 11 human rights, which are abstractly affirmed by politicians such as Bush and Howard as the fruits of "freedom," in practice are routinely abrogated in the pursuit of the "war on terror." The status of the prisoners in the American prison at Guantanamo Bay illustrates this perfectly, designated as "enemy combatants" outside of the bounds of either the Geneva Convention, American domestic law, or the rule of international law. In *Battlestar Galactica*, the legal status of the Cylons is exactly that of the enemy combatants, without recourse to rights. When the (human) Chief is being interrogated by his own people, he says, "I'd like to exercise my Article 21 rights at this time," to which the reply rapidly comes, "I'm sure you would. I guess you haven't heard — Cylons don't have rights" ("Resistance" 2.04). Such post–September 11 extra-legal governmental powers do not extend merely to the "proper subjects" of terror legislation — terrorists — but to potentially anyone so unfortunate as to come to the attention of the military. As Georgio Agamben points out, the Patriot Act enacted in the United States after September 11 effectively creates the "state of exception" as the ground level of functioning for the law, "which radically erase[s] any legal status of the individual, thus producing a legally unnameable and unclassifiable being" (3). *Battlestar Galactica* is canny enough to represent this cultural context, as well as filling out the picture with the continuing ethical negotiations of those in power.

Similarly, the Cylons dramatize a post–September 11 shift in conceptualizing evil. Whereas the Cylons in the 1978 series were entirely synthetic robots and thus not human appearing, the new Cylons appear human. At the beginning of every episode, the following text appears:

> The Cylons were created by Man.
> They Rebelled.
> They evolved.
> They look and feel human.
> Some are even programmed to think they are human.
> There are many copies.
> And they have a plan.[4]

The new "human" Cylons thus dramatize two linked conflicts—first, about identifying evil, and second, about humanity; an identity crisis, if you will. The Cylons, who look and feel human—like "us"—make simple visual identification of evil obsolete. That implied "us" is interesting enough in itself; for the show's interpellated American audience,[5] *Galactica* makes humanity and American-ness synonymous. Yet, evil in *Battlestar Galactica* is no longer visually signified, one cannot look to the scar or other visible signs of "evil." This is not evil as utterly external, the inhuman Other. *Battlestar Galactica* is about the post September 11 shift toward internal vigilance, in which the enemy is already among us. As the opening reads, some even *think* they are human. No one can absolutely guarantee their humanity, even to themselves. Similarly, it exhibits an anxiety about the individuality of subjects—there are many copies—which recalls not only older anxieties about dehumanizing industrialization, but anxieties raised by the prospect of cloning and the proliferation of fundamentalisms and terrorism. After all, terrorism has been constituted as a virus, one that proliferates, multiplies, one that is suggested to erase the subject's own identity.

A kind of spectral Islam thus haunts *Battlestar Galactica*, appearing in the guise of the Cylons only to disappear. The Cylons are not specifically semiotically coded as Muslim through anything besides their monotheism, but it is rather the place of Islam as the paradigmatically "terrorist" religion that works as a source of narrative meaning and tension. But if the emphasis on terrorism and Cylon infiltration seems to suggest that the Cylons are in some sense coded as disguised Muslims, this is hardly total. Except for Sharon, played by Grace Park (an American-Canadian actress of Korean descent), the Cylons are played by white actors like Tricia Helfer and Lucy Lawless (familiar to SF audiences from her role as *Xena: Warrior Princess*). The Cylons are generally not characterized through the expected tropes of Orientalism (say, exoticism in the form of food, music, incense, etc., the veil for Muslim women, feminized masculinity for the men). This paradox is most apparent given that Cylon religion is mediated through the hyper-sexualized body of Number Six. Number Six embodies an excessive feminine sexuality, she is highly sexually coded, often wearing a red dress and red lipstick, and most of her early scenes with Doctor Baltar are sexually charged, if not the sexual act itself. Unsurprisingly perhaps, she suggests to Doctor Baltar that they have a baby, since "procreation is one of God's commandments" ("33" 1.01), a thought which clearly horrifies him. Both human and artificial, sexual and maternal, Number Six is textually overdetermined. It's fitting then that like all the human appearing Cylons, there are multiple copies of her, dramatizing her excessiveness — not only multiple copies in the "real" world, but then there is the phantom Six who appears to Doctor Baltar. That Six could be a sign of Baltar's disintegrating mental state, a Cylon implant in his brain, or even as she suggests, an angel of God. In contrast to the proliferating Sixes, there seems a much clearer demarcation between the two chief Sharons. The Sharon (code-named Boomer) on board Galactica is unaware that she is in fact a Cylon until she shoots Adama, while the one on Caprica for the first series is aware and chooses out of love for Helo to defect to the human cause. Later when the Caprican Sharon joins the crew of Galactica, she is code-named "Athena" rather than Boomer. Not inconsequentially, the two Sharons are involved with different men, one with the chief of the deck crew on Galactica, the other with Helo. While Sharon, who has "always been a flawed model" is the most human of the Cylons, in contrast, Number Six is marked by her indecipherability, slightly human, slightly not — an ambiguity aptly captured in Homi Bhabha's "not quite the same, not quite the Other" formulation (qtd. Ahmed 149).[6] Cylon religion would seem to vacillate between Islam and Christianity (with few specifically Jewish references I think), but more usually, to conflate the religions of the Book together under the rubric of "God."

Battlestar Galactica introduces terrorism as an explicit theme early on; for instance, the episode "Bastille Day" (1.03) sees an interesting discussion between Lee Adama (Apollo) and Tom Zarek over the terminology of terrorism (as opposed to "freedom fighter"). Zarek is initially posed as a freedom fighter, a writer Apollo had greatly admired in college:

ZAREK: I thought you respected me, read my book.

ADAMA: That was before you resorted to violence and hostage taking.

ZAREK: Always better when the oppressed don't fight back, isn't it?

Yet if the episode seems to attempt to make terrorism legible as a political response to oppression, it nevertheless resolves itself in individual pathology, for in the end, Lee comes to believe that "you've been saying that everything you're doing is for freedom but, the truth is, it's all about Tom Zarek and his personal death wish." Unsurprisingly, Zarek remains an enigmatic, untrustworthy figure throughout; his alliance with the traitor Doctor Baltar's disastrous presidential campaign (even with Zarek's being unaware of Baltar's duplicity) is symptomatic of this. "Freedom," then, remains the domain of *Galactica*'s American-coded leaders, *even though* they suspend legal freedoms like elections, the right to abortions and human rights. Similarly, in the "real world," freedom after September 11 has become more a matter of ontological freedom — "we" are always-already free, "they" are always-already not — rather than human rights enshrined in law.

In the third season of *Battlestar Galactica*, the series took an interesting turn in revisiting the terrorism/freedom fighter argument. In the finale of the second season, Doctor Baltar is elected president and decides to settle the fleet permanently on a dank planet called New Caprica. After a year's peace, the Cylons invade, and the human population on New Caprica surrenders. The military on Battlestars Galatica and Pegasus flee with a small number of ships who've managed to escape the invasion. So whereas the first two seasons depict a human, American-coded, race on the run from the Cylons, the third begins with an occupation that uncannily resembles the American invasion of Iraq. "Insurgents" plan suicide bombings and the Cylons "crack down" heavily with imprisonment, torture, and eventually executions. The Cylons detain people indefinitely without charge, a clear reference to the American "state of exception" politics for "enemy combatants." The use of the word "insurgents," a favored euphemism of the Bush administration, makes clear the analogy the series is drawing. We see, for instance, quite graphically, the torture of Colonel Tigh (shades of Abu Ghraib perhaps). Here, *Galactica* abruptly switches the position of identification for the viewer, creating an implicit (and perhaps even unwanted) identification with the people of Iraq — our "heroes" are now the "terrorists." But even here, the series walks an ambivalent line between humanizing "terrorism" and condoning violence. Roslin says "desperate people take desperate measures," but is unable to tell Baltar that she approves of the suicide bombers ("Precipice" 3.02).

But if the bitter fight between humans and Cylons seems all too easily a post–September 11 "clash of civilizations," it is interesting that the series complicates those politics by posing a very real spirituality not exclusively the province of either. The Cylons (particularly Number Six who has taken up residence in Doctor Baltar's head) make similar religious claims to the Ori on *Stargate*. Very early on in the series, Number Six challenges Dr Baltar's scientific rationalist beliefs:

> NUMBER SIX: You have to believe in something.
> BALTAR: I believe in a world I can and do understand, a rational universe, explained through rational means.
> NUMBER SIX: I love you, that's not rational.
> BALTAR: I know. No, but you're not rational ["33" 1.01].

What's interesting here is that it is the artificial, robot race of Cylons, who are espousing a religious creed. Religion, typically regarded as one of the more irrational forms of human experience, meets up with its opposite, the mechanical, the rational. Interestingly, the humans practice a version of Greek polytheism. In "Flesh and Bone" (1.08) Artemis and Aphrodite are specifically mentioned, and humans talk more generally of "the Gods." The Cylon religion, on the other hand, is monotheistic. As the Cylon prisoner says in "Flesh and Bone" (1.08), "I look to one God, not too many." The clash between human and Cylon then seems to be between poly- and mono-theism, which would interestingly ally the American-coded humans with New Age pagan polytheism.

However, this seeming critique of monotheistic religion is scarcely an atheist, rationalist dismissal of the spiritual altogether. Typically for a text of the postmodern sacred, *Battlestar Galactica* also endorses real, usually individual, spiritual experience. In "The Hand of God" (1.10), President Roslin, dying of cancer, begins to hallucinate in seeming fulfillment of a 3,500-year-old prophecy. Under the influence of "kamala extract," a herbal remedy treating her cancer, Roslin discloses to a preacher that she had had prescient dreams of the Cylon prisoner captured in "Flesh and Bone" (1.08) and hallucinates a nest of snakes during a press conference. The preacher tells her that the prophecy foretells of the exile and the renewal of the human species and that the leader of the time would die of a "wasting disease" before they enter the Promised Land. The prophecy clearly recalls the story in Exodus in the Hebrew Bible in which the Jews are exiled to Egypt and return to Israel under Moses' direction, although Moses himself dies before entering the land. Such a reference has an undeniable mythic resonance in our post–Christian world, even as the series makes contemporary revisions such as a female leader, a polytheistic faith of "the Gods," and of course a massive space fleet. Clearly the spirituality of *Battlestar Galactica* is that of the postmodern sacred, drawing on a supplementary relationship between New Age and Christianity spiritual symbols and affirming individualized spiritual experience.

Yet inevitably in drawing on Christian, pagan and New Age symbols, *Battlestar Galactica* puts its human religions in part in dialogue with real-world Christianity. While in general the Cylons present an estranged version of Islamic terrorism (or at least, of American fears engendered by September 11), the coding of the one particular colony, the Geminons, is that of Christian literalists. Roslin, who had publicly declared herself a messianic figure, had been most vociferously supported by the Gemini colony who believe in a literal interpretation of the holy scriptures. In the episode "The Captain's Hand" (2.17), a pregnant girl from the Gemini colony stows aboard the Galactica. The Geminons consider abortion a religious obscenity, and alone among the colonies, have made abortion illegal. Significantly, too, they seem to be a strict patriarchal society — "under Geminon law, the girl is still the property of her parents." Ultimately, and despite her own personal beliefs ("I've fought for a woman's right to control her body my entire political career"), the president makes a ban on abortions in the fleet out of pragmatic concern for the dwindling human population, but to the disappointment of the Gemini representative, allows the girl to escape prosecution for her abortion. Roslin says, bitterly, "You have your pound of flesh, and I suggest you take your victory and move on."

Abortion, of course, has been a hugely divisive issue throughout the Western world, and most violently in the United States among its "fundamentalist" variants (Catholics and Protestants alike). While the episode stops short of truly critiquing fundamentalist Christians, it presents a skeptical attitude toward both pro-choice and pro-life positions and is instead another ethical examination of the rights/survival dichotomy the series has run with. Of course, in the real world, the human race is in danger of *over*-population, not under, but this population boom is occurring largely in non–Western countries such as China and India. So this *Galactica* use of "human" disguises an implicitly Western struggle to reproduce. In Australia, the conservative Liberal government has placed a strong emphasis on "baby bonuses" (that is, financial incentives for Australians to have children), and the UK is considering a tax break for married couples. So the critical interrogation of abortion in *Galactica* is at best flawed, and perhaps more conservative from a feminist perspective than one might expect from a series that typically depicts women in positions of power without much fanfare.

CHAPTER NINE

Good, Evil and Ethics: Morality and All That Stuff

One of the many conservative accusations thrown at popular culture is that it is immoral. Sometimes this is a category mistake — not immorality but rather a different form of morality — but it is true that some texts can be shy about direct statements of morality. To do so can often make for bad business, as when the film adaptation of Philip Pullman's atheist polemic *The Golden Compass* flopped at the cinemas in part due to objections from Catholics and evangelicals. This was despite the film's clear toning down of its religious themes, a move which in turn offended atheists. Textual producers, especially for high-budget visual texts, can be leery of offending any section of their audience, and as it turns out, *The Golden Compass*'s half-hearted changes offended *everyone*. Pullman's "mistake" — if it can be termed that — was in explicitly tying his morality to real-world institutions like the Catholic Magisterium. But many of the texts of the postmodern sacred, however, phrase their morality in more metaphorical ways.

Science fiction and fantasy do not merely feature protagonists, they feature *heroes*. That's a key difference when it comes to discussing morality. While in general we are supposed to identify with heroes, they are nevertheless extraordinary people (or indeed aliens) able to perform feats beyond ordinary human capability. As such, they shoulder a superhuman responsibility to protect the rest of the populace (with great power...). Buffy, we will remember, "stand[s] alone [to] fight the vampires, the demons and the powers of darkness" ("Welcome to the Hellmouth" 1.01). Witches and wizards are a favorite trope of the postmodern sacred (to name just two, *Charmed*, *Harry Potter*). Robots, demons, Slayers, sometimes even traditionally "evil" beings like vampires and werewolves (*Blade*, *Underworld*) may be recruited in the service of fighting evil and protecting the vulnerable.

As we saw in Chapter Three, gods and monsters are far closer than are often thought. They require each other to define themselves against. Both are separated from "ordinary" humanity by virtue of their superior strengths and abilities. Heroes often exist in a liminal space on the edge of society, protecting the world but not necessarily being entirely *of* it. So their separation is often not merely a metaphoric separation, but literal. This is a trope of both "classic" comic books—Clark Kent has his Fortress of Solitude, Batman his cavernous mansion—and of newer texts that have drawn equally from comic book sources as from the mythic (*The League of Extraordinary Gentleman*, for instance, draws characters from 19th century literature like Wilde's *Picture of Dorian Gray*, *Dracula*, and *Tom Sawyer* and refracts them through a postmodern comic sensibility).

The trilogy of films that make up *The Matrix* provide an interesting case of the interplay between religion and ethics in the postmodern sacred—in particular with the way in which they foreground an action-movie Christ-figure in a seeming restatement of pre- or anti-postmodern meta-narratives. For those unfamiliar with the three movies—*The Matrix*, *The Matrix Reloaded* and *Matrix Revolutions*—the story is relatively simple. Sometime in the future, around 2199, mankind has been enslaved by a race of powerful aliens and is living in capsules feeding a giant machine. They're unaware of this however, inhabiting mentally a shared computer simulation of the year 1999. Neo, played by Keanu Reeves, is a hacker who in the first film finds out the nature of "reality" in the Matrix, and then leads a human rebellion against the machines and a rogue computer program called Agent Smith (played by Hugo Weaving).

Like *Star Wars* before it,[7] *The Matrix* draws more or less self-consciously on religious and mythic structures. As such it's unsurprising that it gathered a fanatical response in some fans. While the first movie was a sleeper hit, it seems likely that writer/directors the Wachowskis had hoped the mythic elements would produce the kind of fanatical following for the film that SF and fantasy have been known to produce. The series has been variously read by critics as Buddhist and Christian, as well as a postmodern critique of simulation[8] and dystopic vision of a mechanized future. Given the two-way supplementary relationship between Christianity and the New Age, I believe that both Christian and Buddhist are equally valid readings of *The Matrix* trilogy: the texts are suggestive of both in different ways, as well as significantly influenced by Greek and Roman mythology. The series provides a cornucopia of symbols and names pastiched from various religious and mythic traditions—characters Trinity (Christian) and Morpheus (the God of dreams in Ovid's *Metamorphosis*), the ship Nebuchadnezzar (a Babylonian king mentioned in the Book of Daniel), the ship Osirus (Egyptian), the city Zion (Jewish and Christian), the Oracle (a possible reference to the Greek Oracle at Delphi) and so on. Indeed, philosopher Gregory Bassham criticizes *The Matrix*'s treatment of religious themes for its "cafeteria pluralism" (118) that "while fashionable, is very difficult to make sense of, or to defend" (125). Bassham's critique seems to miss the point, for spiritually inflected pop culture cannot necessarily presume any one religious belief in its mass audience. As a matter of capitalistic pragmatism textual producers often strive to avoid alienating their audiences, as any overt reference is likely to do. Religious pluralism provides a sense of mythic grandeur precisely because of its inability to be pinned to any one religious credo.

The Matrix provides on the one hand a hero in the form of Neo, a properly mythic hero resonant with Christ symbolism. Neo is called "The One" throughout the three movies by Morpheus, the prophesied savior for mankind. The messianic overtones are in the series right from the beginning of the first movie, in Trinity's speech to Neo in the club. She says:

> You're looking for him. I know because I was once looking for the same thing. And when he found me, he told me I wasn't really looking for him, I was looking for an answer. It's the question that drives us, Neo. It's the question that brought you here. You know the question, just as I did.
> NEO: What is the Matrix?
> TRINITY: The answer is out there Neo. It's looking for you, and it will find you if you want it to.

The "him" being referred to in the speech is, of course, Morpheus, the John the Baptist figure to Neo's Jesus (Morpheus, in return, "has spent his entire life looking for [Neo]"). The pre-figuring of the "real" Messiah with another is a common trope in Christianity, in which the coming of Jesus is intuited by Jew and pagan alike, played out in an incomplete fashion. Like most Hollywood Messiahs, Neo is an action-movie Christ ("My own personal Jesus Christ," as a junkie tells him), a gun-toting hero who on one level ignores many of the ethical demands of traditional religion ("Thou shalt not kill," for a start).

On the one hand, though, *The Matrix* seems to present a meta-narrative of morality, a demand for human sovereignty couched in messianic terms. Neo and his compadres struggle on behalf of the ethical values of human freedom and autonomy, attempting to free human consciousness itself from false perceptions. Humankind, as Morpheus puts it, has been "born into a prison that you cannot smell or taste or touch. A prison for your mind."

Slavoj Žižek points out that the first two movies set up a situation in which *Matrix Revolutions* would "have to produce nothing less than the appropriate answer to the dilemmas of revolutionary politics today, a blueprint for the political act the Left is desperately looking for."

The Matrix *and the Postmodern*

While the first *Matrix* movie was made before September 11, the follow-up sequels were released after, meaning that the series reflects an enduring cultural ambivalence toward postmodern simulation that both precedes 9/11 and continues after. On the one hand, much of the force of the first movie derives from its lay-postmodern "revelation" of the simulated world of the matrix (and by inference, the implication that today's world is just as simulated). In that sense, *The Matrix* is a nostalgic, anti-postmodern piece. The fight, after all, is on behalf of a human sovereignty unmediated by simulated technology. That technology is parasitical, draining humans of their energy, literally and metaphorically. The unreality of the simulated world in the first movie is suggested to be a "splinter in your mind" needing to be removed, yet this is increasingly complicated by the following two movies.

The ambivalences in the text run much deeper than a simple rejection of postmodern simulation. It is not merely anti-postmodern, even as it may at times verge toward a trite affirmation of "reality." Baudrillard himself sees that as a sign the films misread his work, keeping a "real" outside of simulation in a way that the theory refuses. Yet the "real" world that the rebels inhabit is often a dank, lifeless existence, scarcely an affirmation of unmediated experience. The traitor Cypher's speech in the first movie about how he would rather eat fake steak than real porridge is a fairly compelling argument for self-deception. Similarly, much of the movies' appeal derives from the spectacular, unreal, effects and abilities that the computer Matrix endows both Neo and Agent Smith with. The computer Matrix provides the pretext for the bending of "real" life — the amazing "bullet time" effect, the famous kung-fu move in which the actors pause mid-air while the camera rotates disorientingly, Neo's ability to fly, the "cool" accoutrements of leather jackets, sunglasses, impressively phallic guns and so on. In short, the action inside the Matrix provides many of the visceral thrills of the series. Such a play of "surfaces" is not to be dismissed easily, for in foregrounding the aesthetic to the point of fetish, *The Matrix* is clearly postmodern in the pleasures it attempts to evoke. And to state the obvious, *The Matrix* pastiches a great many other texts, notably *Blade Runner,* Hong Kong kung-fu flicks and Japanese anime like *Akira* and *Ghost in the Shell.* The Wachowskis, after all, explicitly stated their goal was to create a live action anime (and indeed went on to hire a number of anime directors to create an anime series of short films called *The Animatrix* that bridged the first and second films).[9] Thus, *even as it attempts* to find a way out of the postmodern world of simulations through a heroic Christ figure, *The Matrix* remains profoundly enmeshed in the postmodern, unwilling or even unable to imagine a world outside textual referentiality.

Harry Potter

The immensely successful *Harry Potter* series of books and movies provides an interesting point of comparison to *The Matrix*. While it was initially targeted at children and young adults, *Harry Potter* has since found an enormous, mass market audience and is arguably one of the more influential fantastic texts. While *The Matrix* (especially the first movie) series is arguably one of the key touchstones of contemporary

SF, *Harry Potter*, along with the perennial favorite *Lord of the Rings*, occupies a comparable position in the fantasy genre. An at-times uneasy blend of jolly-hockey-sticks style boarding school stories and fantastic elements, the titular hero Harry fights foes both powerful and mundane, from the evil sorcerer Lord Voldemort to the various childhood and teenage dramas of mean teachers and peers, social exclusion, heterosexual romance and so on. In its blending of source texts like boarding school stories such as Enid Blyton's *Mallory Towers* and *Twins at Saint Claire's* series, Tolkien's *The Hobbit* and *Lord of the Rings*, and the presence of other characteristic fantasy tropes like dragons and magic spells, *Harry Potter* is clearly a postmodern pastiche. And the films take that pastiching impulse in other ways too; for instance, the books describe wizard's clothes as brightly colored, yet the wizards in Diagon Alley are imagined in the first movie (*Harry Potter and the Sorcerer's Stone*) as dressed in the clothes of a Dickensian style London — a pastiche which certainly rang true to Rowling's nostalgic textual impulses. Indeed the literary critic Harold Bloom has criticized the series for its profound lack of originality (which is, I suspect, to miss the point of where a critique of the series could or should be made. The racial and class politics involved in unearthing the merry old days of Empire embedded in the public boarding school story, for instance, are scarcely progressive). Andrew Blake, too, argues that the success of Harry Potter is due to its New Labour style "retro-lutionary" aesthetic, in which the new is sold by simulating the aesthetics of the past. He says, "The stories explore the old, and a little under the surface deal with the new: past literary forms and present concerns exist side by side" (17).

Interestingly, because of its young audience, J.K. Rowling's series has faced numerous criticisms from religious leaders across the globe — evangelical, Anglican, Catholic and even Muslim, though it has primarily centered around the loose movement of evangelical and fundamentalist Protestants in the United States known as the Christian or Religious Right. Sociologist Danielle Souillere (2010) has documented the astounding amount of material devoted to the series by the Christian Right in the United States over the last decade. *Harry Potter* provokes much evangelical anxiety about the evils of "witch-craft" and Satanism — itself a phenomenon worthy of investigation into the kinds of belief involved in construing an innocuous fantasy series as a Satanic "trap" to lure children into temptation (one can only fear devils if one believes in them).

Such readings of the text are fascinating, if highly idiosyncratic, readings of a text which is, ironically, a fairly conventional take on morality. Like *The Matrix*, *Harry Potter* features an apparently preternaturally gifted protagonist fighting the forces of evil. Like many properly mythic heroes, Harry is marked out as special from birth. He is known throughout the wizarding world as "The Boy Who Lived," having survived an attack by Voldemort as a mere infant at a time in which few were able to survive a confrontation with him. Harry's separation from the other students is visually coded with the lightning-bolt scar on his forehead from his attack by Voldemort as a child. When he first begins at the wizard school Hogwarts in *Harry Potter and the Sorcerer's Stone*, Harry is treated with reverence and respect by the other students. Despite her clear superiority in using magic, Hermione's speech to Harry at the end of the first book makes clear that it's *he* who is truly heroic.

And yet while Harry seems at first glance to be innately heroic — he does emerge amazingly unscathed from the abuse of his aunt and uncle — author J.K. Rowling makes that heroism ethical, the product of love and altruism. Although they are by no means perfect, and fall out a number of times, the friendship between Harry, Ron and Hermione is consistently affirmed as one of the series' central themes. And it is in fact the love of Harry's mother, Lily, which prevents Voldemort from killing him, rather than Harry's natural heroism.

Good in *Harry Potter* emerges not merely from heroic action, but from the consequences of those actions. Nicholas Flamel, creator of the Philosopher's Stone of the first book, and his wife both make the ethical choice to die at the ripe old age of 665. As Dumbledore says to Harry:

> To one as young as you, I'm sure it seems incredible, but to Nicholas and Perenelle, it really is like going to bed after a very *very* long day. After all, to the well organized mind, death is but the next great adventure. You know, the [Philosopher's] Stone really was not such a wonderful thing. As much money and life as you could want! The two things most human beings would choose above all — the trouble is, humans do have a knack of choosing precisely those things that are worst for them [297].

Here the desire to artificially extend one's life — what in other circumstances may be desperately fought against in *HP*—is subjected to ethical scrutiny. And of course, for the religious scholar, there seems a clear significance of dying at 665 instead of 666. In what amounts to a magical euthanasia argument, there seems a clear ethical line between the grace of Nicholas and Perenelle's surrender to the inevitable and Voldemort's desperate desire to remain alive.

Unlike Dumbledore, the evil Voldemort is unable to imagine a worse fate than death, as the following exchange in *Harry Potter and The Order of the Phoenix* makes clear:

> "You do not seek to kill me, Dumbledore?" called Voldemort, his scarlet eyes narrowed over the top of the shield. "Above such brutality, are you?"
>
> "We both know there are other ways of destroying a man, Tom." Dumbledore said calmly [...]. "Merely taking your life would not satisfy me, I admit —"
>
> "There is nothing worse than death, Dumbledore!" snarled Voldemort.
>
> "You are quite wrong," said Dumbledore [...] "Indeed your failure to understand that there are things much worse than death has always been your greatest weakness" [814].

Rowling consistently underlines the immorality of Voldemort's magic, which extends his life and power at the expense of innumerable others, and which instrumentalizes people free of love and kindness. As Jerry L. Walls puts it, "Rather than sacrifice himself for others, he is willing to sacrifice innocent beings for his own selfish purposes. This is shown in the fact that he was willing to perform the monstrous act of slaying a unicorn in order to keep himself alive" (75).

But while it makes for exciting and epic battles in fantastic narratives, such an utterly self-centered disregard for others as Voldemort's is rare. Rowling is more suggestive about the varied motives for evil conduct in the series. Evilness at times appears easily readable in the series; there is often a clear slide between unpleasantness and evil in the form of the House of Slytherin. In the films, evil is clearly signaled visually by Voldemort's (played by Ralph Fiennes) effeminacy and monstrous resemblance to a snake. It would therefore be easy to misread *Harry Potter* as positing evil as something Out There and irreducibly different, a kind of demonization of evil as the innate product of Otherness.

Yet J.K. Rowling has a rather more sophisticated moral vision at work. The unpleasant Professor Snape—forever suspect—turns out to have been good out of love for Harry's mother Lily. Harry's father, James, on the other hand, while idolized by his friend Sirius Black, is also seen in an unflattering light as a childhood bully of Snape's. Appearances can be deceiving in the wizarding world no less than our Muggle world.

Rowling's take on evil is strongly related to the Shoah/Holocaust, with the language used to describe human-born wizards as a class echoing that of the Nazis. In particular, the neologism "Mudblood" is in Rowling's lexicon a racialized epithet whose very etymology recalls Social Darwinist ideas of racial "purity." After Draco Malfoy calls Hermione a "filthy little mud blood" in *Harry Potter and the Chamber of Secrets*, Ron explains that "it's a disgusting thing to call someone. Dirty blood, see. Common blood. It's ridiculous" (116). "Mudblood" invokes a familiar form of racial image in which mixing is a kind of metaphysical corruption of purity, formulated through racial or ethnic heredity rather than the Christian ideal of purity as a lack of sinful actions. Despite the hereditary aspect to racialization in *Harry Potter*, as with other forms of racist iconography the term "sticks" as Sara Ahmed would put it (4), with the transitive properties of terms like "Muggle lover" and "blood traitor" easily applied to "pure blood" wizards sympathetic to Muggles—forming in the process a wizarding community defined by its imagined superiority to and rejection of these abjected Others.

But while the stigmatization of human-born wizards is at some points merely an individualist theory of hatred (especially early in the series), Rowling takes this racial imaginary into the modern realm of saturated biopolitics of the totalitarian state. When Voldemort seizes control of the Ministry of Magic, he creates a Muggle-born Registration Commission to create show trials exposing Muggle-borns "stealing" wizard magic.

> RON WEASLEY: "People won't let this happen."
>
> REMUS LUPIN: "It is happening, Ron. Muggle-borns are being rounded up as we speak."
>
> RON WEASLEY: "But how are they supposed to have 'stolen' magic? It's mental, if you could steal magic there wouldn't be any Squibs would there?"

REMUS LUPIN: "I know. Nevertheless, unless you can prove that you have at least one close wizarding relative, you are now deemed to have obtained your magical power illegally and must suffer the punishment."

In a post–Shoah world, the registration of a racialized minority cannot help but raise the memories of the Nazi blood quantum laws in particular (as well as other systems of control in colonial countries). As with the Nazis where "the exception everywhere becomes the rule" (Agamben 1998: 9), the state of exception which makes the Muggles expendable — able to be killed but not sacrificed as in Agamben's *homo sacer*— expands into a broader system to terrorize the general population. And indeed given the indentured servitude that house elves served under pre–Voldemort, it is arguable that the state of exception applied as a means of controlling selected populations is a constitutive element in the institutional regimes of power of the wizarding world.

Wizard-born "pure borns" like the Malfoy and Black families are clearly motivated in part by their racial politics in their enthusiastic participation in Voldemort's genocidal purges. But in Rowling's telling, Voldemort's reign of terror lasts as long as it did not merely because of that human malevolence, but because of inertia and human cowardice. Zygmunt Bauman wrote of the Holocaust, "Evil needs neither enthusiastic followers nor an applauding audience — the instinct of self-preservation will do, encouraged by the thought that it is not my turn yet, thank God: by lying low I can still escape" (2000: 206). This is a perspective confirmed by Primo Levi's Holocaust memoirs, where he describes the inability of contemporary audiences to understand his experiences in Auschwitz. Schoolchildren, he says, would imagine that in the same circumstance they would perform daring prison breaks, though these were in fact relatively rare in the prison camps.

Though it is still certainly far from thinking through the totality of the horror of Nazi biopolitics, Rowling confirms the notion advanced by Susan Nieman that much modern evil stems not from personal malevolence but rather systemically produced violence (as exemplified by the Holocaust, or corporate neglect, and so on), in which good, nice people *nevertheless* contribute to the perpetuation of injustice and even evil. In the context of all this, then, Rowling's dedication to the individualist ideal of the hero is, like that of *The Matrix*, occasionally profoundly unconvincing. However, in contrast to the anonymous capitalist system of the matrix, Lord Voldemort is a charismatic totalitarian leader capable of being defeated—casting Harry as the leader of a revolutionary cell in a sense. Rowling's revolution is certainly not a Marxist revolution of the kind imagined by the Wachowskis though, it is squarely a bourgeois revolution in favor of the autonomous individual's rights and the restoration of the natural order of things. The final chapter of *Harry Potter and the Deathly Hallows* shows the mapping of this order onto compulsory heterosexual futurism (Edelman 4) and the passing of the school community from one generation to another. Rowling's world is an attractive one, modeled on the virtues of friendship, fairness, sacrifice and altruism. But there is no revolutionary, universal dimension of the kind imagined in recent interpretations of the writings of Saint Paul by the likes of Alain Badiou. Harry might save the world from Voldemort, but it is in the name of an order which has, as the extended house elf episodes made clear, been built on inequality and which presumably remains so post-liberation. If Harry is a kind of Christ figure, he is, in the end, a thoroughly modern one, more Privet Drive than the scandal of the Cross.

Conclusion: Is There an Outside to Capital?

In summing up, it seems especially necessary to weigh the ideological implications of the postmodern sacred. Slavoj Žižek in *On Belief* argues that Buddhism works as the ideological supplement to late capitalism. He points out that the Buddhist logic of "letting go" enables its practitioners to surrender to the inevitability of postmodern capital *and* to maintain the illusion of not participating in the game of capitalistic accumulation (2001: 12). Buddhism is, in the Freudian-Lacanian terminology, a fetish by which subjects disavow their own complicity in postmodern capitalism. Buddhism and the New Age, in Žižek's opinion, thus produce apolitical subjects, "who fully participate in the capitalist dynamic while retaining the appearance of mental sanity" (2001: 13). Žižek instead argues through his characteristic use of Hegel and Lacan that one should instead look toward the monism of Christianity.

Now Žižek's initial point is a well-made one, for it is not by accident that Buddhism in the West has been largely popularized by that most capitalistic industry, the entertainment industry (one only has to think of celebrity Buddhists like Richard Gere or the Beastie Boys), and of course, the aforementioned pop New Ageism of Oprah. Yet he arguably overstates his case, for though Buddhism is no longer on the New Age fringe, Christianity remains ideologically hegemonic, especially in the United States—and it is the more fundamentalist forms of Christianity that are, ironically, some of the most capitalistic. What Žižek has overlooked in his haste toward one of his famous reversals of Leftist orthodoxies, of course, is how Christianity itself functions not so much as the ideological supplement of capitalism in the United States but the very precondition for its existence. America, of course, has famously considered itself "God's own country," yet has, traditionally, seen little conflict between rampant capitalism and Christianity. God blesses America with its wealth — therefore, God loves capitalism (and never mind some of those unfortunate commandments in the Bible about justice that might be extended to, say, worker's civil rights). The second Bush administration made explicit the latent connections made between capital, "patriotism," evangelical Protestant Christianity and an aggressive foreign policy, but almost all of those key structural conditions have remained the same during the Obama administration. Žižek suggests playfully that, were he alive today, Max Weber would probably write a sequel to *The Protestant Ethic* on the late capitalist Buddhist ethic (2001:13) — but Weber could just as easily write a sequel on evangelical Christianity and how it informs the American spirit of global capitalism. It is one of the strengths of Žižek's thought that he provocatively questions the presumptions of the intellectual Left, so it is unsurprising that Žižek has mercilessly pilloried the common "respect" for New Age pop spirituality, and conversely the disdain for organized religion, as "watered-down" belief. He suggests that it is true belief, in whatever form that occurs, that is incompatible with the secular West.

Žižek's recent work on religion and belief poses some interesting questions for any consideration of popular culture spirituality — particularly one such as my own, which considers both the New Age and the Christian as entangled in a supplementary relationship. It is doubtful however that the Left could truly engage with the Christian legacy as Žižek suggests (especially through a Hegelian-Lacanian framework). Key Leftist struggles such as feminist and queer rights are, if not irreducibly incompatible with Christianity, then certainly at odds with it. The queer feminist theology of Marcella Althaus-Reid, for instance, is in stark contrast with the all-too-common misogyny and homophobia of the Roman Catholic tradition she writes in. The conservative reigns of Popes John Paul II and Benedict have seen Catholicism retreat from progressive approaches to gender, sexuality and other religions.[1]

Then there is the problem of actually believing in God under postmodernity. It is arguable that the secular and religious in postmodernity have become difficult to tell apart. It is not merely that Christian belief has become "watered down" into New Age obscurantism — many people who once called themselves atheists now prefer agnostic. Recall once again Mark C. Taylor's work. Taylor argues that the problem of postmodernity is not merely belief or unbelief; it is that, for many people, they are caught somewhere in between. The postmodern religious culture finds itself somewhere between a fundamentalist belief in a singular God, a pagan belief in *everything*, and a modern skeptical disbelief in *anything*— three often incompatible belief systems. Yet, even given the significant differences among those positions, it is interesting to see how they begin to incorporate elements of each other — Oprah's spirituality which speaks of "'karma' and 'grace' in equal parts" (Parkins 149). And even with their oft-stated antipathy toward the New Age, it is not unusual to even hear evangelical Christian fundamentalists speak of their faith in characteristically New Age terms (as "self-fulfilment" and so on).

It is unsurprising then that a fictional popular culture has evolved which makes equal use of the New Age, of Enlightenment skepticism, and the traditions of Judaism and Christianity. I have argued throughout this book that, while eclectic in its use of spiritual symbols, the postmodern sacred persistently draws on a New Age style method of consumption, one in which spiritual experience and truth "come by way of one's own experience" (Heelas 21). As we saw in the case of Peter Jackson's *The Lord of the Rings* adaptations, the New Age is retrospectively rewriting Christian figures like sacraments, angels, and even God. But, if it seems to more strongly depend on a New Age framework, the postmodern sacred is not reducible to it, and it is hardly necessarily an indicator of real-world belief or practice. As I have argued throughout, an engagement with popular culture requires neither belief nor unbelief. Those people systematically excluded from organized religion can find themselves, through acts of adept reading, the fragments of an inclusive postmodern spirituality. Those who do have religious beliefs can find echoes of their beliefs in popular culture. Yet this consumerist shift is not unproblematic, given that it is individually focused and driven by the logic of postmodern global capitalism.

Sociologist Zygmunt Bauman asks the question of whether "one can legitimately recognize the orgasmic experience of postmodern sensation-gatherers as essentially religious?" (180). There are striking similarities to be sure, yet I am hesitant to uncritically equate the transcendent experiences of saints and the like with the various postmodern ecstasies fuelled by the needs of the market. It is debatable whether "orgasmic experience" is necessarily *essentially* religious; it tends to be one aspect of religious cultures among many. The question for me, is not so much, is postmodern sensation-gathering religious, as is postmodern sensation-gathering being consumed *as* religious? That question seeks to find not the ontological status of postmodern consumption — is pop culture spirituality *really* religious — but the functionality of it, what it does. Bauman says that

> postmodern cultural pressures, while intensifying the search for "peak experiences," have at the same time uncoupled it from religion-prone interests and concerns, privatized it, and cast mainly non-religious institutions in the role of purveyors of relevant services. The "whole experience" of revelation, ecstasy, breaking the boundaries of the self and total transcendence, once the privilege of the selected "aristocracy of culture" — saints, hermits, mystics, ascetic monks, *tsadiks* or dervishes — and coming either as an unsolicited miracle, in no obvious fashion related to what the receiver of grace has done to earn it, or as an act of grace rewarding the life of self-immolation and denial, has been put by postmodern culture in every individual's reach, recast as a realistic target and plausible prospect of each individual's self-training, and relocated at the product of life devoted to the art of consumer self-indulgence [180].

As he rightly points out, one can hardly regard the process of spiritual consumption as religious in and of itself. There is nothing very otherworldly about the everyday practices of global capitalism. If the postmodern sacred provides a vicarious experience of belief, or the supernatural, then it is only that. One cannot presume consumption to necessarily be an affirmation of realworld belief in any faith, but neither can one presume the opposite.

One form that this search for "peak" experience takes is the search for "real" life. If "real experience" seems so difficult to access in postmodernity that subjects feel compelled to raid the cultural artifacts of the past, even the cultural representations of the unreal, then it should be hardly surprising that "the real" begins to take on a quasi-spiritual aura. As Baudrillard says, "Paradoxically, it is the real which has become our true utopia — but a utopia that is no longer in the realm of the possible, that can only be dreamt of as one would dream of a lost object" (1994:123). But if this search for the real seems to have some similarities with classical theology — God as pure Being — then it differs equally, looking for this-worldly authenticity rather than otherworldly transcendence. It is *also* the reverse, pure Being as God, a way of rendering consumerism as spiritual. Once again, then, the spiritual seems to appear in postmodernity, only to dart away upon closer examination.

So the utopic dream of truly recovering the real through consumption, in the form of the postmodern sacred, is simply not possible. That it is not should be unsurprising, considering the considerable paradoxes at work here — and most especially, consuming to treat the alienation produced by postmodernist consumerism. Yet this hardly discounts the postmodern sacred from being culturally vital or significant. It might seem slightly bizarre that contemporary subjects would aim at experiencing the sacred through popular culture; however, such are the paradoxes of postmodern life, in which consuming the spiritual appears to make perfect capitalist sense. Most especially after September 11, religion and spirituality are important concerns for every subject, whether one believes or not, and it is in the popular culture of the postmodern sacred that we find the contradictions of contemporary spiritual life coming together in an important, if not unproblematic, way. Searching for the transcendental, lost heroes, authenticity and meta-narratives, the postmodern sacred finds only fragments and traces of the transcendental, and the endless deferral of spiritual satisfaction to another episode, another show, another movie.

Exiting Postmodernism?

Yet though the virtual postmodern media culture assimilates almost everything in its path, there remain some elements of human culture that need not be an object of capitalist exchange. In his *The Cost of Discipleship*, Lutheran minister and theologian Dietrich Bonhoeffer isolated "cheap grace" as the "deadly enemy of the Church," meaning a grace "sold on the market" (43). Bonhoeffer notes that cheap grace does not require anything of its adherents, that it allows the world to go on functioning as it is. He considers this to be a kind of heresy, anti–Christian.

Conclusion

So what is the alternative to this "cheap grace"? Bonhoeffer puts forth a theory of "costly grace," which may appeal to Christians but have limited appeal for others.

One particular theme that might present a viable alternative is that of the gift, which has provoked the thoughts of many anthropologists, philosophers and theologians over the course of the twentieth century in a discussion which brings out the difficulty of an anti- or post-capitalist economy. Jacques Derrida's work on the gift fleshes out the discussion considerably. In *Given Time*, Derrida discusses the impossibility of the gift, arguing that for a gift to be truly a gift, it must not appear as an object in the economy of exchange. If a gift appears *as* a gift, it immediately enters its recipient into a cycle of debt and repayment—a gift must either be returned in kind, or one remains in the giver's debt. Derrida questions, "How is one to speak reasonably [...] of a gift that could not be what it was except on the condition of not being what it was?" (1992: 35).

In various ways, then, Derrida draws our attention to the linguistic economies of sacrifice. Any gift must not appear to be a gift, must not appear to be a sacrifice, for that is the usual state of economic exchange. *Given Time* makes clear that the very method of circulation is cut through with anxieties about the counterfeit, the simulacrum. Paradoxically too, counterfeit money for Derrida can only be what it is by virtue of appearing to be what it is not—real money, "good and true money" (59). "The enigma of the simulacrum should orient us toward the triple and indissociable question of the *gift*, of *forgiveness*, and of the *excuse*. And to question whether a gift can or *ought* to *secure itself* against counterfeit money" (59). But dissimulation is a risk that must be taken by any potential gift giver: "*[o]ught* they not—but beyond duty and debt—*deprive themselves* of any security against the counterfeit, or any mistrust regarding counterfeit money, so as to preserve the chance of being what they *ought to be*, but ought to be beyond duty and debt?" (70). Yet, if on one level the gift appears to be outside the sphere of economic circulation, Derrida suggests that it is "anecomomic" (7), that it is not completely foreign to the circle of economy, but that it "must *keep* a relation of foreignness" (7).

And thus Derrida argues, in his other meditation on the subject in *The Gift of Death* (1994) that the only true gift is death itself, which is unreturnable. Death exits (or appears to) the economic in all its anxieties about the counterfeit, the true, the authentic. For while death is certainly not foreign to capital (86), it maintains a relation of foreignness. Like Søren Kierkegaard in *Fear and Trembling*, Derrida finds in Genesis 22 a story of fidelity, of silence, of sacrifice — Abraham's "gift of death" as he so evocatively terms it. If the economic is fraught with the danger of the simulacrum, a gift must instead be given in silence. Derrida underlines the secret nature of Abraham's actions and its incommunicability to the social. To speak is to be social, to enter the economic sphere.

But though he follows Kierkegaard's argument for some distance, what separates Derrida from Kierkegaard is his recognition that the infinite alterity of God differs little in the end from the infinite alterity of any other Other. Derrida suggests that "everyone else [...] is infinitely other in its absolute singularity, inaccessibility, solitary, transcendent" (1994: 78). Therefore, "what can be said about Abraham's relation to God can be said about my relation without relation to every one (one) as every (bit) other" (78). In typical fashion, Derrida collapses the distinction between ethical and religious, opening the religious up to a generalized responsibility, a universal singularity.[2]

For Derrida, therefore, the opacity of the Other —*any* Other — prevents us from making any firm distinctions between God and any Other. The gift therefore has a close relation to hospitality, as when Derrida says that

> for pure hospitality or pure gift to occur there must be absolute surprise [...] an opening without horizon of expectation [...] to this newcomer whoever he [sic] be. The newcomer may be good or evil, but if you exclude the possibility that the newcomer is coming to destroy your house, if you wish to control this and exclude this terrible possibility, there is no hospitality [1999: 70].

Derrida preempts objections to this theme of absolute openness to the Other, when he acknowledges that the undecidability of openness to the Other is a risky move. There is after all a volatility in the very etymology of the word "hospitality" in Latin, which signals both hostility *and* hospitality. In a very real sense, then the guest *is* God, and our responsibility is to be open to every form of alterity, unconditionally, without guarantees.

Much of my point with this book has been not only to discuss reli-

Conclusion

gion in the media, but about how "organized" religion is so thoroughly mediated and hence commoditized and individualized itself. The challenge in postmodern culture, therefore, is to begin from the impossibility that Derrida raises, to look for moments of the impossible and bring them into the realm of the possible, to be open to alterity. Derrida sees a true gift only in silence, but as the theme of hospitality suggests, there are yet perhaps other cultural moments of the impossible that we can isolate.

Political theorists Michael Hardt and Antonio Negri have discussed "the multitude," a chaotic mass, drawn together in solidarity across difference. These are "innumerable internal differences that can never be reduced to a unity of single identity—different cultures, races, ethnicities, gender, sexual orientations; different forms of labor; different views of the world and different desires" (2004: xiv). This multitude emerges from the global, networked virtual culture, as a kind of swarm, premised on structural difference but common interest and purpose. Hardt and Negri argue passionately and compellingly about the need for the resuscitation of the commons, of recognizing humanity's common inheritances—the material world of air, water, earth, and the shared social productions of language, codes, knowledge.

The recent development of the Occupy movement in late 2011 has seen a multitude much like that described by Hardt and Negri assemble in solidarity against marked income inequality, the dismantling of the welfare state and the increasingly authoritarian rule over ostensible democracies in the United States, Europe, Australia and elsewhere by markets and the politicians they have bought off. This movement has been frequently dismissed by the political classes and mainstream media as incoherent, lacking demands, confused by a movement premised on a mass rather than charismatic individuals. Hardt and Negri anticipate the challenges posed by such a political movement, noting the difficulty "for a social multiplicity to manage to communicate and act in common while remaining internally different" (2004: xiv). Yet it is also arguable that Occupy has been glossed as incoherent not because its demands are so difficult to translate into political policy (in its U.S. incarnation for instance, common demands include the repeal of the Bush tax cuts for the wealthy and a repeal of the doctrine of "corporate personhood," as well as broader demands for a return to the social democratic programs of the mid-twentieth century) but because of the unwillingness on the part of either center Left or Right to consider such demands politically viable.

But if we follow Marx's basic insight that capital sows the seeds of its own destruction, and Hardt and Negri's suggestion that the resistant multitude emerges from the networked society itself, then we must consider the religious connotations of such a move. It's telling that Hardt and Negri turn to the Christian figure of Legion recounted in Mark, Luke and Matthew, a possessed man whose "demons" are removed by Jesus and transferred to a group of pigs. Legion represents the power of the multitude, which is "at once both 'we' and 'I'" (2004: 138). Though Legion recalls the mighty Roman legions, for Hardt and Negri,

> perhaps the real threat of this demonic multitude is more metaphysical: since it is at once singular and plural, it destroys numerical distinction itself. Think of the great lengths to which theologians have gone to prove there are not many gods but only one [138].

Here the religious and the supernatural meld into the one figure, with the demonic figure of Legion obliquely echoing Marx's infamous usage of the vampire to describe Capital. The metaphysics of the play between many and one capture not merely the tension between polytheism and monotheism that I have described throughout this book, but need for both unanimity of purpose (as seen in the consensus model of the Occupy General Assemblies) and diversity.

Though Hardt and Negri suggest in *Commonwealth* that we should "abandon all [...] 'higher values' that would allow us to remain outside [of Empire]" (2009: vii), it is my belief that movements such as Occupy demand a substantial religious element, one that includes a critique of the systems of oppression *as well as* a plausible vision of a better one. It would need to draw together, in totality, the spirituality of the New Age with their skepticism for corrupt institutions and the liberatory aspects of the Abrahamic religions, those that foreground hospitality and demand justice. And in moving from the capitalist world of mediated consumption, it would demand fidelity and commitment without homogeneity.

Though quite obviously real-world religions are being practiced by the likes of Occupy Judaism (who held services for Yom Kippur in Zuccotti Park during the initial stage of Occupation in New York in October

2011), the seeds of this vision of another world may also well be found in the popular culture texts produced through the mechanics of global capitalism — as with the use of the iconic Guy Fawkes mask from the Wachowskis' *V For Vendetta* as a symbol of anonymous resistance at protests. One might find, in *Children of Men*'s uncertain creativity, a trajectory out from the twin problems of climate change and the biopolitical political state. Even a conservative text like *Twilight* might allow us to reflect critically on the kinds of desires that a capitalist economy solicits from us, even as inevitably these exceed the margins of the text.

In a symbolic economy, like Derrida's gift, no text will be completely outside the sphere of economic circulation. But it is the opacity, the unpredictability of the sacred, that we must insist upon, and look to isolate moments in culture that "*keep* a relation of foreignness" (1991: 7) to the insistent normalizing of the commodification of the sacred. We must practice radical hospitality to one another, to usher in the stranger and the strange. To look for true liberation, or even lasting spiritual solace in popular culture then is insufficient — for that, we must form a multitude united in difference with which to create a better world.

Chapter Notes

Introduction

1. Hindu, Buddhism and Confucianism represent special cases given their relationship to the New Age in the West. Although I argue that the New Age is particularly receptive to those traditions because of their perceived liberal approaches to gender and sexuality, as Karen Armstrong notes, "There are Buddhist, Hindu and even Confucian fundamentalisms, which also cast aside many of the painfully acquired insights of liberal culture, which fight and kill in the name of religion and seek to bring the sacred into the realm of politics and national struggle" (2004:ix). So the separation between fundamentalism and spirituality becomes slightly strained, and depends on the national context in which one is talking — Buddhism as practiced in the U.S. or the U.K. varies significantly from its practice in Tibet.
2. This is a phrase Harvey takes from the editors of PRECIS 6, a journal from the Columbia Graduate School of Architecture.
3. I have developed this idea more fully in my Ph.D. dissertation "The Postmodern Sacred: Popular Culture Spirituality in the Genres of Science Fiction, Fantasy and Fantastic Horror" (2007).
4. My thanks to the anonymous reviewer in *The Journal of Religion and Popular Culture* who suggested this point.
5. See Chapter One for an in-depth analysis of Eliade's work on the sacred and profane.
6. Kuhn defines cultural instrumentality briefly as "what, in cultural terms, it [the text] *does*" (1).

Chapter 1

1. See David Harvey, *The Condition of Postmodernity*.
2. Notably Edward Soja's *Postmodern Geographies*, which draws interestingly on some of Foucault's speculations about heterotopic space.
3. See, for instance, Ihab Hassan's pioneering work, Brian McHale, *Postmodernist Fiction* and Linda Hutcheon's *A Poetics of Postmodernism: History, Theory, Fiction*.
4. The evangelizing ideas behind fundamentalist and evangelical texts like *The Passion of the Christ* are a notable exception to this.

5. In which the Danish newspaper Jyllands-Posten published pictures of the Prophet Muhammad, provoking protests across the world by Muslims, as well as the republication of the offending cartoons by other newspapers as "free speech."

Chapter 2

1. This has played out in both scientific discussions and popular culture. Recent popular culture examples of these include Mayan-referencing apocalypse in *2012*, nuclear apocalypse on TV series *Gideon*, environmental apocalypse in movies like *Armageddon* (giant meteor heading toward Earth), *The Day After Tomorrow* (global warming), and viral apocalypse in *Outbreak* and *28 Days Later*.
2. This even in the midst of the Catholic Church's increased drive to canonize new saints under the last two Popes, though one is tempted to point out that it is precisely the lack of an epistemological sustainable supernatural element in contemporary Christianity that these saints are suppose to fill — the transcendent in the immanent.
3. Although conversely, the media framing of the event suggests the intrinsic role of the media simulacra — events strike as "real" only so far as they have been always-already mediated through the TV coverage. Hyperreality is base level of the real now.
4. The BBC website carried the story at the time: http://news.bbc.co.uk/1/hi/uk/1589133.stm.
5. This is an idea played with in the finale of the first season of *Joan of Arcadia*. Joan, a teenage girl who has been talking throughout the series with a very literal God, is diagnosed with Lyme disease and realizes that the visitations may have just been a symptom of her illness.

Chapter 3

1. He says, "At the very moment when, at the level of the 'economic infrastructure,' 'European' technology and capitalism is triumphing world-wide, at the level of 'ideological superstructure,' the Judeo-Christian legacy is threatened in the European space itself by the onslaught of the New Age 'Asiatic' thought, which [...] is establishing itself as the hegemonic ideology of global capitalism" (12).
2. The one recurring guest who perhaps fits this New Age list the least is tough-talking psychologist Dr. Phil, whose brand of "common-sense" pop therapy holds the individual entirely responsible for the course of their lives. It's arguable that the Texan Dr. Phil is the Republican Red State counterpart to Oprah's Blue State Democrat, yet the commonality between the two is the above-all primacy of the individual — which suggests that perhaps neo-conservative individualism and liberal New Ageism are not so far apart.
3. I should also note that Oprah's brand of spirituality also, as Wendy Parkins points out, emerges as a response to the disenchantment of heterosexual women with the self-sacrificing ethic encouraged in discourses of romance and motherhood.
4. Derrida suggests that one cannot make absolute distinctions between signifier and signified. However, "that this opposition cannot be radical or absolute does not prevent it from functioning, and even from being indispensable within certain limits — very wide limits" (19).
5. Derrida in "Des Tour de Babel" suggests the Tower of Babel story in the Hebrew Bible has traditionally worked as "the myth of the origin of myth, the metaphor of

metaphor, the narrative of narrative, the translation of translation, and so on" (104). Curiously, however, he argues the sacred, however, is "transferable and untranslatable. There is only letter, and it is the truth of pure language, the truth as pure language" (133). He gives the example of prophecy, in which the event of the sacred merges with the act of language. This article is puzzling given Derrida's penchant for demystifying the meta-narratives of a "pure" language; he seems in the concluding passages to reestablish ground for the sacred as transcendental signifier, as an untranslatable signature.

6. Though of course, some New Age movements will pastiche together some rather elaborate cosmologies to give themselves an ontological foundation.

7. Although it is arguable that a New Age transcendental signifier is at times like God, a sort of god after one has discarded the God of Judaism, Christianity and Islam. The question of whether those Gods *are*, in fact, the same is one for those better suited to theological discourse; suffice to say, for the purposes of the average postmodern subject, the three are usually considered as one.

8. Though one should also note at this point the concurrent perception of New Age teachers as rip-off artists—cult leaders intent on fleecing their followers for money, power and sex. How this relates to the postmodern sacred is an interesting question, though the postmodern sacred is perhaps more comfortable in talking in a New Age vocabulary of personal happiness and fulfillment, it nevertheless must retain some skepticism toward the occasional attempt at a New Age meta-narrative.

9. The title of the series itself is interesting enough in positing a pop Buddhist or Hindu cyclical notion of time. Indeed, the central premise of the series is the that hero Rand is the reincarnation of a legendary hero from another Age called The Dragon, who, now half-mad, has taken up residence in his brain. One should note the capitalization of the names of Things and People is one formal feature of generic fantasy aimed at producing a greater sense of meaning, and is often tied to transcendental gesturing in the genre.

10. We're told exceptions do occasionally occur, that sometimes people don't show up for their "appointment" with the Reapers. Rube says, "It's rare but it happens" ("Reapercussions" 1.04).

11. Roswell has become clearly the most recognizable of UFO locations, a fact played out for instance, in the television series *Roswell* which ran from 1999 to 2002. Set in the present, *Roswell* is the story of three alien teens with supernatural powers living in Roswell, New Mexico. The trio believe themselves to have been involved in the infamous alien incident, having been "incubated" on Earth for 40 years and found as human-appearing 6-year-olds 10 years prior to the action of the series commencing. The series reads like a mixture of *The X- Files* and *Buffy the Vampire Slayer*'s teenage angst, albeit without the texture of either.

12. See Darcee McLaren and Jennifer Porter's "(Re)Covering Sacred Ground" article, for a discussion of New Age spirituality in *Star Trek: Voyager*. Chronologically, *Voyager* was brought into production after *Deep Space Nine*.

13. Robert Asa, for instance, suggests that "classic *Star Trek*, like the radical theologians of the 1960s, declared that God was dead and enthroned science in the Deity" (51).

14. Of course, the following series suggest other changes. While *Voyager* (1995–2001) is a return to *Next Generation* style adventuring, and is largely devoid of originality, the most recent Star Trek spin-off, *Enterprise* (2001–2005), is interesting for another reason. *Enterprise* is a prequel to the original series, set several hundred years before, before the foundation of The Federation. As such, it avoids the utopian elements of the original series, and instead raises *Star Trek*'s usual subtextual imperialism into

an explicitly American, jingoistic narrative. Having thus turned into its opposite, it's little wonder that the original *Trek* characters were thus rebooted afterwards in the 2009 film.

Chapter 4

1. Fans of Matt Groenig's other more famous series *The Simpsons* will note the similarity of this episode to one of the vignettes in "Treehouse of Horror VII" (8.01), in which Lisa becomes God to a small race of people living on a tooth she had been doing a science experiment on.

2. Interestingly, this episode of *Futurama* in some ways recalls Terry Gilliam's 1981 science fiction comedy *Time Bandits*, which features a bumbling God. In *Time Bandits*, God "refuses to let on whether He has a design in everything, or is just making it up as He goes along" (Worley 142). A similar kind of ambivalence to the divine is clearly at work in "Godfellas."

3. A key touchpoint is the science fiction series *Star Trek*. The first *Futurama* episode begins with a *Star Trek* referencing monologue: "Space. It seems to go on and on forever. But then you get to the end and the monkey starts throwing barrels at you" ("Space Pilot 3000" 1.01). The series 4 episode, "Where No Fan Has Gone Before" (4.11), features many of the cast members from the original series.

4. It is interesting to note that the effect of the vocal device on the female Goa'uld renders their voices decidedly masculine. Given that the Goa'uld are generally coded as innately evil in the series, it is possible to read such an effect as either mobilizing a fear of female masculinity, or of transgender femininity—in either case, the anxiety is clearly about "inappropriate" gender performances.

5. There are a number of examples of *Stargate*'s dubious racial politics besides the racial Othering of the Goa'uld. The episode "The Warrior" features the Jaffa rebellion leader Kytano (later revealed to be the Goa'uld Imotep), whose language recalls Martin Luther King and whose "fanatic" tactics simultaneously recall Malcolm X and suicide bombers. Also, one of the other chief enemies of SG-1, the intergalactic mechanical pests the "Replicators," are revealed to be the creation of Reese, an android who "turned out wrong" (played by African American actress Danielle Nicolet).

6. The episode "Threshold" (5.02) sees the brain-washed Teal'c regress back to his earlier belief that the Goa'uld Apothis is his God. He has a conversation with Major Carter that deftly dodges critiquing the Christian God:

TEAL'C: Do you believe in a God, Major Carter?
CARTER: This isn't about me.
TEAL'C: How would it be if you were punished for loving your God as I love mine?
CARTER: It's not the same.
TEAL'C: I can't help what I believe.
CARTER: You believe in freedom, Teal'c, in justice, in protecting people from false Gods. You despise everything Apothis was.

7. Kushner is himself Jewish and gay, though *Angels in America* clearly also draws on a certain tradition of Christian apocalypticism, as well as representing the Church of the Latter Day Saints. These religions are not alone in featuring angels; the Qu'ran too contains angels. However, in the West at least, representations of angels are largely in dialogue with Christian traditions on the subject.

8. Religious scholar Karen Armstrong notes the polytheistic belief implicit in early Judaism. She argues that the covenant between God and the Jews only makes

sense in a polytheistic setting — "The Israelites did not believe that Yahweh, the God of Sinai, was the *only* God, but promised, in their covenant, that they would ignore all the deities and worship him alone" (1999: 31).

Chapter 5

1. Clip shows are television episodes cut largely together out of other older episodes.

2. One group, Ellinais, claims to have 2,000 followers and up to 100,000 sympathizers within Greece. http://www.guardian.co.uk/world/2007/feb/01/religion.uk

3. This contemporary heteronormativity is obvious too in Xena's parent series *Hercules: The Legendary Journeys*, which transmutes the relationship between Hercules and his lover Iolus into friendship.

4. Creator Joss Whedon states in the commentaries of the pilot "Welcome to the Hellmouth" (1.01) that the premise of the show was based upon a reversal of the standard horror movie formula in which a blond girl walks into a dark alley and is attacked by something monstrous. Whedon's revision has attracted praise from some feminists, although others have their reservations.

5. For instance, this exchange:
BUFFY: Ok, what do *I* want?
ANGEL: To kill them, to kill them all.
BUFFY: Sorry that's incorrect, but you do get this lovely watch and a year's supply of Turtle Wax. What I want is to be left alone ["Welcome to the Hellmouth" 1.01].

6. CORDELIA: You, you, you. What about me? It's one thing to be dating the lame unpopular guy, but it's another to be dating the creature from the Blue Lagoon. XANDER: Black Lagoon. The creature from the Blue Lagoon was Brooke Shields.

7. See Richard S. Albright's article "'Breakaway pop hit ... or book number?': 'Once More with Feeling' and Genre" for a more in-depth look at the episode's use of the musical genre. See also Jeffrey Middents for a look at how the episode configures race.

8. See for instance Michael Adams' book *Slayer Slang: A Buffy the Vampire Slayer Lexicon*.

9. Buffy's inability to take a human life has already been established in "The Gift" (5.22), when Giles kills the innocent Ben, who shares his body periodically with the evil hell-god Glory. Giles tells us, "sooner or later Glory will reemerge and make Buffy pay for that mercy [of not killing Ben] ... and the world with her. Buffy knows that, and she still couldn't take a human life. She's a hero, you see." Giles himself then makes the pragmatic decision to kill Ben, to do what Buffy could not.

10. Interestingly, the *Buffy* spin-off *Angel* features an episode almost entirely set in the 1950s ("Are You Now, Or Have You Ever Been" 2.02), which shows the darkest sides of the period — McCarthyism, racial discrimination, homophobia and a lynching. Those aspects of the 1950s are, needless to say, rarely featured fully in nostalgic depictions, even in such feted texts as *Mad Men*.

Chapter 6

1. In particular, see the response by some Catholic clergy on the website Jesus Decoded: http://www.jesusdecoded.com.

2. Interestingly, Kabbalah Center director Michael Berger's book *Becoming Like God*, never specifically mentions Judaism. On the relationship between Kabbalah and Judaism he gives a typically New Age perennialist response: "I don't know too much about Buddhism, but I know that there certainly are similarities. Of course since Kabbalah is such an inter-spiritual wisdom, it makes a lot of sense that there are a lot of similarities between it and other spiritual teachings" (Phillips, n.pag).

3. See theologian Marcella Althaus-Reid for a take on the misogyny and homophobia inherent in the sex negativity of much Christianity, as well as a nuanced queer theology.

4. In particular, see the "Gnosticism? No Thanks!" section in *On Belief*. Žižek moves there from a discussion of Gnosticism to a discussion of New Age Buddhism as the "ideological supplement" of late capitalism (2001: 16). Interestingly, Žižek sees posthuman cyberspace as fulfilling the Gnostic dream of "the self getting rid of the decay and inertia of material reality" (33).

Chapter 7

1. See Em McAvan, "Sacramentality Between Catholicism and the New Age in *Lord of the Rings*." *Roman Catholicism in Fantastic Film* (ed. Regina Hansen), Jefferson, NC: McFarland, 2011.

2. The Gospel of Mark has two alternative endings. The so called "shorter ending of Mark" in the second half of verse 8 that begins "and all that..." did not appear in manuscripts earlier than the fourth C.E., while the traditional longer ending from verses 9 to 19 is assumed by most scholars to be a second century c.e. pastiche of other Gospels added to give the Gospel a more conclusive ending than the ghost story suggested by verse 8's "So they went out and fled from the tomb, for terror and amazement had seized them; and they said nothing to anyone, for they were afraid."

3. Matthew, by contrast, simply has Mary Magdalene and "the other Mary" being greeted by Jesus, holding his feet and worshiping him.

4. And simultaneously also opening the text up to a queer reading. The possibility of a queer Christ, while undeniably scandalous to a great many Christians, is taken up in theologian Marcella Althaus-Reid's *Indecent Theology*.

Chapter 9

1. See Jan Johnson-Smith's chapter in her *American Science Fiction TV* (153–184) for more on the wormhole in *Stargate* and other series like *Farscape*. In particular, she looks at the ways in which the CGI involved in creating the wormhole reconfigures audience reception of SF. She says that *Stargate* "points to and denies its artifice, creating in its wake a new kind of formal engagement for the audience" (180).

2. This is a familiar enough plot in *Stargate*. Alternate universes feature in "There But For The Grace of God" (1.19), "Point of View" (3.06), "2010" (4.16) and "The Changeling" (6.19).

3. The suspension of democratic elections on *Galactica*, not the U.S.—though perhaps the dubious legality of George Bush's election in 2000 lingers somewhere in the American unconscious.

4. This text is modified in series 2 and 3 removing the "look and feel human/some are even programmed" aspects of the text.

Notes — Chapter 10 and Conclusion

5. Like a great deal of contemporary shows and movies (*Stargate* among them), *Battlestar Galactica* is in fact shot in Vancouver, Canada, and screened worldwide. Nevertheless, it remains clearly within the domain of American popular culture. If not specifically American, it is hard to place anywhere else.

6. Bhabha makes this statement about mixed-race subjects, but it captures the ambiguity of other liminal subjects equally well — Sara Ahmed, for instance, applies the phrase to queerness as "almost normal, but not quite" (149).

Chapter 10

1. George Lucas, of course, infamously used Joseph Campbell's theories on myth in structuring his original trilogy. Interestingly, Lucas had the courage to include incest in the form of the Luke/Leia relationship, which while suitably mythic was scarcely likely to endear him to many audiences. And in keeping with the mythic overtones, the first *Star Wars* series has sometimes been called, mock seriously, "the holy trilogy" by fans.

2. The first movie directly references Baudrillard's theories of simulation. We see Neo with a copy of *Simulations*, and Morpheus cites Baudrillard's "Welcome to the desert of the real." Needless to say, this has generated some interest in the movies among postmodern critics.

3. See Carl Silvio's work on *The Animatrix* for how the anime films handle the questions of post-humanity raised by the films.

Conclusion

1. For instance, the announcement of Pope Benedict in July 2007 that Protestants do not worship in "real" churches, and the decision to resuscitate a form of liturgy that had been removed by the Vatican II council. This outraged Jewish leaders, for the understandable reason that the liturgy calls for the conversion of Jews. See John Hooper and Stephen Bates for more on the Protestant comment, and Jason Burke on the liturgy revival.

2. Here Derrida is close to Levinas (1996), who in his few brief but poignant notes on Kierkegaard in *Proper Names* argues that ethics must be marked by singularity.

Bibliography

Primary Texts

Adams, Douglas. 1979. *The Hitch-hiker's Guide to the Universe*. London: Pan.
Brown, Dan. 2003. *The Da Vinci Code*. New York: Random House Large Print.
LaHaye, Timothy, and Jerry B. Jenkins. 1995. *Left Behind: A Novel of the Earth's Last Days*. Colorado Springs: Tyndale House.
LeGuin, Ursula. 1979. *Earthsea Trilogy*. Harmondsworth: Penguin.
Lewis, C. S. 1980. *The Last Battle*. 1956. London: Lions.
_____. 1980. *The Voyage of the Dawn Treader*. New York: HarperCollins.
Meyer, Stephenie. 2005. *Twilight*. New York: Little, Brown.
_____. 2008. *Breaking Dawn*. New York: Little Brown.
Pulman, Philip. 2002. *His Dark Materials (Trilogy Anthology)*. 1995, 1997, 2000. London: Scholastic.
Rowling, J. K. 1997. *Harry Potter and the Philosopher's Stone*. London: Bloomsbury.
_____. 1998. *Harry Potter and the Chamber of Secrets*. London: Bloomsbury.
_____. 1999. *Harry Potter and the Prisoner of Azkaban*. London: Bloomsbury.
_____. 2000. *Harry Potter and the Goblet of Fire*. London: Bloomsbury.
_____. 2004. *Harry Potter and the Order of the Phoenix*. London: Bloomsbury.
Tolkien, J. R. R. 1964. *Leaf by Niggle*. London: Allen & Unwin.
_____. 2001. *The Lord of the Rings*. London: HarperCollins.

Visual Texts

Angel. 1999–2004. Creat. Joss Whedon. Dir. Joss Whedon. The WB. DVD. Warner Brothers, 2006.
Battlestar Galactica. 2003–2007. Creat. Ronald D. Moore. Sci-Fi Channel. DVD. Universal, 2007.
Buffy the Vampire Slayer. 1997–2003. Creat. Joss Whedon. Dir. Joss Whedon. The WB. DVD. Warner Brothers, 2005.
Charmed. 1998–2006. Creat. Constance M. Burge. The WB. DVD. Warner Brothers, 2006.
Constantine. 2005. Dir. Francis Lawrence. Perf. Keanu Reeves, Rachel Weisz, Shia LaBeouf, Tilda Swinton, Pruitt Taylor Vince, Djimon Hounsou, Gavin Rossdale, Peter Stormare. DVD. Warner Brothers, 2006.

Dark Angel. 2000–2002. Creat. James Cameron and Charles H. Eglee. Fox. DVD. 20th Century–Fox, 2003.
Dead Like Me. 2003–2004. Creat. Bryan Fuller. Dir. Bryan Fuller. Showtime. DVD. MGM, 2005.
Eragon. 2006. Dir. Stefen Fangmeier. Perf. Ed Speleers, Jeremy Irons, Sienna Guillory, Robert Carlyle, Djimon Houson, Garrett Hedlund, Joss Stone, Rachel Weisz, John Malkovich. DVD. Twentieth Century–Fox, 2007.
Firefly. 2002–2003. Creat. Joss Whedon. Dir. Joss Whedon. Fox. DVD. Fox, 2004.
The 4400. 2004–2007. Creat. René Echevarria and Scott Peters. USA Network. DVD. Paramount, 2006.
Gilmore Girls. 2000–2007. Creat. Amy Sherman-Palladino. Dir. Amy Sherman-Palladino. The WB and CW. DVD. Warner Brothers, 2006.
"Godfellas," *Futurama.* 2002. Writ. Ken Keelar. Dir. Susan Dietter. Fox. DVD. Fox, 2003.
Harry Potter and the Sorcerer's Stone. 2001. Dir. Chris Columbus. Perf. Daniel Radcliffe, Rupert Grint, Emma Watson, Robbie Coltrane, Alan Rickman, Richard Harris. DVD. Twentieth Century–Fox, 2002.
Harry Potter and the Chamber of Secrets. 2002. Dir. Chris Columbus. Perf. Daniel Radcliffe, Rupert Grint, Emma Watson, Robbie Coltrane, Alan Rickman, Richard Harris. DVD. Twentieth Century–Fox, 2003.
Harry Potter and the Prisoner of Azkaban. 2004. Dir. Alfonso Cuaron. Perf. Daniel Radcliffe, Rupert Grint, Emma Watson, Robbie Coltrane, Alan Rickman, Michael Gambon. DVD. Twentieth Century–Fox, 2004.
Harry Potter and the Goblet of Fire. 2005. Dir. Mike Newell. Perf. Daniel Radcliffe, Rupert Grint, Emma Watson, Robbie Coltrane, Alan Rickman, Michael Gambon. DVD. Twentieth Century–Fox, 2006.
Hellboy. 2004. Dir. Guillermo del Toro. Perf. Ron Perlman, Doug Jones, Selma Blair, John Hurt, Rupert Evans, Jeffrey Tambor. DVD. Columbia, 2005.
Hercules: The Legendary Journeys. 1995–1999. Creat. Christian Williams. USA network. DVD. Paramount, 2001.
"Homer the Heretic," *The Simpsons.* 1992. Writ. George Meyer. Dir. Jim Reardon. Fox. DVD. Fox, 2004.
Joan of Arcadia. 2003–2004. Creat. Barbara Hall. CBS. DVD. Paramount, 2005.
"The Long Dark," *Babylon 5.* 1994. Writ. Scott Frost. Dir. Mario Dileo. Fox. DVD. Warner Brothers, 2003.
The Lord of the Rings: The Fellowship of the Ring. 2001. Dir. Peter Jackson. Perf. Elijah Wood, Viggo Mortenson, Sean Astin, Ian MacKellen, Sean Bean. DVD. New Line, 2002.
The Lord of the Rings: The Two Towers. 2002. Dir. Peter Jackson. Perf. Elijah Wood, Viggo Mortenson, Sean Astin, Ian MacKellen, Andy Sirkis, Cate Blanchett. DVD. New Line, 2003.
The Lord of the Rings: The Return of the King. 2003. Dir. Peter Jackson. Perf. Elijah Wood, Viggo Mortenson, Sean Astin, Ian MacKellen, Andy Sirkis, Miranda Otto. DVD. New Line, 2004.
The Matrix. 1999. Dir. Larry Wachowski and Andy Wachowski. Perf. Keanu Reeves, Laurence Fishburne, Carrie-Anne Moss, Joe Pantoliano, Hugo Weaving. DVD. Warner Brothers, 1999.
The Matrix Reloaded. 2003. Dir. Larry Wachowski and Andy Wachowski. Perf. Keanu Reeves, Laurence Fishburne, Carrie-Anne Moss, Hugo Weaving, Gloria Foster, Jada Pinkett-Smith. DVD. Warner Brothers, 2003.
The Matrix Revolutions. 2003. Dir. Larry Wachowski and Andy Wachowski. Perf. Keanu

Reeves, Laurence Fishburne, Carrie-Anne Moss, Hugo Weaving, Mary Alice, Jada Pinkett-Smith. DVD. Warner Brothers, 2004.

The Oprah Winfrey Show. 1986–2011.Creat. Oprah Winfrey. Perf. Oprah Winfrey. Syndication.

The Passion of the Christ. 2004. Dir. Mel Gibson. Perf. Jim Cazaviel, Maia Morgenstern, Christo Jivkov, Francesco De Vito, Monica Belluci. DVD. Warner Brothers, 2004.

Roswell. 1999–2002. Writ. Jason Katims. Dir. Jason Katims. The WB and UPN. DVD. Warner Bros, 2006.

Serenity. 2005. Dir. Joss Whedon. Perf. Nathan Fillion, Alan Tudyk, Adam Baldwin, Summer Glau and Chiwetel Ejiofor. DVD. Universal, 2005.

Shrek. 2001. Dir. Andrew Adamson and Vicky Jensen. Perf. Mike Myers, Eddie Murphy, Cameron Diaz and John Lithgow. DVD. Dreamworks, 2002.

Smallville. 2000–2007. Writ. Alfred Gough and Robert J. Cooper. The WB and CW. DVD. MGM, 2007.

The Sopranos. 1997–2007. Writ. David Chase. Dir. David Chase. HBO. DVD. HBO, 2007.

Stargate Atlantis. 2004–2007. Writ. Brad Wright and Robert J. Cooper. Sci-Fi Channel. DVD. MGM, 2007.

Stargate SG-1. 1997–2007. Writ. Jonathon Glassner and Brad Wright. Showtime and Sci-Fi Channel. DVD. MGM, 2007.

Star Trek: Deep Space Nine. 1993–1999. Writ. Rick Berman and Michael Piller. Syndication. DVD. Paramount, 2002.

Star Wars: A New Hope. 1977. Dir. George Lucas. Perf. Mark Hamill, Harrison Ford, Carrie Fisher, Peter Cushing, Alec Guinness. DVD. 20th Century–Fox, 2004.

Star Wars: Revenge of the Sith. 2005. Dir. George Lucas. Perf. Ewan MacGregor, Natalie Portman, Hayden Christensen, Ian McDiarmid, Samuel L. Jackson, Christopher Lee. DVD. 20th Century–Fox, 2005.

Star Wars: The Phantom Menace. 1999. Dir. George Lucas. Perf. Liam Neeson, Samuel L. Jackson, Ewan MacGregor, Natalie Portman, Jake Lloyd, Ian McDiarmid. DVD. 20th Century–Fox, 2000.

Time Bandits. 1981. Dir. Terry Gilliam. Perf. Craig Warnock, John Cleese, Kenny Baker, Tiny Ross, Mike Edwards, David Rappaport, Malcolm Dixon, Jack Purvis, Sean Connery, Ian Holm. DVD. Warner Bros, 2002.

Torchwood. 2006–2007. Writ. Russell T. Davies. Dir. Russell T. Davies. BBC Three. DVD. BBC 2007.

Touched by an Angel. 1994–2003. Creat. John Masius and Martha Williamson. CBS. DVD. Paramount, 2005.

Troy. 2004. Dir. Wolfgang Peterson. Perf. Brad Pitt, Eric Bana, Orlando Bloom, Diane Kruger, Brian Cox, Sean Bean, Brendan Gleeson and Peter O'Toole. DVD. Warner Bros, 2004.

Underworld. 2003. Dir. Len Wiseman. Perf. Kate Beckinsale, Scott Speedman, Michael Sheen, Shane Brolly, Erwin Leder and Bill Nighy. DVD. Columbia TriStar, 2004.

Xena: Warrior Princess. 1995–2001. Writ. John Schulian and Robert Taper. Syndication. DVD. Universal, 2002.

The X-Files. 1993–2002. Writ. Chris Carter. Dir. Chris Carter. Fox. DVD. Fox, 2005.

X-Men. 2000. Dir. Bryan Singer. Perf. Patrick Stewart, Hugh Jackman, Ian MacKellen, Halle Berry, Famke Jansen, James Marsden, Bruce Davidson, Rebecca Romijn-Stamos, Ray Park and Anna Paquin. DVD. Twentieth Century–Fox, 2003.

X-Men 2. 2003. Dir. Bryan Singer. Perf. Patrick Stewart, Hugh Jackman, Ian MacKellen, Halle Berry, Famke Jansen, Bruce Davidson, Rebecca Romijn-Stamos, Brian Cox, Alan Cumming, James Marsden and Anna Paquin. DVD. Twentieth Century–Fox, 2003.

BIBLIOGRAPHY

Secondary Texts

Adams, Michael. 2004. *Slayer Slang: A Buffy the Vampire Slayer Lexicon.* New York: Oxford University Press.
Adcock, David. 2000. "*Xena Warrior Princess* and the Texture of the Religious: Reimagining the Role of Popular Culture in Academic Discourse." *Journal of Culture and Religious Theory* 2.1.
Agamben, Giorgio. 1998. *Homo Sacer: Sovereign Power and Bare Life.* Trans. Daniel Heller-Roazen. Stanford: Stanford University Press.
_____. 2005. *State of Exception.* Trans. Kevin Attell. Chicago: Chicago University Press.
Ahmed, Sara. 2004. *The Cultural Politics of Emotion.* Edinburgh: Edinburgh University Press.
Aichelle, George, and Richard Walsh, eds. 2002. *Screening Scripture: Intertextual Connections between Scripture and Film.* Harrisburg, PA: Trinity Press International.
Albright, Richard S. 2005. "'[B]reakaway Pop Hit Or ... Book Number?': 'Once More, with Feeling' and Genre." *Slayage* 5.1: 63–80.
Alfred, Lisa. 2000. "Plastic Shamans and Astroturf Sun Dances: New Age Commercialization of Native American Spirituality." *American Indian Quarterly* 24.3: 329–352.
Althaus-Reid, Marcella. 2000. *Indecent Theology: Theological Perversions in Sex, Gender and Politics.* London: Routledge.
Althusser, Louis. 1971. "Ideology and Ideological State Apparatuses (Notes Toward an Investigation)." Trans. Ben Brewster. In *Lenin and Philosophy and Other Essays,* 127–86. New York: Monthly Review.
Anderson, Perry. 1998. *The Origins of Postmodernity.* London and New York: Verso.
Anderson, Wendy Love. 2003. "Prophecy Girl and the Powers That Be: The Philosophy of Religion in the Buffyverse." In *Buffy the Vampire Slayer and Philosophy: Fear and Trembling in Sunnydale,* edited by James B. South, 212–27. Chicago: Open Court.
Armstrong, Karen. 1999. *A History of God.* London: Vintage.
_____. 2004. *The Battle for God: Fundamentalism in Judaism, Christianity and Islam.* London: Harper Perennial.
Asa, Robert. 1999. "Classic *Star Trek* and the Death of God." In *Star Trek and Sacred Ground: Explorations of* Star Trek, *Religion and American Culture,* edited by Jennifer E. Porter and Darcee L. McLaren, 33–59. Albany: State University of New York Press.
Attebery, Brian. 1992. *Strategies of Fantasy.* Bloomington: Indiana University Press.
Auerbach, Nina. 1995. *Our Vampires, Ourselves.* Chicago: Chicago University Press.
Augustine, Saint. 1961. *The Confessions.* Trans. R. S. Pine-Coffin. London: Penguin.
Badiou, Alain. 2003. *Saint Paul: The Foundation of Universalism.* Trans. Ray Brassier. Stanford: Stanford University Press.
Bakutman, Scott. 1993. *Terminal Identity: The Virtual Subject in Postmodern Science Fiction.* Durham, NC: Duke University Press.
Barthes, Roland. 2000. *Mythologies.* Trans. Annette Lavers. London: Vintage.
Bassham, Gregory. 2002. "The Religion of *The Matrix* and the Problems of Pluralism." In *The Matrix and Philosophy,* edited by William Irwin, 111–26. Chicago: Open Court.
Battis, Jes. 2004. "Gazing Upon Sauron: Hobbits, Elves, and the Queering of the Postcolonial Optic." *MFS Modern Fiction Studies* 50.4: 908–25.
Baudrillard, Jean. 1983. *Simulations.* Trans. Paul Foss, Paul Patton and Philip Beitchman. United States: Semiotext[e].
_____. 1988. *America.* 1986. Trans. Chris Turner. London: Verso.

Bibliography

———. 1994. *Simulacra and Simulation*. Trans. Sheila Faria Glaser. Ann Arbor: Michigan University Press.
———. 1995. *The Gulf War Did Not Take Place*. 1991. Trans. Paul Patton. Sydney: Power.
———. 2003. *The Spirit of Terrorism and Other Essays*. Trans. Chris Turner. London: Verso.
———. 2007. *Forget Foucault*. 1977. Trans. Nicole Sufresne. Cambridge, MA: Semiotext(e).
Baudrillard, Jean, and Aude Lancelin. 2004. "The Matrix Decoded: Le Nouvel Observateur Interview with Jean Baudrillard." *International Journal of Baudrillard Studies* 1.2: n.pag.
Bauman, Zygmunt. 1992. *Intimations of Postmodernity*. London: Routledge.
———. 1996. "Morality in the Age of Contingency." In *Detraditionalization*, edited by Paul Heelas, Scott Lash and Paul Morris, 49–59. Cambridge, MA: Blackwell.
———. 1997. *Postmodernity and Its Discontents*. New York: New York University Press.
———. 2000. *Modernity and the Holocaust*. New York: Cornell University Press.
Baumgartner, Frederic J. 1999. *Longing for the End: A History of Millennialism in Western Civilization*. New York: St. Martin's.
Beaudoin, Tom. 1998. *Virtual Faith: The Irreverent Spiritual Quest of Generation X*. San Francisco: Jossey-Bass.
Beaumont, Matthew. 2007. "Baudrillard and the End of Postmodernism: What Next?" blog post. *The Guardian*. Accessed 31 May 2007. <http://blogs.guardian.co.uk/books/2007/03/baudrillard_and_the_end_of_pos.html>.
Bebbington, David William. 2002. *Evangelicalism in Modern Britain: A History from the 1730s to the 1980s*. London: Routledge.
Beck, Ulrich, and Elisabeth Beck-Gernsheim. 2002. *Individualization: Institutional Individualism and Its Social and Political Consequences*. Trans. Patrick Camiller. London: Sage.
Beck, Ulrich, Anthony Giddens, and Scott Lash. 1994. *Reflexive Modernization: Politics, Tradition and Aesthetic in the Modern Social Order*. Cambridge: Polity.
Bennett, Jane. 2001. *The Enchantment of Modern Life*. Princeton, NJ: Princeton University Press.
Bennington, Geoffrey, and Jacques Derrida. 1993. *Jacques Derrida*. Trans. Geoffrey Bennington. Chicago: Chicago University Press.
Berger, James. 1999. *After the End: Representations of Post-Apocalypse*. Minneapolis: Minnesota University Press.
Bertolin, Matthew. 2005. *The Dharma of Star Wars*. Boston: Wisdom.
Billington, Ray. 2002. *Religion Without God*. London: Routledge.
Blake, Andrew. 2002. *The Irresistible Rise of Harry Potter*. London: Verso.
Bloom, Harold. 1988. "Introduction." In *Modern Critical Interpretations: The Revelation of Saint John the Divine*, edited by Harold Bloom, 1–6. New York: Chelsea House.
Boesel, Chris, and Catherine Keller. 2009. "Introduction." In *Apophatic Bodies: Negative Theology, Incarnation, and Relationality*, edited by Boesel and Keller. New York: Fordham University Press.
Bourdieu, Pierre. 1984. *Distinction : A Social Critique of the Judgement of Taste*. Trans. Richard Nice. London: Routledge & Kegan Paul.
Brock, Rita Nakashima, and Rebecca Ann Parker. 2001. *Proverbs of Ashes: Violence, Redemptive Suffering and the Search for What Saves Us*. Boston: Beacon.
Brown, Wendy. 2005. *Edgework: Critical Essays on Knowledge and Power*. Princeton, NJ: Princeton University Press.
———. 2006. *Regulating Aversion: Tolerance in the Age of Identity and Empire*. Princeton, NJ: Princeton University Press.

BIBLIOGRAPHY

Bruce, Steve. 2002. *God Is Dead: Secularization in the West*. Oxford: Blackwell.
Burke, Jason. July 8, 2007. "Pope's Move on Latin Mass 'a Blow to Jews.'" *The Observer*. Accessed 26 July 2007. <http://www.guardian.co.uk/pope/story/0,,2121355,00.html>
Butler, Judith. 1993. *Bodies That Matter: On the Discursive Limits of "Sex."* New York: Routledge.
———. 1999. *Gender Trouble: Feminism and the Subversion of Identity*. 1990. New York: Routledge.
———. 2004a. "Is Kinship Always Already Heterosexual?" In *Undoing Gender*, 102–31. New York: Routledge.
———. 2004b. *Precarious Life: The Powers of Mourning and Violence*. London: Verso.
Caldecott, Stratford. 2003. *Secret Fire: The Spiritual Vision of J. R. R. Tolkien*. London: Darton, Longman and Todd.
Calvert-Koyzis, Nancy. 2006. "Re-sexualizing the Magdane: Dan Brown's Misuse of Early Christian Documents in The Da Vinci Code." *Journal of Religion and Popular Culture* 12.
Caputo, John D. 1997. *The Prayers and Tears of Jacques Derrida: Religion Without Religion*. Bloomington: Indiana University Press.
———. 2001. *On Religion*. New York: Routledge,.
———. 2006. *The Weakness of God: A Theology of the Event*. Bloomington: Indiana University Press.
———, Kevin Hart, and Yvonne Sherwood. 2005. "Epoché and Faith: An Interview with Jacques Derrida." In *Derrida and Religion: Other Testaments*, edited by Yvonne Sherwood and Kevin Hart, 27–53. New York: Routledge.
———, and Gianni Vattimo. 2007. *After the Death of God*. New York: Columbia University Press.
Carey, Frances. 1999. "The Apocalyptic Imagination: Between Tradition and Modernity." In *Apocalypse and the Shape of Things to Come*, edited by Frances Carey, 270–320. Toronto: Toronto University Press.
Chambers, Joseph. 2009. "The Harry Potter Series: A Vision of the Antichrist." Accessed 17 September 2010. http://www.pawcreek.org/end-times/harry-potter-antichrist.
Chopra, Deepak. June 23, 2010. "Insights into Sex and Spirituality." *The Huffington Post*. http://www.huffingtonpost.com/deepak-chopra/kama-sutra-insights-into_b_623177.html
Cixous, Hélène. 2004. *Portrait of Jacques Derrida as a Young Jewish Saint*. Trans. Beverley Bie Brahic. New York: Columbia University Press.
Clark, Lynn Schofield. 2003. *From Angels to Aliens: Teenagers, the Media, and the Supernatural*. New York: Oxford University Press.
Cohen, Patricia. March 6, 2007. "Jean Baudrillard, 77, Critic and Theorist of Hyperreality, Dies." *New York Times*. Accessed 31 May 2007. http://www.nytimes.com/2007/03/07/books/07baudrillard.html?ex=1180756800&en=f083c64b9b2d995e&ei=5070.
Cohn, Norman. 1999. "Biblical Origins of the Apocalyptic Tradition." In *Apocalypse and the Shape of Things to Come*, edited by Frances Carey, 28–43. Toronto: Toronto University Press.
Curry, Agnes. 2005. "Is Joss Becoming a Thomist?" *Slayage* 4.4: 38–55.
DeLamotte, Eugenia. 2004. "White Terror, Black Dreams: Gothic Constructions of Race in the Nineteenth Century." In *The Gothic Other: Racial and Social Constructions in the Literary Imagination*, edited by Ruth Bienstock Anolik and Douglas L. Howard, 17–31. Jefferson, NC: McFarland.
De La Torre, Miguel, and Albert Hernandez. 2011. *The Quest For the Historical Satan*. Minneapolis: Fortress.

Bibliography

Demos, John. 2008. *The Enemy Within: 2000 Years of Witch-hunting in the Western World*. New York: Viking.
Derrida, Jacques. 1976. *Of Grammatology*. Trans. Gayatri Chakravorty Spivak. Baltimore: Johns Hopkins University Press.
———. 1981. *Positions*. Trans. Alan Bass. London: Athlone.
———. 1982. *Margins of Philosophy*. Trans. Alan Bass. Brighton: Harvester.
———. 1994a. *The Gift of Death*. Trans. David Wills. Chicago: University of Chicago.
———. 1994b. *Given Time: 1. Counterfeit Money*. Trans. Peggy Kamuf. Chicago: University of Chicago.
———. 1994c. *Specters of Marx: The State of the Debt, the Work of Mourning, and the New International*. Trans. Peggy Kamuf. New York: Routledge.
———. 1999. "Hospitality, Justice and Responsibility: A Dialogue with Jacques Derrida." In *Questioning Ethics,* edited by Richard Kearney and Mark Dooley, 65–83. New York: Routledge.
———. 2001a. *Writing and Difference*. 1978. Trans. Alan Bass. London: Routledge.
———. 2001b. "Above All No Journalists!" In *Religion and Media*, edited by Hent De Vries and Samuel Weber, 56–93. Stanford: Stanford University Press.
———. 2002. "Des Tours de Babel." Trans. Joseph F. Graham. In *Acts of Religion*, edited by Gil Anidjar, 102–34. New York: Routledge.
Detweiler, Craig, and Barry Taylor. 2003. *A Matrix of Meanings*. Grand Rapids, MI: Baker Academic.
Dulles, Avery. 1992. *Models of Revelation*. 1983. Maryknoll, NY: Orbis.
Eagleton, Terry. 2004. *After Theory*. London: Allen Lane.
Edelman, Lee. 2004. *No Future: Queer Theory and the Death Drive*. Durham, NC: Duke University Press.
Edmundson, Mark. 1997. *Nightmare on Main Street: Angels, Sadomasochism, and the Culture of the Gothic*. Cambridge, MA: Harvard University Press.
Eliade, Mercea. 1959. *The Sacred and the Profane: The Nature of Religion*. Trans. William R. Trask. New York: Harper & Brothers.
Faludi, Susan. 1992. *Backlash: The Undeclared War Against Women*. London: Vintage.
Featherstone, Mike. 1991. *Consumer Culture & Postmodernism*. London: SAGE.
Fiorenza, Elisabeth Schüssler. 1985. *The Book of Revelation: Justice and Judgment*. Philadelphia: Fortress Press.
Fish, Stanley. 2002. "Don't Blame Relativism." *The Responsive Community* 12.3: 27–31.
Fisher, Mark. 2009. *Capitalist Realism: Is There No Alternative?* Winchester, UK: O Books.
Fontana, Paul. 2004. "Finding God in *The Matrix*." In *Taking the Red Pill: Science, Philosophy and Religion in the Matrix,* edited by Glenn Yeffeth, 183–214. Camberwell: Penguin.
Ford, James L. 2004. "Buddhism, Mythology and *The Matrix*." In *Taking the Red Pill: Science, Philosophy and Religion in the Matrix*, Edited by Glenn Yeffeth, 144–68. Camberwell: Penguin.
Forsyth, Neil. 2003. *The Satanic Epic*. Princeton, NJ: Princeton University Press.
Foucault, Michel. 1979. *Discipline and Punish: The Birth of the Prison*. London: Peregrine.
———. 1980. "What Is an Author?" In *Textual Strategies*, edited by Josné Harrari, 141–160. London: Methuen.
Fouché, Gwylands. January 2, 2006. *Cartoon Row Spreads across Europe*. The Guardian. Accessed 31 May 2007. <http://www.guardian.co.uk/international/story/0,,16998 11,00.html. 28th March 2006.>
Freedman, Carl. 1998. "A Note On Fantasy." *Historical Materialism* 10.4: 260–71.

Bibliography

Frost, Laura. 2002. *Sex Drives: Fantasies of Fascism in Literary Modernism*. Ithaca, NY: Cornell University Press.
Frye, Northrop. 1957. *Anatomy of Criticism*. Princeton, NJ: Princeton University Press.
Frykholm, Amy Johnson. 2004. *Rapture Culture: Left Behind in Evangelical America*. Oxford: Oxford University Press.
Gane, Nicholas. 2002. "Rationalization and Disenchantment, 1: From the Origins of Religion to the Death of God." In *Max Weber and Postmodern Theory: Rationalization Versus Re-Enchantment*, 15–27. Basingstoke: Palgrave.
Gilbertson, Michael. 2003. *God and History in the Book of Revelation*. Cambridge: Cambridge University Press.
Gills, Stacy, ed. 2005. *The Matrix Trilogy: Cyberpunk Reloaded*. London: Wallflower.
Goldberg, Michelle. 2006. *Kingdom Coming: The Rise of Christian Nationalism*. New York: W. W. Norton.
Gooderham, David. 2003. "Fantasizing It as It Is: Religious Language in Philip Pullman's Trilogy, *His Dark Materials*." *Children's Literature* 31: 155–75.
Grant, John. 2000. "Gulliver Unravels: Generic Fantasy and the Loss of Subversion." *Extrapolation* 41.1.
Green, William H. 1998. "'Where's Mama?': The Construction of the Feminine in *The Hobbit*." *The Lion and the Unicorn* 22.2: 188–95.
Greenwood, Linda. 2005. "Love: 'The Gift of Death.'" *Tolkien Studies* 2.1: 171–95.
Gribben, Crawford. 2004. "Rapture Fictions and the Changing Evangelical Condition." *Literature & Theology* 18.1: 77–94.
Grosz, Elizabeth. 1989. *Sexual Subversions: Three French Feminists*. Sydney: Allen & Unwin.
Halberstam, Judith. 1995. *Skin Shows: Gothic Horror and the Technology of Monsters*. Durham, NC: Duke University Press.
Haley, Christopher, and Davis, Creston. 2008. "The Cultural Logic of Evangelical Christianity." In *The Sleeping Giant Has Awoken: The New Politics of Religion in the United States*, edited by Jeffrey Robbins and Neal Macgee, 65–85. New York: Continuum.
Harding, James, and Loveday Alexander. May 28, 1999. "Dating the Testament of Solomon." Lecture, University of St. Andrews. Accessed 1 December 2011. http://www.st-andrews.ac.uk/divinity/rt/otp/guestlectures/harding/
Hardt, Michael, and Antonio Negri. 2000. *Empire*. Cambridge, MA: Harvard University Press.
_____. 2004. *Multitude: War and Democracy in the Age of Empire*. New York: Penguin.
_____. 2009. *Commonwealth*. Cambridge: Harvard University Press.
Hart, Kevin. 1989. *Trespass of the Sign: Deconstruction, Theology and Philosophy*. Cambridge: Cambridge University Press.
Harvey, David. 1987. *The Condition of Postmodernity: An Enquiry into the Conditions of Cultural Change*. Cambridge, MA: Blackwell.
Hassan, Ihab. 1987. *The Postmodern Turn: Essays in Postmodern Theory and Culture*. Columbus: Ohio State University Press.
Heelas, Paul. 1996a. "Introduction: Detraditionalization and Its Rivals." In *Detraditionalization: Critical Reflections on Authority and Identity*, edited by Paul Heelas, Thomas Luckmann and Paul Morris. Cambridge, MA: Blackwell.
_____. 1996b. *The New Age Movement: The Celebration of the Self and the Sacralization of Modernity*. Oxford: Blackwell.
Heelas, Paul, and Linda Woodhead. 2005. *The Spiritual Revolution: Why Religion is Giving Way to Spirituality*. Malden, MA: Blackwell.
Hiley, Margaret. 2004. "Stolen Language, Cosmic Models: Myth and Mythology in Tolkien." *MFS Modern Fiction Studies* 50.4: 838–60.

Bibliography

Hinlicky, Sarah E. 2002. "The End of Magic." *First Things: A Monthly Journal of Religion and Public Life* 13.2: n.pag.

Hooper, John, and Stephen Bates. July 11, 2007. "Dismay and Anger as Pope Declares Protestants Cannot Have Churches." *The Guardian.* Accessed 26 July 2007. <http://www.guardian.co.uk/international/story/0,,2123171,00.html>

Huntington, Samuel P. 1993. "The Clash of Civilizations?" *Foreign Affairs* 72.3: 22–49.

———. 1996. *The Clash of Civilizations and the Remaking of World Order.* New Delhi: Penguin.

Hutcheon, Linda. 1988. *A Poetics of Postmodernism: History, Theory, Fiction.* New York: Routledge.

Ingebretson, Edward J. 1996. *Maps of Heaven, Maps of Hell.* Armonk, NY: M.E. Sharpe.

———. 2001. *At Stake: Monsters and the Rhetoric of Fear in Public Culture.* Chicago: Chicago University Press.

Introvigne, Massimo. 2000. "God, New Religious Movements and *Buffy the Vampire Slayer.*" In *Expanding Concepts of God.* Lecture, Harvard.

Irigaray, Luce. 1991. "Women-Mothers, the Silent Substratum of the Social Order." Trans. David Macey. In *The Irigaray Reader,* edited by Margaret Whitford, 47–53. Oxford: Blackwell.

———. 1993. *Marine Lover of Friedrich Nietzsche.* Trans. Gillian C. Gill. New York: Columbia University Press.

Iwabuchi, Koichi. 2002. *Recentering Globalization: Popular Culture and Japanese Transnationalizm.* Durham, NC: Duke University Press.

Jackson, Rosemary. 1981. *Fantasy: The Literature of Subversion.* London: Methuen.

Jameson, Fredric. 1991. *Postmodernism, or, the Cultural Logic of Late Capitalism.* London: Verso.

———. 2002. *A Singular Modernity: Essay on the Ontology of the Present.* London: Verso.

———. 2003. "The End of Temporality." *Critical Inquiry* 29.4: 695–718.

———. 2005. *Archaeologies of the Future: The Desire Called Utopia and Other Science Fictions.* London: Verso.

———. 2007. *Signatures of the Visible.* New York: Routledge.

Jenkins, Henry. 1992. *Textual Poachers: Television Fans and Participatory Culture.* New York: Routledge.

Johnson, Elizabeth. 2003. *Truly Our Sister: A Theology in the Communion of Saints.* New York: Continuum.

Johnson-Smith, Jan. 2005. *American Science Fiction TV: Star Trek, Stargate and Beyond.* London: I. B. Tauris.

Kaveney, Roz. 2005. *From Alien to the Matrix: Reading Science Fiction Film.* London: I. B. Tauris.

Kehoe, Alice. 1996. "Eliade and Hultkrantz: The European Primitivist Tradition." *American Indian Quarterly* 20.3/4: 377–93.

Keller, Catherine. 2003. *Face of the Deep: A Theology of Becoming.* London: Routledge.

———. 2005. *God and Power: Counter-Apocalyptic Journeys.* Minneapolis: Fortress.

———. 2008. *In the Mystery: Discerning Divinity in Process.* Minneapolis: Fortress.

Kierkegaard, Søren. 1985. *Fear and Trembling.* Trans. Alistair Hannay. London: Penguin.

Kim, Sue. 2004. "Beyond Black and White: Race and Postmodernism in the *Lord of the Rings* Films." *MFS Modern Fiction Studies* 40.4: 875–907.

Klein, Naomi. 2002. *Fences and Windows: Dispatches from the Front Lines of the Globalization Debate.* London: Flamingo.

Kontos, Alkis. 1994. "The World Disenchanted, and the Return of Gods and Demons." In *The Barbarism of Reason: Max Weber and the Twilight of Enlightenment,* edited by Asher Horowitz and Terry Maley, 223–47. Toronto: Toronto University Press.

Kotsko, Adam. 2010. *The Politics of Redemption: The Social Logic of Salvation.* New York: Continuum.
Kuhn, Annette. 1990. "Introduction: Cultural Theory and Science Fiction Cinema." In *Alien Zone: Cultural Theory and Science Fiction Cinema,* edited by Annette Kuhn, 1–15. London: Verso.
Kuhn, Annette, ed. 1990. *Alien Zone: Cultural Theory and Contemporary Science Fiction Cinema.* London: Verso.
_____. 1999. *Alien Zone II: The Spaces of Science Fiction Cinema.* London: Verso.
Kvistad, Ivar. 2005. "*Xena*'s Double-edged Sword: Sapphic Love and the Judeo-Christian Tradition." *Refractory* 8.1: n.pag.
Landa, Ishay. 1998. "Slaves of the Ring: Tolkien's Political Unconscious." *Historical Materialism* 10.4: 113–33.
Larbalestier, Justine. 2004. "The Only Thing Better Than Killing a Slayer: Heterosexuality and Sex in *Buffy the Vampire Slayer*." In *Reading the Vampire Slayer: The New, Updated Unofficial Guide to Buffy and Angel,* edited by Roz Kaveney, 195–219. London: Tauris.
Lavery, David, Angela Hague, and Marta Cartwright. 1996. "Introduction: Generation X — *The X-Files* and the Cultural Moment." In *Deny All Knowledge: Reading the X-Files,* edited by David Lavery, Angela Hague and Marta Cartwright. London: Faber & Faber.
LeGuin, Ursula. 1989. "From Elfland to Poughkeepsie." In *The Language of the Night: Essays on Fantasy and Science Fiction,* 70–82. London: Women's Press.
Levi, Antonia. 2006. "The Americanization of Anime and Manga: Negotiating Popular Culture." In *Cinema Anime: Critical Engagements With Japanese Animation,* edited by Stephen T. Brown, 43–65. New York: Palgrave Macmillan.
Linford, Peter. 1999. "Deeds of Power: Respect for Religion in *Star Trek: Deep Space Nine*." In *Star Trek and Sacred Ground: Explorations of Star Trek, Religion and American Culture,* edited by Jennifer E. Porter and Darcee L. McLaren, 77–100. Albany: State University of New York Press.
Lobell, Jared. 2004. *The World of the Rings: Language, Religion and Adventure in Tolkein.* Chicago: Open Court.
Lofton, Kathryn. 2006. "Practicing Oprah; or, the Prescriptive Compulsion of a Spiritual Capitalism." *Journal of Popular Culture* 39.4: 599–622.
Long, Ronald E. 2004. *Men, Homosexuality, and the Gods: An Exploration into the Religious Significance of Male Homosexuality in World Perspective.* New York: Harrington Park Press.
López, José, and Garry Potter, eds. 2005. *After Postmodernism: An Introduction to Critical Realism.* London: Continuum.
Lyotard, Jean-François. 1984a. "Answering the Question: What Is Postmodernism?" Trans. Régis Durand. In *The Postmodern Condition: A Report on Knowledge,* 71–85. *Critique,* number 419 (April 1982). Minneapolis: Minnesota University Press.
_____. 1984b. *The Postmodern Condition : A Report on Knowledge.* Trans. Geoff Bennington and Brian Massumi. Minneapolis: Minnesota University Press.
_____. 1993. *Toward the Postmodern.* Trans. Humanities Press International. New Jersey: Humanities Press International.
_____. 1999. "On a Hyphen." Trans. P. Brault & M. Naas (eds.). In *The Hyphen: Between Judaism and Christianity,* edited by J. Lyotard & E. Gruber. Amherst: Humanity.
Maddox, Marion. 2005. *God Under Howard: The Rise of the Religious Right in Australian Politics.* Sydney: Allen & Unwin.
Maier, Harry O. 2002. *Apocalypse Recalled: The Book of Revelation after Christendom.* Minneapolis: Fortress Press.

Maresco, Peter A. 2004. "Mel Gibson's *The Passion of the Christ*: Market Segmentation, Mass Marketing and Promotion, and the Internet." *Journal of Religion and Popular Culture* 8: n.pag.

Martin, Joel W. 1995. "Introduction: Seeing the Sacred on Screen." In *Screening the Sacred: Religion, Myth and Ideology in Popular American Film*, edited by Joel W. Martin and Conrad E. Ostwalt, Jr., 1–13. Boulder, CO: Westview.

_____, and Conrad E. Ostwalt, Jr., eds. 1995. *Screening the Sacred: Religion, Myth and Ideology in Popular American Film*. Boulder, CO: Westview.

Marx, Karl. 1988. *The Communist Manifesto (a Norton Critical Edition)*. 1872. Ed. Frederic L. Bender. New York: Norton.

Mather, Cotton. 2010. *Wonders of the Invisible World: Being an Account of the Trials of Several Witches Lately Executed in New England*. Whitefish, MT: Kessinger.

McAvan, Em. 2007. "The Postmodern Sacred: Popular Culture Spirituality in the Genres of Science Fiction, Fantasy and Fantastic Horror." Ph.D. diss., Murdoch University.

McGrath, Alister. 2004. *The Twilight of Atheism: The Rise and Fall of Disbelief in the Modern World*. London: Rider.

McHale, Brian. 1987. *Postmodernist Fiction*. New York and London: Methuen.

McKenna, Elise. 2007. "To Sex Up *The Lord of the Rings*: Jackson's Feminine Approach in His 'Sub-creation.'" *How We Became Middle-earth: A Collection of Essays on The Lord of the Rings*, edited by Adam Lam and Nataliya Oryshchuk. Zollikofen: Walking Tree.

McLaren, Darcee, and Jennifer E. Porter. 1999. "(Re)Covering Sacred Ground: New Age Spirituality in *Star Trek: Voyager*." In *Star Trek and Sacred Ground: Explorations of Star Trek, Religion and American Culture*, edited by Jennifer E. Porter and Darcee L. McLaren, 101–115. Albany: State University of New York Press.

Middents, Jeffrey. 2005. "A Sweet Vamp: Critiquing the Treatment of Race on *Buffy* and the American Musical Once More (with Feeling)." *Slayage* 5.1: 51–62.

Milbank, Allison. 2007. *Chesterton and Tolkien as Theologians: The Fantasy of the Real*. London: T & T Clark.

Miller, Vincent. 2003. *Consuming Religion: Christian Faith and Practice in a Consumer Culture*. New York: Continuum.

Mishra, Vijay. 1994. *The Gothic Sublime*. Albany: State University Press of New York.

_____. Forthcoming. "The Religious Sublime." In *The Oxford Handbook of Religion and the Arts*, edited by Frank Burch Brown. Oxford: Oxford University Press.

Morreale, Joanne. 1998."*Xena: Warrior Princess* as Feminist Camp." *Journal of Popular Culture* 8.1: 79–86.

Nakashima Brock, Rita, and Rebecca Ann Parker. 2001. *Proverbs of Ashes: Violence, Redemptive Suffering, and the Search for What Saves Us*. Boston: Beacon.

Napier, Susan. 2005. *Anime: From Akira to Howl's Moving Castle*. New York: Palgrave MacMillan.

Nieman, Susan. 2002. *Evil in Modern Thought: An Alternative History of Philosophy*. Princeton, NJ: Princeton University Press.

Nietzsche, Friedrich. 1956. *The Birth of Tragedy and The Genealogy of Morals*. 1872 and 1887. Trans. Francis Golfling. New York: Doubleday Anchor.

_____. 1990. *Twilight of the Idols; and, The Anti-Christ*. Trans. R. J. Hollingdale. London: Penguin.

Olson, Carl. 1998."The Fore-Structure of Eliade's Hermeneutics." *Philosophy Today* 32.1: 43–52.

Ostwalt, Conrad E. 1995. "Hollywood and Armageddon: Apocalyptic themes in recent cinematic presentation." In Screening the Sacred: Religion, Myth, and Ideology in Popular American Film, edited by Joel W. Martin and Conrad E. Ostwalt, Jr., 55–65. Boulder, CO: Westview Press.

Otto, Rudolph. 1923. *The Idea of the Holy: An Inquiry into the Non-rational Factor of the Divine and Its Relation to the Rational*. Trans. John W. Harvey. London: Oxford University Press.

Pagels, Elaine. 1979. *The Gnostic Gospels*. New York: Vintage.

_____. 1989. *Adam, Eve and the Serpent*. New York: Vintage.

Pagels, Elaine, and Karen L. King. 2007. *Reading Judas: The Gospel of Judas and the Shaping of Christianity*. New York: Viking.

Parkins, Wendy. 2001. "Oprah Winfrey's Change Your Life TV and the Spiritual Everyday." *Continuum* 15.2: 145–57.

Parsons, Michael. October 10, 2010. "Interview: Wired meets William Gibson." *Wired UK*. Accessed 15 December 2011. <http://www.wired.co.uk/news/archive/2010-10/13/william-gibson-interview>

Passakos, Demetrios. 2002. "Clean and Unclean in the New Testament: Implications for Contemporary Liturgical Practices." *Greek Orthodox Theological Review* 47.1–4: 277–93.

Pennington, John. 2002. "From Elfland to Hogwarts, or the Aesthetic Trouble with Harry Potter." *Lion and the Unicorn* 26.1: n.pag.

Pitts, Victoria L. 2003. *In the Flesh: The Cultural Politics of Body Modification*. New York: Palgrave MacMillan.

Rashi. 1970. *Commentaries on the Pentateuch*. Trans. Chaim Pearl. New York: Viking.

Riess, Jana. 2004. *What Would Buffy Do? The Vampire Slayer as Spiritual Guide*. San Francisco: Jossey-Bass.

Ritzer, George. 1998. *The McDonaldization Thesis: Explorations and Extensions*. London: SAGE.

_____. 1999. *Enchanting a Disenchanted World: Revolutionizing the Means of Consumption*. Thousand Oaks, CA: Pine Forge.

Ruppersberg, Hugh. 1990. "The Alien Messiah." In *Alien Zone: Cultural Theory and Science Fiction Cinema*, edited by Annette Kuhn, 32–39. London: Verso.

Said, Edward. October 22, 2001. "The Clash of Ignorance." *The Nation*.

Saussure, Ferdinand de. 1959. *Course in General Linguistics*. Trans. Charles Bally and Albert Sechehaye. New York: McGraw-Hill.

Schuyler, William. 1986. "The Ethical Status of Magic." In *Forms of the Fantastic: Selected Essays from the Third International Conference on the Fantastic in Literature and Film*, edited by Jan Hokenson and Howard Pearce, 25–29. New York: Greenwood.

Schwartzman, Sarah. 2009. "*Children of Men* and a Plural Messianism." *Journal of Religion and Film* 13.1: n.pag.

Sedgwick, Eve Kosofsky. 1990. *Epistemology of the Closet*. Berkeley: University of California Press.

Seifart, Christine. 2008. "Bite Me! (Or Don't)." *Bitch Magazine*. Web. <http://bitchmagazine.org/article/bite-me-or-dont>

Shuck, Glenn W. 2005. *Marks of the Beast: The* Left Behind *series and the Struggle for Evangelical Identity*. New York: New York University Press.

Silver, Anna. 2010. "Twilight is Not Good for Maidens: Gender, Sexuality and the Family in Stephenie Meyer's *Twilight* series." *Studies in the Novel* 42.1–2: 121–138.

Silvio, Carl. 2006. "Animated Bodies and Cybernetic Selves: *The Animatrix* and the Question of Post-Humanity." In *Cinema Anime: Critical Engagements With Japanese Animation*, edited by Stephen T. Brown, 113–139. New York: Palgrave Macmillan.

Bibliography

Smith, James K. A. 2006. *Who's Afraid of Postmodernism? Taking Derrida, Lyotard and Foucault to Church.* Grand Rapids: Baker Academic.
Smol, Anna. 2004. "'Oh...Oh...Frodo!': Readings of Male Intimacy in *The Lord of the Rings*." *MFS Modern Fiction Studies* 50.4: 949–79.
Soja, Edward. 1989. *Postmodern Geographies: The Appraisal of Space in Critical Social Theory.* London: Verso.
Soulliere, Danielle. 2010. "Much Ado About Harry: The Creation of a Moral Panic." *Journal of Religion and Popular Culture* 22.1: n.pag. Accessed 17 September 2010. http://www.usask.ca/relst/jrpc/pdfs/art22%281%29-PotterPanic.pdf
Spargo, Tamsin. 1999. *Foucault and Queer Theory.* Cambridge: Icon.
Spivak, Gayatri Chakravorty. 1999. *A Critique of Postcolonial Reason: Toward a History of the Vanishing Present.* Cambridge, MA: Harvard University Press.
Stark, Rodney. 1999. "Secularization, R.I.P." *Sociology* 60.3: 249–73.
Stewart, Susan. 1993. *On Longing.* Durham, NC: Duke University Press.
Stigliano, Tony. 2002. "Fascism's Mythologist: Mircea Eliade and the Politics of Myth." *ReVision* 24.3: 32–38.
Stroumsa, Guy Gedaliahu. 1984. *Another Seed: Studies in Gnostic Mythology.* Leiden, Netherlands: Brill.
Summers-Bremner, Elenor. 2000. "Reading Irigaray, Dancing." *Hypatia* 15.1: 90–124.
Suvin, Darko. 1979. *Metamorphoses of Science Fiction.* New Haven, CT: Yale University Press.
_____. 2000. "Considering the Sense of 'Fantasy' or 'Fantastic Fiction': An Effusion." *Extrapolation* 41.3: 209–49.
Taylor, Mark C. 1984. *Erring: A Postmodern a/Theology.* Chicago: Chicago University Press.
_____. 1993. *Nots.* Chicago: Chicago University Press.
_____. 1997. *Hiding.* Chicago: University of Chicago Press.
_____. 1999. *About Religion: Economies of Faith in Virtual Culture.* Chicago: University of Chicago Press.
_____. 2004. *Confidence Games: Money and Markets in a World Without Redemption.* Chicago: University of Chicago Press.
_____. 2007. *After God.* Chicago: University of Chicago Press.
Thompson, Kristin. 2003. "Fantasy, Franchises and Frodo Baggins: *The Lord of the Rings* and Modern Hollywood." *Velvet Light Trap* 52: 45–63.
Todorov, Tzvetan. 1973. *The Fantastic: A Structural Approach to a Literary Genre.* Trans. Richard Howard. Cleveland: Case Western Reserve University Press.
Torre, Michael. 2002. "The Portrait of Evil in *The Lord of the Rings*: Reflections Personal, Literary, and Theological." *Logos: A Journal of Catholic Thought and Culture* 5.4: 65–74.
Tramell, James. 2010. "Who Does God Want Me to Invite to See *The Passion of the Christ?*: Marketing Movies to Evangelicals." *Journal of Religion and Media* 9.1: 19–29.
Vanita, Ruth. 1996. *Sappho and the Virgin Mary: Same-Sex Love and the English Literary Imagination.* New York: Columbia University Press.
Vattimo, Gianni. 1998. "Trace of the Trace." Trans. David Webb. In *Religion*, edited by Jaques Derrida and Gianni Vattimo, 79–95. Polity.
Walsh, Richard. 2005. "Wrestling with *Passion of the Christ*: At the Movies with Roland Barthes and Mel Gibson." *Bible and Critical Theory* 1.2: 1–16.
_____. 2008. "The Passion as Horror Film: St. Mel of the Cross." *The Journal of Religion and Popular Culture* 20: n.p.
Weber, Max. 1971. *The Protestant Ethic and the Spirit of Capitalism.* 1930. Trans. Talcott Parsons. London: Unwin University Press.

Webster, Tracey Wright. 2009. "The Glittering World: Female Youth, Nightclubs and Lifestyle Choices." Journal of Gender, Technology and Development.
Winslade, J. Lawton. 2001. "Teen Witches, Wiccans and 'Wanna-Blessed-Be's': Pop-Culture Magic in *Buffy the Vampire Slayer*." *Slayage* 1.1: 31–40.
Woods, Ralph C. 1993. "Traveling the One Road: *The Lord of the Rings* as a 'Pre-Christian Classic.'" *The Christian Century* 110.6: 208–12.
Worley, Alec. 2005. *Empires of the Imagination: A Critical Survey of Fantasy Cinema from Georges Méliès to* The Lord of the Rings. Jefferson, NC: McFarland.
Wright, Melanie J. 2007. *Religion and Film: An Introduction.* London: I. B. Tauris.
Zanger, Jules, and Robert G. Wolf. 1986. "The Disenchantment of Magic." In *Forms of the Fantastic: Selected Essays from the Third International Conference on the Fantastic in Literature and Film,* edited by Jan Hokenson and Howard Pearce, 31–39. New York: Greenwood.
Zengotita, Thomas de. 2005. *Mediated: How the Media Shape Your World and the Way You Live In It.* London: Bloomsbury.
Zipes, Jack, ed. 1986. *Don't Bet on the Prince: Contemporary Feminist Fairy Tales of North America and England.* Hants, England: Scholar.
Žižek, Slavoj. 1989. *The Sublime Object of Ideology.* London: Verso.
_____. 1999a. "*The Matrix* or Malebranche in Hollywood." *Philosophy Today* 43.1: 11–27.
_____. 1999b. "'You May.'" *London Review of Books* 21.6: n.pag.
_____. 2000. *The Fragile Absolute: Or, Why Is the Christian Legacy Worth Fighting For?* London: Verso.
_____. 2001. *On Belief.* London: Routledge.
_____. 2002. "Welcome to the Desert of the Real." *The Symptom* 2 (Spring).
_____. 2004a. *Iraq: The Borrowed Kettle.* New York: Verso.
_____. 2004b. *Organs Without Bodies: On Deleuze and Consequences.* New York: Routledge.
_____. 2006. *The Parallax View.* Cambridge, MA: MIT University Press.
_____. 2008a. *In Defense of Lost Causes.* London: Verso.
_____. 2008b. "Postface: Better Red than Dead!" In *The Sleeping Giant Has Awoken: The New Politics of Religion in the United State,* edited by Jeffrey Robbins and Neal Macgee, 221–231. New York: Continuum.
Zournazi, Mary, and Brian Massumi. 2002. "Navigating Movements: A Conversation with Brian Massumi." In *Hope,* edited by Mary Zournazi, 210–244. Annandale: Pluto Press Australia.

Index

abortion 128, 141–142
abstinence-only sex education 125–127
Adcock, David 80, 84, 176
Ahmed, Sara 134, 151, 176
anime 147, 171
Anderson, Perry 21, 176
Angel 15, 35, 36, 37, 51, 64, 73, 169, 173
Angels in America 77
Armstrong, Karen 47, 165, 168, 176
atheism 143
Auerbach, Nina 73, 126, 176
Avatar 32–33

Barthes, Roland 121, 123, 176
Bassham, Gregory 145, 176
Battlestar Galactica 6, 19, 61, 130, 135–141, 171
Baudrillard, Jean 11, 14, 17, 21, 22, 24, 25, 31, 33, 35, 39, 41, 78, 80, 87, 94, 147, 157, 171, 176, 177, 178
Bauman, Zygmunt 29, 44, 97, 120, 152, 156–157, 177
Beck, Ulrich 10, 177
Beck-Gernsheim, Elisabeth 10, 177
Bennett, Jane 10
Billington, Ray 7, 177
Blake, Andrew 148, 177
Bortolin, Matthew 50
Brown, Wendy 9, 10, 117, 118, 134, 177
Buddhism 7, 8, 26, 43, 60, 61, 68, 78, 95–97
Buffy the Vampire Slayer 8, 9, 15, 36, 37, 51, 59, 60, 61, 64, 80, 88–97
Bush, George W. 22, 117, 133, 136, 139, 155, 170

Calvert-Koyzis, Nancy 101, 178
Caputo, John D. 1, 38, 47, 116, 178
CGI (Computer Generated Imagery) 24, 32–35

Christianity 8, 34–38, 45, 54, 59–61, 77–79, 85–86, 89, 117–129, 141, 145–146, 154–156, 166–168, 170; Catholicism 35–36, 45, 60, 98, 105–108, 114, 122–124, 143, 155, 166, 169, 170; and the Devil 64; and evangelical Protestantism 3, 6, 8–9, 57, 107, 117–128, 148, 155–156; and Gnosticism 18, 78, 98–107, 170
Clarke, Lynne Schofield 56, 178
Constantine 18, 35–37, 64, 82, 123, 173

Dark Angel 72–73, 174
Dead Like Me 15, 18, 52–53, 71, 81, 174
Derrida, Jacques 8, 11, 17, 21, 34, 38, 39, 46, 47, 48, 61, 62, 123, 126, 127, 129, 159, 160, 161, 163, 166, 167, 171
Dracula 71, 74, 89, 144
Dulles, Avery 54, 61, 179

Eagleton, Terry 21
Edmundson, Mark 70, 71, 72, 77, 179
Eliade, Mircea 17, 22, 26–29, 54, 56, 57, 165, 179
enchantment 58, 84, 93–94
ethics 143–153
Eucharist 39

Farscape 130, 170
Fiorenza, Elisabeth Schussler 121, 179
The 4400 40, 41, 54, 174
Freud, Sigmund 1, 112, 127
Frykholm, Amy Johnson 121, 180
Futurama 18, 43, 64–67, 132, 168, 174

Gay, lesbian, bisexual and transgender 2, 9, 12, 75, 78, 86–87, 112, 155, 170; and marriage equality 2, 118
Gibson, Mel 6, 18, 122, 124, 175
Gibson, William 4, 184
Gooderham, David 108, 180

Index

Gothic 70–76
Graham, Billy 122

Halberstam, Judith 72, 74–76, 180
Hardt, Michael 4, 134, 161–162, 180
Harry Potter series. 5, 9, 15, 16, 19, 32, 87, 88, 130, 144, 147–153
Harvey, David 3
Heelas, Paul 6, 44, 98, 100, 101, 106, 120, 156, 177, 180
Hinduism 8, 33, 52–53, 67, 82
The Holocaust 152
Huntington, Samuel 66

Ingebretson, Edward J. 37, 64, 71, 72, 77, 181
Islam 25, 130, 135–142

Jameson, Fredric 4, 11, 17, 22, 25, 31, 62, 91, 95, 181
Jesus 47, 99–103; and Christ figures 36, 60–61, 67, 77, 93, 108–116, 122–124, 144–146, 153; and sacrifice 93
Judaism 79, 85; and anti-Semitism 122; and Occupy Judaism 162

Keller, Catherine 3, 177, 181
Kotsko, Adam 124, 182
Kuhn, Annette 12, 34, 165, 182
Kvistad, Ivar 85–87, 182

Lavery, David 55, 91, 182
Left Behind 6, 9, 18, 119, 121, 171
Lofton, Kathryn 44, 182
The Lord of the Rings 15, 16, 17, 18, 32, 51, 63, 76, 87, 108–116
Lyotard, Jean-Francois 11, 17, 22, 23, 55, 72, 85, 182

Marx, Karl 1, 74, 162, 183
Mary Magdalene 98–102
The Matrix series 9, 13, 15, 17, 19, 32, 35, 123, 130, 144–147, 149, 152, 171, 174
Milbank, Alison 110, 183
Mishra, Vijay 23, 183
monstrosity 71–79
Morreale, Joanne 80, 86, 183

negative theology 39, 49
Negri, Antonio 4, 134, 161, 162, 180
New Age 6–8, 12, 23, 24, 26, 37–38, 43–70
Nietzsche, Friedrich 1, 181, 183

nostalgia 87–88, 95–96, 120

Occupy movement 161–162; and Judaism 162

Pagels, Elaine 73, 100, 102, 105, 184
Parkins, Wendy 8, 45, 156, 166, 184
Passion of the Christ 3, 122–124, 165
polytheism 58, 78–79, 80–95; modern paganism 82
Pope John Paul II 123, 155, 166
postmodernism: and metanarrative 22–24, 55; and music 81–82; and pastiche 59, 62, 66, 91
Pullman, Philip 143, 180

Ruppersberg, Hugh 57, 68, 184

Seifart, Christine 126, 184
sexuality 126–128
Shepard, Matthew 77
Shuck, Glenn 121, 184
Silver, Anna 125, 128, 184
Spivak, Gayatri 4, 185
Star Trek: Deep Space Nine 59–60, 167
Star Wars 12, 32, 41, 42, 50, 51, 60, 85, 90, 144, 171, 175
Stargate franchise 9, 18, 19, 64, 68–70, 82, 130–135, 168, 170, 175
Superman 54, 72, 90
Suvin, Darko 14, 26, 29, 51, 78, 185

Taylor, Mark C 11, 23, 31, 48, 62, 77, 87, 96, 106, 117, 118, 120, 156, 185
Todorov, Tvetzan 13, 18, 93, 106, 185
Tolkien, J.R.R 62, 108–116
Twilight 18, 124–129, 163, 173

Walls, Jerry L 150
Warren, Rick 8, 120
Weber, Max 3, 29, 155, 185
Winfrey, Oprah 8, 23, 43, 44, 45, 104, 154, 156, 166n2–3, 175
Woodhead, Linda 120, 180
Wright, Melanie 10, 11, 15, 186

The X-Files 6, 9, 15, 18, 22, 40, 54–58, 72, 76, 93, 167, 175
Xena: Warrior Princess 18, 64, 80–87, 169, 175

Žižek, Slavoj 3, 21, 23, 43, 60, 100, 102–103, 117, 118, 136, 146, 154, 155

188

www.ingramcontent.com/pod-product-compliance
Ingram Content Group UK Ltd.
Pitfield, Milton Keynes, MK11 3LW, UK
UKHW041919140426
5217IPUK00013B/227